HOW THE OTHER HALF LEARNS

HOW THE OTHER HALF LEARNS

EQUALITY, EXCELLENCE, AND
THE BATTLE OVER SCHOOL CHOICE

ROBERT PONDISCIO

AVERY

an imprint of Penguin Random House
New York

AVERY

An imprint of Penguin Random House LLC
penguinrandomhouse.com

First trade paperback edition 2020

Names: Pondiscio, Robert, author.
Title: How the other half learns : equality, excellence, and
the battle over school choice / Robert Pondiscio.
Description: New York : Avery, an imprint of Penguin Random House, LLC, [2019] |
Includes bibliographical references and index.
Identifiers: LCCN 2019021574 | ISBN 9780525533733 (hardcover) |
ISBN 9780525533740 (ebook)
Subjects: LCSH: Educational equalization—United States. |
Charter schools—United States. | School choice—United States. |
Education and state—United States. | Public schools—Social aspects—United States.
Classification: LCC LC213.2 .P66 2019 | DDC 379.2/6—dc23
LC record available at https://lccn.loc.gov/2019021574
p.   cm.

ISBN 9780525533757 (paperback)

Book design by Elke Sigal

147429898

For Liza and Katie, and for Don Hirsch

CONTENTS

CONTENTS

HOW THE
OTHER HALF
LEARNS

Prologue

THE LEADERSHIP TEAM AT SUCCESS ACADEMY BRONX 1 ELEMENTARY school is making its morning round of classroom visits. Principal Elizabeth Vandlik started the day by announcing "deliverables" for every teacher, which she and her assistant principals expect to see when they enter a classroom: Students should be "on task" at least 95 percent of the time. Teachers are expected to notice off-task behavior 100 percent of the time and, without prompting, take corrective action to refocus and reengage inattentive students. Every time.

After each classroom visit, Vandlik and her team strategize in the hallway, rehearsing the feedback each teacher should get. One of the assistant principals goes back inside and whispers into the teacher's ear. Changes are made immediately, in real time, and without interrupting classroom instruction.

After the walk-through, the school leadership team huddles to discuss both teachers and students who need their immediate attention. The meeting concludes with a discussion of "whole-school improvements" that need to be made.

For tomorrow.

Two assistant principals take out their cell phones and start calling parents to ask for "brief chats" in person at that afternoon's dismissal to address concerns that have come up with their children.

It's August 15. The school year is three hours old.

CHAPTER 1

The Tiffany Test

THE PERSON WHO HAS HAD THE GREATEST INFLUENCE ON MY career in education was not a professor, policymaker, researcher, or fellow teacher. It was a ten-year-old girl named Tiffany, a fifth grader in my class during my second year of teaching at PS 277, a low-performing elementary school in the South Bronx. Walk into any classroom in any struggling urban school in the United States and you will spot a child like Tiffany. Her eyes are on the teacher, paying careful attention and following directions. She is bright and pleasant, happy to help and eager to please. Her desk is clean and well organized; her homework neat and complete. She has grown up hearing about the importance of education. She believes it, and her behavior shows it. She gets praise and good grades.

She also gets screwed.

Because she goes to a school where most of her classmates read and do math well below their grade level, Tiffany is "not your problem," as an assistant principal pointedly told me when I expressed concern about how little of my attention she was getting.

The message to a new teacher could not have been clearer: Focus your efforts on the low achievers, the disruptive, and the disengaged. Get them in the game. Tiffany will be fine.

Since leaving the classroom, I have applied the "Tiffany test" to any new education reform initiative, policy prescription, or innovative teaching idea: Will this make it more likely or less likely that kids like Tiffany—promising low-income children of color in places like the South Bronx—will get what they need to reach their full academic and life potential? The answer rarely comes back in the affirmative. The broad thrust of education reform efforts, stretching back decades, has been aimed at closing achievement gaps between children of color and white and Asian children, between those who grow up in poverty and those who are more fortunate. The biggest losers in classrooms shaped by these well-intended policies are children like Tiffany. Children who are ready for new intellectual challenges pay a price when they sit in classrooms focused on their less proficient and less engaged peers. We can insist that the answer is "differentiated instruction," personalized learning, or policies that valorize student "growth" over proficiency on standardized tests, making every student the teacher's problem. But these remedies are unsatisfying and naive, mere homilies. If the vast majority of America's nearly four million teachers cannot easily and effectively implement a proposal, it is no solution at all. It fails the Tiffany test.

When you have a "not your problem" child sitting in your class in the age of testing, accountability, and gap-closing, you understand that despite her good grades and rock-steady performance on state tests, she is subsisting on starvation rations in history, geography, science, art, and music—the stuff that makes education interesting and engaging. Her finish line—read on grade level; graduate on time—is the starting line for more fortunate children, including your own. Tiffany and the multitude of children like her represent the low-hanging fruit the typical struggling school leaves dying on the vine. But she is maddeningly, damnably, *undemocratically* not your problem.

A question has gnawed at me ever since I was Tiffany's fifth-grade teacher. If we are committed to equity and social justice, if we wish to keep faith with the American dream and believe that education is the indispensable engine of upward mobility, should we attempt to serve all disadvantaged children equally and labor to close the achievement gap because that is what's fair? Or should we do all in our power to ensure that receptive and motivated students can reap the full benefit of their talents and ambitions because that is what's just? The latter, of course, is what well-off families effortlessly secure for their children, either by paying tuition to opt out of the public school system or by buying homes in affluent zip codes where their property taxes function as de facto tuition for excellent neighborhood schools.

What might it look like—what might America look like—if parents' ability to steer their children into the best possible school setting was not a function of money and privilege but was something closer to the default setting in K–12 education in the United States?

Give a focused low-income kid a superior education and you improve the odds that she is on the path to upward mobility and that her children will not grow up in poverty. Give the same kid a bland, *good-enough* education and she is prepared mostly to march in place. A false dichotomy? Of course it is. The promise of an American education is excellence for all. But that promise has seldom been kept for those who are poor, black, or brown. Worse, our humane and laudable efforts to increase educational equity have made educational excellence largely available only to those with the means to purchase it. Low-income black and brown children who are ready for greater academic challenges or who are simply buying what schools are selling? Not your problem.

After leaving my classroom, Tiffany, with her reliably solid performance on state reading and math tests, continued her dutiful march onward and upward, eventually moving with her mother to Pennsylvania, where she attended high school and a state university. Given the long odds at birth against the child of a Hispanic single mother ever becoming a college graduate, she is a success story. But I'm haunted to this day by what I know the data cannot show. Tiffany was neglected by me, by other teachers, and by the systems we have created to ostensibly benefit children like her. And that neglect was not an accident; it was a policy. There is little doubt in my mind that had she attended my daughter's school, two subway stops and a world away on Manhattan's Upper East Side, she easily could have found her way to Harvard, Princeton, Stanford, or any of the top-echelon universities whose admissions offices search and compete for students like her. From there, it's a short distance to diversifying the leadership class—America's ultimate achievement gap. With her limitless grit and desire to learn, her deep investment in education, and the devoted support of her hardworking mother, Tiffany at age ten had as much potential as any kid in this country. With luck, those natural gifts will fuel her rise for the next several decades. But if she becomes all that it was obvious to me she could be—sitting patient, alert, and expectant in my fifth-grade classroom—it will not be because of what I and other teachers did for her. It will be in spite of it.

People who write about education and our decades-long attempts to improve it invariably bring their personal interests, experiences, and biases to the task. The reader deserves to know mine and something about the lens I brought to my yearlong examination of Success Academy, the nation's most successful and controversial network of charter schools, and the lessons from it that we might apply to American education, particularly schools serving children growing up in poverty.

In 2002, I began working as a fifth-grade teacher in a low-performing South Bronx elementary school. My midcareer decision to become a public school teacher was closer to an impulse purchase than to answering a call to service. It was the year I would turn forty. I was the father of a three-year-old daughter. I was working as the communications director for *BusinessWeek* magazine after serving in a similar capacity for *Time*. The magazine industry had been disrupted by the Internet and the bursting of the dot-com advertising bubble. In a little more than a year, *BusinessWeek* went from running a record number of advertising pages to losing money for the first time since the Great Depression. I was ripe for the plucking a few months after the 9/11 terrorist attacks when, riding the downtown N train home from Rockefeller Center, I sat across from an ad for the New York City Teaching Fellows, an "alternative certification" program aimed at luring midcareer professionals into hard-to-staff inner-city public school classrooms. "You remember your first-grade teacher's name," read the ad across the aisle. "Who will remember yours?"

Fools rush in. I had been (and still am) a longtime board member of East Side House Settlement, a community-based organization in the Mott Haven neighborhood of the South Bronx. Under its executive director, John Sanchez,[1] the organization had evolved from providing cradle-to-grave social services to putting education at the core of its mission and programs. Undoubtedly my involvement with East Side House made me more receptive to the subway ad's pitch. It was through Sanchez's advice that I found myself one spring afternoon in the main office of PS 277, on St. Ann's Avenue and 148th Street, across the street from St. Mary's Park, asking to speak with the school's principal, Carol Pertchik.

New York City Community School District 7 was, then and now, the city's lowest-performing school district. PS 277 was the lowest-performing school in District 7. But as I toured the building with Pertchik, I was struck by its relative calm. When I told her I was hoping to teach fifth grade, typically the oldest, rowdiest, and hardest-to-staff year in most New York City elementary schools, she raised an eyebrow and offered me a job. I received six weeks of training from the New York City Department of Education, District 7, and the United Federation of Teachers, the teachers' union. I taught summer school. In the fall, I was assigned to a fifth-grade "collaborative team teaching" classroom, which serves both general and special education students in the same room. While teaching, I attended required graduate school classes in elementary education as part of my Teaching Fellows training. What was supposed to be a two-year midcareer public service stint became a five-year commitment—and then education became my second career.

Teaching is the easiest job in the world to do badly. If you wanted to go through the motions and head home at the end of your contractually obligated six-hour-and-twenty-minute workday, you could get away with it forever—particularly in a school like mine, where I had only two formal observations in five years. But it's the hardest job to do well. Most days, to be blunt, it defeated me. Like every new teacher, I struggled with classroom management. There was no set curriculum, and the techniques I was trained to use to teach reading, writing, and math bore scant resemblance to what I remembered as a child. I was surprised at how little of my school's curriculum was codified in any way. Plenty of people were telling me how to teach, but when I asked *what* I should be teaching, the question was greeted with either amusement or dismissal. "Mr. Pondiscio," a staff developer from the Teachers College Reading and Writing Project told me early in my career, "you're the best person to know what your students need!" I found that answer unhelpful and almost certainly incorrect. I was in no position to decide unilaterally what a ten-year-old in the South Bronx needed to know to become a well-educated, upwardly mobile, happily productive, and engaged citizen of the United States of America.

I became deeply interested in curriculum, which has guided much of my work since leaving the classroom. I was particularly persuaded by the work of E.D. Hirsch Jr., the author of the Core Knowledge curriculum and the nonprofit foundation that publishes and promotes it.[2] Hirsch alone among educational theorists accurately described and diagnosed what I saw every day in my South Bronx classroom: children who could "decode" printed text but often struggled to answer basic questions about what they had just read. Hirsch ascribed reading-comprehension struggles to a lack of a shared knowledge base, particularly among low-income children, driven by American education's indifference, if not outright hostility, to establishing a set curriculum in schools. This was the subject of Hirsch's best-known book, *Cultural Literacy*,[3] as well as several other subsequent works.

Because Hirsch's insights were so readily observable in my school, where fewer than one in five students read at or above grade level, I became an advocate for his vision of literacy instruction and a knowledge-rich core curriculum, particularly for low-income children. After leaving the classroom, I sought out Dr. Hirsch and worked for his Core Knowledge Foundation for several years. I also developed a keen interest in civic education and the civic mission of schools. This led me to work on civic education initiatives at Democracy Prep Public Schools, a network of charter schools based in Harlem, where I returned to the classroom, teaching a high school seminar in civics and citizenship. Since 2014, I have been a senior fellow at the Thomas B. Fordham Institute, an education policy think tank based in Washington, DC. In short, my roles have evolved, but my interests in education have not changed at all from my first day as a fifth-grade teacher: I remain focused entirely on what it takes to improve educational outcomes for our most disadvantaged children—those whom America's schools continue to fail.

Education policymakers can be oddly incurious about what students actually do all day. Analysts and researchers typically look at whether school choice, charter schools, or traditional public schools "work." But from the perspective of a teacher, such sweeping conclusions are of little value—unless we also know what curriculum or instructional tactics are being used or something about the school's setting, adult culture, and other factors that shape classroom life and practice. That said, I try to avoid falling into the trap of teachers who wave the bloody shirt and insist that those who have never stood in front of students have no business setting policies that affect their daily lives. As long as public education runs primarily on tax dollars, public scrutiny, transparency, and accountability are inevitable and essential. It will not do to say simply, "Trust teachers and send more money." Thus, I occupy an odd place in education policy debates, which tend to focus on structures: academic standards such as Common Core,[4] accountability, teacher quality, testing, school funding, and the like. What happens inside classrooms remains largely beneath the notice of education policymakers and pundits. I have long believed that this indifference to curriculum and instruction is a significant impediment to progress.

———

This was the spirit in which I first approached Eva Moskowitz in spring 2016 to seek access to her network of Success Academy charter schools for the coming school year. For all the attention, much of it negative, that they had received in the media, I felt I knew very little and wanted to know much more about a very simple question: What do the kids do all day? This has long seemed to me the only question worth asking if we are serious about improving the outcome of American education, particularly for low-income children of color, the only children I've ever taught.

I confess that I came to Success Academy at least somewhat skeptically. In an August 2014 *New York Daily News* op-ed that took note of the network's astonishing test scores, I wrote, "Is Eva Moskowitz the Michael Jordan of education reform, or is she Mark McGwire?"—invoking the names of one of our most transcendent athletes and a notorious steroids-taking cheater. Privately, I was inclined to think there was at least *something* unholy going on. I do not believe in miracles in education. I have a complicated relationship with testing and accountability. The data from standardized testing is the lifeblood of education reform. Without it, we would not be fully aware of the pernicious and persistent gaps between affluent and white children and low-income students and children of color. At the same time, we can't turn a blind eye to the deleterious effects of testing on American education: narrowing schooling to reading, math, and little else, and the drudgery of reducing a child's education to a dull regimen of test prep.

There's only so much that can be learned visiting schools for a "drive-by." Teachers and school administrators are not actors. When you spend hundreds of hours observing, they reveal who they are. Once Moskowitz agreed, albeit reluctantly, to allow me to "embed" in one of her schools, Ann Powell, the network's communications chief, suggested Success Academy Bronx 1 and escorted me on an initial visit. My first summer in the New York City Teaching Fellows program, I taught summer school at PS 18, an elementary school just up the block. The prospect of embedding in a school in the same neighborhood where I taught was appealing. Having secured Moskowitz's cooperation, I asked Elizabeth Vandlik, Bronx 1's principal, for hers. She assented and, throughout the course of my year of observations, was both welcoming and forthcoming. We were in immediate agreement that the interest of Bronx 1's students would come first and that my observations must not distract from the work of teachers. I would tread lightly.

Very few restrictions were placed on my observations. Vandlik suggested classrooms where I might see the best examples of Success Academy's curriculum and pedagogy. I regularly sat in on her meetings with the leadership team to better understand her priorities and leadership style. I was not barred from any classrooms, although Vandlik—appropriately, in my opinion—asked me to avoid those with teachers who were new or uncomfortable with an outsider sitting in their rooms for hours at a time. Most of the restrictions I faced were self-imposed: If I sensed a teacher was ill at ease with me there, I tended to avoid returning. I never attended meetings on disciplinary matters between Success Academy staff, students, and family members, nor did I ask to. I was, however, privy to many meetings where disciplinary issues were discussed.

Candor increased the closer I got to the ground. Moskowitz allowed me access to most of her schools and some, but not all, of Success Academy's teacher training and professional development. Most requests for access to schools or interviews with network personnel were granted, though some were not. I signed up independently for several Success Academy–led trainings that were open to interested educators. Parents were unfiltered in their willingness to talk, inviting me to visit with them in their homes, workplaces, and churches. Success Academy suggested several families for me to interview; however, I formed most of my impressions from parents I came to know independently simply by being present.

Even with my regular and unmonitored access, this book does not purport to be a complete record of a year at Success Academy. There is simply too much going on in any school for one person to observe. The vast majority of names of the adults in this book are real. However, when what I observed, in my judgment, might cast a negative light on an individual, particularly a teacher, I have reserved the right to use a pseudonym. This decision was mine alone; it was not requested or even suggested by Success Academy. It was made out of empathy for the enormous challenge of teaching well in neighborhoods that have seen multiple generations of educational neglect, disappointment, or failure. The purpose of this book is to describe what happens inside one of the nation's most successful charter school networks, evaluate the student experience, and see whether there are lessons that can translate to American education at large. There is nothing to be gained nor any value in calling out by name someone who tried their best and failed, as some do inevitably in every school.

Most important, I have maintained complete and total editorial control throughout this project. The contents of this book have not been subject to oversight by Success Academy, its employees, its board members, or others. Nor was I asked by anyone at Success Academy to provide it.

CHAPTER 2

"We Have an Army Coming"

"IF YOU WERE HERE IN 2006, RAISE YOUR HAND!" SOMEONE shouts from the stage.

From the look of the crowd, it's likely that most of the Success Academy staff gathered under a massive tent on a stifling August afternoon were still in high school in 2006. Many were probably in middle school. It is the first day of August 2016, and the entire team—more than two thousand teachers, administrators, support staff, network employees, and CEO Eva Moskowitz herself—are at Liberty House in Jersey City, New Jersey, across the Hudson River from downtown Manhattan, to kick off the new school year and celebrate Success Academy's tenth anniversary. The first day of class for fourteen thousand students of the nation's most controversial charter school network is still two weeks away. The tent is a fitting venue for a revival meeting, to reenergize the network's young staff and welcome hundreds of newcomers into the faith.

If any ten-year Success Academy veterans have raised their hands, they are lost in the throng of cheering bodies, all wearing identical orange T-shirts bearing the names of each of Success Academy's forty-one schools and the Twitter hashtag #PathToPossible. When those who are new to Success this year are asked to raise their hands, a forest of arms goes up: some nine hundred new teachers and staffers have been hired for the coming year.

Chief academic officer Michele Caracappa tells the sea of faces arrayed before her, "There is no one doing what we're doing." It's no idle boast. Days before the tent rally, New York State released the results of statewide tests in reading and math. More than 4,200 Success Academy students in grades three through eight were required to sit for the exams, most of them black and brown children from low-income homes.[1] Eighty-two percent passed the English Language Arts (ELA) test by earning at least a Level 3, indicating grade-level proficiency; 29 percent earned a Level 4, the highest possible score. "Our performance puts us in the top one point five percent in the state in ELA," Caracappa announces.[2] "Two of the top five schools in the state are Success Academy schools—Crown Heights and Bed-Stuy," she adds, drawing a loud cheer from the crowd and delighted screams from the staff of those two schools, located in two of the city's poorest neighborhoods.

There is more—much more. New York City is home to some of the most highly regarded and successful charter schools in the nation, including KIPP, Achievement First, and Uncommon Schools. Most of these "no excuses" charter schools—a name born of the conviction that there should be no excuses made by schools or society to explain away the achievement gap between poor minority students and their more affluent white peers—easily outperform the district-operated schools in Gotham's poorest neighborhoods. Success Academy easily outperforms its high-flying charter school peers.

The immense daylight between Success Academy and longer-established charter schools has opened a second front in the nation's education reform wars, which typically pit figures like Moskowitz against teachers' unions and others who favor strengthening traditional public schools rather than authorizing charter schools to compete with them. Pushing thousands of low-income children to unprecedented academic heights should make Moskowitz a hero to those committed to social justice and closing the achievement gap. But her abrasive public persona and combative style have made her a divisive figure even among putative charter school allies, who seem more inclined to explain away her results, even as they try, and mostly fail, to duplicate them.

Everyone has a theory about how she does it: Success Academy engages in "creaming," recruiting the easiest students to teach from neighborhood schools while "counseling out" laggards and kids with behavior problems or special needs.[3] Moskowitz's schools are joyless and militaristic test-prep mills that push kids so relentlessly that they literally soil themselves from the pressure. Or it's the millions she raises at glittering fund-raisers from deep-pocketed Wall Street titans eager to humiliate the teachers' unions. The darkest and simplest theory is that she's cheating—her test scores are just too good to be true. Perhaps it's unsurprising how few friends Moskowitz has in traditional public education circles or among education reformers. She is an existential threat, a rebuke, or a humiliation to nearly all of them.

But the question remains unanswered: How *does* she do it?

If the attacks and skepticism bother Moskowitz, she seldom shows it, at least in public. She and Success Academy are hunting bigger game: to entirely close the achievement gap between white kids and children of color.[4] This has been a dewy-eyed dream for decades among education reformers, who insist that the only difference between minority youth and their more affluent white peers is the quality of their schools and teachers.

Others dream; Moskowitz appears to have cracked the code. But her methods, however effective, may not work in all schools, and not all parents would want to send their child to a Success Academy even if they could. The extraordinary demands the schools place not just on students but also on their parents to be active participants in educating their children reaches a level that can be uncomfortable; for some it borders on harassment. It smacks of paternalism. But so far, at least, Success Academy keeps getting bigger and adding more schools every year without any obvious growing pains or visible signs of weakness—a gravity-defying act that only reinforces critics' and competitors' assumption that there must be some nefarious explanation for the results achieved in Moskowitz's schools.

Success Academy appears to have not merely closed the achievement gap but *reversed* it.[5] Schools in New York State's most affluent districts are now chasing Success Academy. Invoking the name of one of suburban Westchester's richest towns, Caracappa announces, "Our results outpace Scarsdale on English Language Arts by nine percent." But even this data fails to capture the scope of Success Academy's apparent accomplishment. Three-fourths of its pupils are eligible for a free or reduced-price lunch,[6] the standard proxy for low-income status. Over 90 percent are children of color. If you are a black or Hispanic child in a New York City public school, you have a one-in-four chance of passing the state English Language Arts exam. At Success, 82 percent of black and Hispanic students passed in 2016—a rate that easily outpaces even the 59 percent rate for Asian and white students citywide. In math, 93 percent of Success Academy's black students and 95 percent of its Hispanic students passed their math tests, with 73 percent scoring at Level 4, the very highest level. "And this is truly phenomenal," Caracappa crows. "The top five schools in the state of New York [in math] are all Success Academy schools."

The tent explodes in cheers.

In New York City, Wall Street titans, well-heeled lawyers and real estate developers, high-profile hedge-fund tycoons, and bold-faced names in entertainment and the arts pay upwards of forty thousand dollars a year to send their sons and daughters to some of the nation's most exclusive private schools. The children who attend those schools are not required to sit for state tests, but if they did, it would be fascinating to know whether three-fourths of them, blessed with every possible advantage of money, parental engagement, social capital, and all conceivable forms of personal enrichment, could score a Level 4 on New York State's tests. It is entirely possible that Success Academy is running the highest-performing schools, public *or* private, in New York City. Or anywhere.

It should not be assumed that standardized test scores are the singular measure of a good education, that strong scores correlate with positive long-term life outcomes, or that poor children who score the highest are on a glide path to break free of generational poverty. But for the last two decades, a muscular testing regime has been how we hold both traditional public schools and charter schools nationwide accountable for taxpayers' considerable investment in public education. For good or for ill, it's the name of the game. And no one has played the game as well as Eva Moskowitz and Success Academy.

When she takes the stage, speaking without notes, Moskowitz's biggest applause comes when she talks about Success Academy's educational endgame: the work of getting poor kids into college. But she has not come here to pile on facts and figures about academic results. Her role is to conscript the young staffers sheltering under the tent from the brutal August sun as foot soldiers in the other half of Success Academy's dual mission: its aggressive political advocacy to open more schools, mostly in "co-located" space already occupied by existing New York City public schools. "We advocate a lot," she remarks drily. "We've brought it to an art form. It's kinda like breathing to us."

If it's an art, it's the art of war. Charter schools nationwide are locked in battles in state capitals for the right to expand, or even to exist. Critics accuse charter schools of bleeding resources away from traditional public schools; proponents counter that charter schools *are* public schools. Publicly funded but privately run, charters offer a lifeboat to low-income kids from failing schools while in theory creating choice-driven market pressures that force bad schools— charter and traditional public schools alike—to improve or die. Playing politics is the price of admission for many charter school leaders and education reformers, but Moskowitz seems to relish combat. Her high-profile clashes with critics from teachers' union head Randi Weingarten to New York mayor Bill de Blasio have made her, without question, one of the most polarizing and divisive figures in American education today. Donald Trump even interviewed Moskowitz, a lifelong liberal Democrat, to be his education secretary. She turned him down.[7]

Now Moskowitz shows off a pedantic speaking style prone to lecturing. A former history professor and the child of academics, she does not project arrogance exactly, but rather the tone of someone who is accustomed to being listened to—and who expects to be heard. A few minutes into her pep talk to her troops, Moskowitz has wound herself up discussing the "three *f*'s" of Success Academy's political agenda: "facilities, funding, and freedom." Every staffer, she insists, has an obligation to fight for these things. "Where is the leadership on education?" she demands. "If there were more leadership, we wouldn't have hundreds of thousands of kids in New York City alone stuck in failing schools. *We* are the leadership. If we don't do it, it's not going to get done." This kind of rhetoric has made Moskowitz the darling of deep-pocketed donors, many from the financial industry, who have pledged tens of millions to Success Academy in the past decade, whether in the spirit of noblesse oblige, a heartfelt commitment to education reform, or merely an antipathy to teachers' unions.

Her staff applauds warmly, but not wildly, for Moskowitz's political stemwinder. They are much more excited about promoting social justice, closing achievement gaps, and getting poor kids into college than fighting over facilities and funding. Moskowitz reads her audience and connects the dots for them. "Whether you like it or not, you are disruptors," she says, borrowing language from venture capitalists and the tech industry. "We have to fight for the three *f*'s because the political class isn't naturally going to give us equal funding."

She's an expatriate of that political class herself. A former New York City Council member known to have her eye on New York City's mayoral mansion, Moskowitz's fights are far from over. As the 2016–17 school year opened, Success Academy had twenty-nine elementary schools, eleven middle schools, and a high school. Her rapid expansion and oft-stated ambition to grow to one hundred schools in New York City forces Success Academy into inevitable fights for space and seats. As it is, she warns, the network will not be able to accommodate the students they've already enrolled through high school.

"We have an army coming," Moskowitz declares.

She winds down but not before trying one last time to make her struggle theirs. "I'm an ed reform warrior. I was one before we opened Success Academy," she declares. "So you are not only a teacher. You're an ed reform warrior." The line gets no response. "You might not feel totally comfortable with that yet. But I can assure you that if you want what's best for your children and all children, we're gonna have to fight to get it."

There's one last bit of business to attend to before the meeting breaks up. Two thousand teachers and staffers wander out from under the tent and into the brutal August sun to pose for a photograph. Ten years ago Moskowitz and the entire staff of Harlem 1, her original school, could have taken a cell phone selfie. Today, she and her growing army of ed reform warriors stand on the lawn with lower Manhattan looming behind them. They look up and grin.

The picture is taken from a drone.

CHAPTER 3

Bronx 1

DURING THE SECOND INNING OF GAME TWO OF THE 1977 WORLD Series between the New York Yankees and the Los Angeles Dodgers, an ABC Sports aerial camera zoomed in on a fire at PS 3, an abandoned elementary school a few blocks from Yankee Stadium. "My *goodness*, that's a huge blaze!"[1] exclaimed sportscaster Keith Jackson in his trademark Georgia drawl. "That's the very area where President Carter trod just a few days ago,"[2] added Howard Cosell, alluding to the president's visit to the neighborhood following a speech at the United Nations.[3] Cosell never actually uttered the line famously but erroneously attributed to him: "Ladies and gentlemen, the Bronx is burning."

By the end of the decade, nearly half the neighborhood's buildings had been lost to fire, primarily arson. What the fires didn't destroy, the crack epidemic claimed in the 1980s. Crime soared. The words "South Bronx" became synonymous nationwide with urban squalor, a reputation the neighborhood struggles with to this day, even as neat rows of one- and two-family homes have filled in the gaps between the towering housing projects. The area is now largely Hispanic, heavily populated with immigrants from Central America and West Africa, and still deeply impoverished. Nearly nowhere in the United States is poverty deeper or more widespread than in Mott Haven, the neighborhood where Success Academy's Bronx 1 campus occupies two floors of a nondescript four-story building adjacent to a Western Beef supermarket and across the street from the Patterson Houses, one of the largest of the dismal 1950s-era housing projects that are a ubiquitous feature of the skyline.

From the curb, there is little evidence of a Success Academy. The signage above the small courtyard is a public school pentimento. Permanently affixed to the building are brushed metal letters spelling out THE PAUL ROBESON SCHOOL. Directly below it hangs a large banner, burgundy with gold letters, updating the name to the PAUL ROBESON COMPLEX, and below that BRONX ACADEMY OF LETTERS, PUBLIC SCHOOL 168. Under an overhang, an easily overlooked sign, too small to see from the street, reads, SUCCESS ACADEMY, BRONX 1 ELEMENTARY AND MIDDLE SCHOOL, in the network's trademark orange and white.

The bodegas a few doors down stock Starbucks Frappuccinos and Naked Juices for the doctors and nurses who work at Lincoln Hospital, a massive medical center just up the street. Murders, car thefts, and shootings are a fraction of what they were when the South Bronx was given up for dead in its "Bronx is burning" days. Optimistic real estate developers, trying to lure would-be home-owners priced out of Manhattan, have tried to rebrand the neigh-borhood "SoBro," but the name hasn't stuck. The neighborhood's poor public schools surely haven't helped redevelopment efforts. Community School District 7, the public schools of the South Bronx operated by the New York City Department of Education, remains the sick man of the city's school system—the lowest-performing dis-trict in the five boroughs.[4] By the end of third grade, a mere 26 percent of South Bronx children read on grade level. That's the high-water mark. By sixth grade, it's 15 percent.

For decades, Mott Haven has been ground zero in America's

battles over the education given to the nation's poorest children and attempts to reform it. The author and activist Jonathan Kozol wrote a series of heart-wrenching books about the neighborhood's struggles with drugs, violence, and racism. In Kozol's vivid telling, public schools in the South Bronx are segregated and starved for resources, which explains their chronic failure stretching back over generations. Ironically, his books helped spur a generation of idealistic teachers and education reformers to flock to the charter schools that did not exist in the South Bronx when his best-known book, *Amazing Grace*,[5] was published in 1995. Kozol is a reliably strident critic of education reform efforts and charter schools, which he says are "far more segregated" than most other public schools, guaranteeing "a swift and vicious deepening of class and racial separation."[6]

Bronx 1 principal Elizabeth Vandlik is a former kindergarten teacher and Teach For America corps member, whose shoulder-length light brown hair and angular features give her a passing re-semblance to the actress Kyra Sedgwick. In one conversation, she mentioned that she had spent time doing construction work as a member of Local 1 in Chicago, where she grew up. It would be less surprising if she said she'd been a member of Navy SEAL Team Six and hunted down Osama bin Laden. With her taste for tailored skirts and pumps, Vandlik would blend in seamlessly as a partner at a Manhattan law firm or an investment bank. She doesn't look like someone you would find hanging drywall on a construction site. Or running a South Bronx elementary school.

Bronx 1 is a highly successful school in a neighborhood that hasn't had many, and Vandlik is a rising star at Success Academy. It is highly unlikely that Eva Moskowitz would allow an outside ob-server to make a year's worth of unstructured and unmonitored observations in one of her schools if she were less than confident that the school's principal was a strong representative of the network and someone whose work would stand up to close scrutiny. One teacher who has worked with Liz Vandlik for years says she is "by the book." It was meant as praise.

But the school year that's about to start will be a stiff challenge for Vandlik. She is surrounded by strangers. More than two-thirds of her staff is new—either in new roles at Bronx 1 or in their first year at Success Academy. Even as the school year opens, she is scrambling to fill holes. A first-grade lead teacher she had expected to return left without notice. A new kindergarten staffer named Matt Carnaghi, hired as an assistant teacher, has been pressed into emergency service as a classroom lead to fill another unanticipated vacancy. But Vandlik's first priority in the days before students arrive is the school's leadership. Her junior leaders, the assistant principals, or APs, who are responsible for directly managing and coaching the entire faculty, are each new to Bronx 1 and unknown quantities.

A week before school starts, Vandlik is feeling out her untested deputies while teachers busy themselves decorating their classrooms, putting children's names on behavior charts, hanging posters, and sorting books into classroom libraries. In the school leadership office adjacent to the third-grade wing, Vandlik prepares to lead her direct reports on a walk-through of classrooms. "We're going to start by going in, observing, then pop out of the room. 'What did you see?' 'What did you see?'" she says, pointing as she speaks to Kerrie Riley, Amy Young, and Nick Carton, the three assistant principals who, along with Kellie Grant, who oversees special education, and business operations manager Jennifer Fuoco, make up the school's administration. A fourth assistant principal, Noreen Cooke-Coleman, also new to her role, is starting the school year on maternity leave. Vandlik is in her fourth year as principal at Bronx 1; at age thirty-four, with eight years at Success Academy, she is the most senior member of the team. "I want to see that you're noticing the same things I'm noticing," she explains to nodding heads.

The exercise is only nominally about ensuring that rooms will be ready for children, who will start arriving next week. Vandlik's main purpose is to ensure that everyone in a position of authority at Bronx 1 sees things the same way she does. "We want as quickly as possible for me to be, like, 'Amy, go. What did you notice? What would you prioritize? What are you going to do?' And for all of us to say, 'Thumbs-up. We're all on the same page,'" she instructs. "Does that make sense? Sound right?" Vandlik seldom gives direct orders. Her instructions come wrapped in questions—an inquiry-based style of coaching that mirrors the way Success Academy teachers are trained to run their classrooms. She is running a school but at the same time leading a seminar for her team, none of whom have even a single day of administrative experience.

"What sorts of things can we learn about individuals or the team just from the health of their classroom?" she challenges her staff. "Name some things."

"Organization?" suggests Nick Carton. It comes out as a question. Perhaps hearing a lack of confidence in his voice, he repeats himself with more conviction. "Their level of organization." Carton will be responsible for overseeing second-grade teachers and "scholar talent," the term Success Academy uses for art, music, chess, and other "specials." He is new to school leadership, Success Academy, and New York City. This time last year he was starting his third year as a classroom teacher in Key Largo, Florida. Success Academy promotes school principals exclusively from within its ranks, but promising outsiders like Carton are occasionally brought in as junior leaders if they show "skill and will"—a strong belief in Success Academy's mission and approach, along with the ability to take feedback and grow quickly in their roles.

"Time management," adds Kerrie Riley, who is also in her first year in school leadership. Last year she was a third-grade teacher in the network's Crown Heights, Brooklyn, school, and one of eighty-five teachers from across the network to win a Success Academy Excellence Award for classroom teaching. She will be supervising Bronx 1's third- and fourth-grade teachers.

"Frazzledness," adds Amy Young, another newcomer, who was a dean of students at a different Success Academy campus last year; she will be overseeing kindergarten and first grade. Vandlik seizes on the word, affirming and adding on. "Their mental state. Their level of noticing," she elaborates. "Is everything in the room crooked?" If teachers aren't attentive to those small details, they won't notice when a student fails to put his name on his paper, the strategies kids use to solve a math problem, or whether a scholar is daydreaming or off task. Children at Success Academy are invariably referred to as "scholars"—not children, students, or "boys and girls"—even when teachers are speaking among themselves with no children present. She alerts her team to look for evidence that shows teachers are focused on systems and routines. Vandlik also instructs her APs to look for clues that suggest strong or weak team dynamics. "Have grade-level teams come together with a plan?" she asks, "Or do they feel random and not united?"

Vandlik calls this exercise "lensing," and it's her first priority in the days before the school year starts. This focus on consistency of vision and execution is right out of the Success Academy playbook. There are dozens of Success Academy elementary schools, but there is one model for all of them. The curriculum, pedagogy, schedule, furniture, and hallway and classroom décor are virtually identical in each. So are the results. Based on standardized test scores, there is—so far—no such thing as an observably "weak" Success Academy school. No other charter school network in the nation of its size can make a similar claim.

"So again, 'What do you notice? What do you prioritize?'" Vandlik reiterates. "Fix your face. Say why you're there," she continues as the group moves toward the kindergarten wing. "This is also going to get them used to seeing us all move around like this, in and out of their space." Business operations manager Jennifer Fuoco reminds the junior leaders, "Make sure you have something good to say to them, because they're working hard."

The first stop is Carolyn Syskowski's kindergarten classroom. No one needs to fix their face and say why they're here, since the classroom is empty. She is a Success veteran whose room serves as a "lab site" where new teachers come to observe, and it already looks ready to receive children. Tables and chairs are neatly arranged and posters hung; the library is stocked with a collection of picture books artfully arranged within easy reach of four- and five-year-olds' hands. Syskowski, the only returning lead kindergarten teacher, is off helping her new grade-level teammates set up their rooms. "This is a great room to bring people into," Vandlik says to her team. "Do you guys feel like you have a sense now of what you would actually want to point out to people instead of just, 'Come into this room—it's so pretty'?"

Syskowski walks in. I recognize her from a brief encounter this morning. I was sitting alone in the hallway in a child-size chair, scribbling in my notebook, when she walked up to me before most of the staff had arrived. "Who are you?" she asked. She smiled and quickly added, "I didn't ask if I could help you because you don't look like you need help." Another staffer, whom I now recognize as Fuoco, breezed by and complimented Syskowski for following safety protocol. "Know who's in your building!" she called without breaking stride as she cruised down the hall toward the main office.

Vandlik lets slip that Syskowski, who is in her fifth year at Bronx 1, has expressed interest in rising to the leadership ranks. "We could start that today," Vandlik says, suggesting to Young that she arrange Syskowski's schedule so she's not always teaching at the same time as the rest of her team, giving her colleagues the opportunity to observe her and for her to coach them. "Let's make matches," she adds as the walk-through continues. "We're going to see a room where something is not going well. We're going to see a room where that's done at a really high level. Part of your follow-up should be, 'This person's doing it better than you. Go and see what they did.'"

———

Next Vandlik calls a meeting with science teachers and scholar talent—the art, dance, chess, and physical education teachers at Bronx 1—to discuss student discipline. Success Academy uses an identical color-coded "stoplight" behavior-management system in all its schools. At the start of each day, every scholar is "on green." If a student is off task, misbehaving, or not following instructions, teachers give them multiple reminders, redirections, or corrections before changing their color to "yellow" on a plastic pocket chart. If a child continues to misbehave, they may end up "on red." Misbehavior is dealt with swiftly, with consequences that run the gamut from an in-classroom time-out lasting several minutes, to being sent to another classroom for a cooldown, to a teacher calling a parent in the moment, either to intervene with the child over the phone or to arrange to meet at the end of the school day.

This year Vandlik wants the behavior-management system and the student's "color" to travel with the child throughout the building, including to specials and science class. "The last couple of years you guys did your own thing in your own room," Vandlik begins after the group assembles in the art room. "You know that one of our big concerns is the level of inconsistency across the building, right?" Vandlik frequently ends sentences with a rhetorical "right?" It's a habit she developed as a kindergarten teacher and while "checking for understanding" among her students. "We want it to travel with the child throughout the whole day. From science to the homeroom to scholar talent, back again. So that's what we're going to do," she says. It's a decision, not a discussion. "I see people processing," she pauses. "Obviously we wouldn't make this decision if we didn't think it was good for children and good for adults. So what's good about this? Then we'll talk about what's hard about it."

It's an awkward moment for the dozen teachers assembled. They are young, mostly new, and eager to be perceived as team players, but they could be disadvantaged by the new system, which might force them to play bad cop if a child comes into their room with previous infractions. A single trivial transgression could put a child "on red," triggering a mandatory parent meeting. Scholar talent teachers spend far less time with students than their homeroom teachers do, sometimes seeing children as little as once a week; it's in their self-interest to start every class with a clean slate. Amanda Sommi, a first-year assistant science teacher, breaks the uneasy silence and suggests that if behavior norms are building-wide, students don't have to keep track of multiple teachers' expectations.

"They don't get the idea there are some places where they can get away with more things, and some that are more strict," sports teacher Justin Wingard chimes in. Vandlik reinforces Wingard's comment. "It makes me think of parents," she notes. "Like, 'Mom said no, so I'm going to Dad.'"

Nick Carton, who supervises this group of teachers, points out that a single set of expectations makes it less likely that parents with kids in different grades will get mixed messages about Success Academy's school culture: an offense that brings detention in one class shouldn't be permissible in another. In his old school, he observes, "everyone had different behavior-management plans. They would try to play us off each other." His description reflects standard practice and outcome in most US elementary schools. Novice teachers are typically encouraged to collaborate with students in making classroom rules, on the theory that children will be more invested in rules they helped write. In practice, it can lead to chaos when behavior that one teacher condones or ignores is deemed unacceptable by another. Children quickly develop a keen sense about teachers, much like base runners in baseball know which outfielders have weak throwing arms. They know what they can get away with in one teacher's class, and which ones "don't play."

Amy Young has been growing visibly irritated as the teachers discuss the advantages and disadvantages of having the student's behavior color follow the child; she seems eager to weigh in. "If a scholar is getting his or her fifth correction of the day in your room, you should be bothered, even if they came in with four," she says. "It's not, 'Well, you had four there and one here.'" Teachers, she insists, need to lift their own expectations for student behavior. One of two African American women on the school leadership team, Young, who has a serious mien, suggests that allowing children to evade the consequences of "bad decisions" by leaving one classroom for another doesn't do them any favors. "It's a disservice to teach our children that they can restart. Because that's not real life," she says. "Especially the population we serve. They're not coming from money. They're not coming from things that can save them. We have to teach them to save themselves."

———

In the hallway just outside the art room, chess teacher Matthew Morales lines up a dozen teachers, who are pretending to be students, to demonstrate the proper way to escort children through the halls. He is "modeling," a widespread training technique where teachers role-play how to perform a routine. "We're going to go downstairs silently, safely, and efficiently," he instructs his colleagues. "Our voices are off and our hands at our sides. Stop at number three," he orders, referring to a series of numbers permanently affixed to the floor in the hallway—another standard feature in every Success elementary school, along with "sight words" like "my," "up," and "they." Few opportunities for reading and counting are missed, even when children are on their way to lunch or the bathroom. "Line leaders go through the double doors and find a safe stopping spot," he continues, then adds, momentarily breaking out of character, "That's not what I would normally say to kids, but I don't have any spots on the floor out there yet." His aside is purposeful: directions should be clear and precise, not subject to interpretation.

"When you're leading a class, you want to be in position so that you can see the scholars that are walking as well as the scholars that are still in the classroom," Morales explains to the new teachers. "If you walk ahead at the beginning of the line, you won't see the scholars that are still in the classroom. That's when things go bad."

The sight of adults walking in two straight lines like small children is faintly ridiculous. Actual Bronx 1 students would laugh themselves silly at the sight. But elementary school teachers quickly get used to role-playing in training settings and professional development. The anxious first-year teachers, doubtlessly terrified that the instructions they give will be ignored or mocked, are determined to anticipate every conceivable stumbling block before they have to move real live students through hallways, upstairs to science, or downstairs to lunch and recess. They pepper Morales with questions: Where do you stand on the stairs? Can you fit more than one class in that stairwell? Morales patiently answers each one.

Vandlik, who has been watching the demonstration, thanks Morales and then asks everyone, even the rawest newbies who have yet to lay eyes on an actual student, to give feedback. "What did he do well that he should keep doing?" One teacher comments on the clarity of his directions. Another notes that he speaks with authority and purpose. "It's funny. The kids are way too scared to act up with Mr. Morales," Albert Barabas, a veteran fourth-grade teacher, says with a mischievous grin. "And the teachers are way too scared to act up with Mr. Morales."

"I wasn't scared!" says Syskowski, hands on her hips in mock indignation.

"Did he sound mean?" Vandlik asks. Everyone agrees he didn't. "Mean doesn't make kids listen," says Morales, who radiates competence and calm. If you turned the wrong way on 149th Street, Morales is the guy you'd instinctively ask for directions. But it's more likely he'd notice you first and ask if you needed help. "I talk to children the same way I talk to adults. I don't talk to them like they're little babies," he coaches. With six years in the building, he has long-running relationships with families who have had multiple children at Success Academy. "Same expectations for all parts of the day, whether you're walking down to recess or to dance and specials," he says, echoing the conversation from the behavior-management meeting. "Parents appreciate when you talk to their child with respect."

His new colleagues will inevitably make mistakes, especially during transitions. Morales encourages them to be honest. "If you make a mistake, own it. Say, 'I'm sorry. That was a mistake. We're gonna make sure tomorrow we do that better. I'm gonna give you more clear directions.' They respect you more that way." The newcomers soak in the advice, nodding and jotting notes.

"There was a reason for everything Mr. Morales was doing,"

Vandlik tells her teachers. "It's purposeful. When you practice with your groups, and you should run your routes, you need to figure out your positioning. Where are you going to stand at every moment to see every single kid? If you see them and they know that you see them all the time, you've cut out 99 percent of your problems."

Watching Morales drill his new colleagues, I'm reminded of my first day as a student teacher at PS 18, just up the street. If these new teachers are anything like I was, they are probably petrified their students will ignore them, refuse to comply, or ask disdainfully, "Are you a real teacher?" I could have used a Matthew Morales. I wasn't trained with anything like this level of specificity or attention to detail. It would not have occurred to anyone to role-play and practice transitioning from place to place. My own classroom management practice improved dramatically when I happened upon a copy of *The Essential 55*, a collection of recommended rules, strategies, and tips penned by a charismatic North Carolina teacher named Ron Clark, whose approach was condemned as behavioristic and authoritarian, much as Success Academy is now, even as grateful teachers made the book a bestseller. Oprah Winfrey hosted Clark on her show in 2001 and wrote him a check for $365,000 when he opened his own school a few years later. If I hadn't discovered his book toward the middle of my first year of teaching, I might not have made it to a second year.

"When I say, 'Go,' we're going to turn our lines and stop at the double doors following the line leaders," Morales commands, back in character and in control. "Remember, we are silent at all times and our hands stay at our sides. Eyes forward.

"Go."

———

The Thursday before the school year begins, Vandlik, Nick Carton, and Kellie Grant meet with second-grade teacher Elena Ortiz in her classroom, named "Hunter College," to hammer out a behavior plan for Adama, a troubled and challenging student slated to be in her class. No issue is more volatile than student discipline for Success

Academy and Eva Moskowitz, who has repeatedly found herself in the crosshairs over charges that her schools are little more than a sorting mechanism, luring away the best and brightest students from neighborhood schools while counseling out low achievers and those with disabilities and behavior problems. In 2016, Success Academy was left reeling when *New York Times* reporter Kate Taylor posted a surreptitiously recorded video of a teacher verbally berating a first-grade child and exiling her to a "calm-down chair" away from the rest of her classmates.[7] The video came on the heels of another damning story that seemed to provide a smoking gun to Moskowitz's enemies: Taylor revealed the existence of a principal's "Got to Go" list naming sixteen students to be pushed out of his school in Fort Greene, Brooklyn.[8] Success Academy has "long been dogged by accusations that its remarkable accomplishments are due, in part, to a practice of weeding out weak or difficult students," Taylor wrote. "The network has always denied it. But documents obtained by *The New York Times* and interviews with 10 current and former Success employees at five schools suggest that some administrators in the network have singled out children they would like to see leave."

The meeting in Ortiz's classroom is not aimed at figuring out how to marginalize or get rid of Adama, however, but how to bring the boy in for a landing. "We are trying to win him over to our side. He's having a very negative experience of school. We need to change it over to a very positive experience and something he likes," Vandlik tells Ortiz, who listens intently as the principal, Carton, and Grant coach her on an extensive behavior plan. "The point of this is you are giving him positive reinforcement for every tiny little wonderful thing that he does," Vandlik tells Ortiz. "You ask him to come to the rug? Star. He sits in Magic Five? Star," she says, referring to Success Academy's expectation that children should sit on the classroom rug during instructional time with legs crossed and hands folded, listening and silently tracking the speaker. "If he gets ten stars in the first five minutes of the day, that actually would be a success."

The meeting turns into an ad hoc seminar on elementary school behavior management. Vandlik cautions Ortiz not to bribe the boy to behave himself. "You're like, 'Class, fold your hands. Adama, you folded your hands. Star!' It's not 'If you fold your hands, I'll give you a star.'" The idea is to recognize and praise children's positive behavior, not to bargain with them. The overarching goal is to keep the child from being removed from the classroom "for safety reasons, which was happening so much last year," Vandlik explains. "We're going to do whatever we need to fix that problem, and when he's in a better place, then move on to a new goal."

Success Academy is unabashedly behavioristic, and every tool in the teachers' bags of tricks finds its way onto the table now, including "verbal redirection," or interrupting misbehavior by pointing the child back to the lesson or desired behavior, and "planned ignoring" of undesirable actions combined with "positive praise" of children who are doing the right thing to signal the kind of behavior the teacher expects to see. Ortiz worked with Adama in first grade and notes that he loves being a classroom helper, so Vandlik encourages her to use a technique called "antiseptic bouncing"—sending him off on a classroom errand when she senses a meltdown coming. "When you start to see him going in whatever direction, you might say, 'Adama, Ms. Vandlik desperately needs this red marker.'" They decide to keep a color-coded envelope on hand for when there's trouble brewing and Adama needs to "bounce." "If that envelope comes to us, we'll know why," Vandlik explains.

Dealing with chronic disruptive behavior is a challenge for any teacher. It will be particularly difficult for Ortiz, who is relatively inexperienced but nonetheless a lead teacher in one of Bronx 1's three second-grade classrooms. Virtually the entire second-grade team is new to the school, with the exception of returning lead teacher Laura Belkin, a five-year Success Academy veteran and second-career teacher who used to work for a New York auction house. In fact, more than two-thirds of the classroom teachers at Bronx 1 are either new to Success or new to their roles, which is surprising given its status as one of Success Academy's most successful schools and one of the highest-ranked in the entire state.

Second grade is a particularly critical year for disadvantaged children, the last chance to make it to the academic starting line. Three out of four struggling third-grade readers are still struggling in ninth grade,[9] and one in six children who are not reading proficiently in third grade do not graduate from high school on time—a rate four times greater than that for proficient readers.[10] It's also a critical year for those who run schools, as second grade is the last year before federally mandated state testing begins—and the public scrutiny that comes with it. This raises the stakes precipitously for Ortiz, Adama and his classmates, Bronx 1, and Success Academy. A disruptive student can have a deleterious impact on an entire class, placing at risk the academic progress and test scores of dozens of children.

"Are you worried about what the rest of your kids will think?" Vandlik asks Ortiz, who nods. "Do I explain this to my children when they're out of the room?" she asks. "I don't want my kids to see him as a problem." Vandlik compliments Ortiz for her "nice perspective" and suggests it might not be necessary to address it at all. "Kids are smart," she says. "Usually it's the adults who are worried about fairness." As the meeting winds down, Vandlik cautions Ortiz that the relationship with Adama's parents became contentious last year and that his parents "are desperate for him to be successful here." I draw several stars alongside Adama's name in my notebook, a reminder to keep an eye out for him when school starts the following week and to monitor his progress—and the success or failure of Ortiz, Vandlik, and the others to bring this child, whom I've not yet laid eyes on, into the fold. "Right now, he's probably our highest priority for our young kids," Vandlik tells Ortiz.

"I got this," says Ortiz, and quickly corrects herself. "Not 'I got this,' but I totally get what you guys are saying and I'm totally on board."

—

Early Monday morning, Elena Ortiz's room crackles with nervous energy and the excited buzz of dozens of twentysomething teachers.

Her classroom is a large, centrally located space across the hall from the main office at Bronx 1, and the default meeting room for team "huddles," professional development sessions, and any other whole-staff gatherings. When the faculty meets as a group at Bronx 1, the location is specified only if it's not in this room.

A few minutes after 7:00 a.m., Liz Vandlik raises her hand over her head, a universal signal for silence and attention throughout Success Academy, taught to students and followed even when no children are present. The room falls silent. When Vandlik offers a cheerful "Good morning," the staff answers back in unison, at more than double her volume. Vandlik goes wide-eyed. "Good energy for 7:05 in the morning! That's great, that's what we're going to need to bring it today. So . . ." she pauses and inhales audibly. "Happy first day of school, everyone." The room breaks into claps, nervous laughter, and a smattering of *woo-hoo*s.

Vandlik is not prone to locker room–style motivational speeches, but she has a sense of the moment and what it means for her young and largely inexperienced staff. "It's a big day, right? Two weeks ago, we came together and talked about our dual mission and why we care so much about running our school and doing that work here in this neighborhood. And today's the day when we open the doors and really make it happen. So, as tiring as today will be, I want us to really keep in mind why we're all here and why we're all doing this." When the doors open a few minutes from now, she says, they will be "opening the door to opportunity" for 475 South Bronx kids and their families.

In most elementary schools, the first day's focus would be on icebreakers, writing and reviewing classroom rules, practicing classroom-management routines, and assorted getting-to-know-you activities aimed at smoothing the transition, enabling students and teachers alike to get their school heads back on. At Success Academy, it's shock and awe. The high expectations begin even before the students walk in the door. Vandlik reminds her staff to keep their "excellence-training deliverables" top of mind. Launching into a pop quiz, she calls on Mandisa Brudey, a new lead first-grade teacher, to remind the staff "what excellence training is about." Brudey answers that it's about the adults, not the children. Vandlik nods and adds, "We're not here to train and practice and turn kids into robots. We're training and practicing so that we get better, right? If we want an excellent school, if we want to change things and get better and better, we're the ones who need to change to get better and better."

To underscore the point, Vandlik announces that she and the leadership team will be coming into every classroom this morning looking for the "behavior-management deliverables." At any given time, from the first moments of the school year, 95 percent of students are expected to be observably on task and engaged in the lesson or activity in the classroom. "I don't expect that the kids are going to be perfect," Vandlik explains. "But do I expect that you're going to notice and address it 100 percent of the time? Absolutely. And in doing so, you'll get 95 percent of your kids on task and engaged."

The principal peppers the teachers with questions about classroom management and "outlier scholars," those children with behavioral problems. They are to be identified quickly; teachers should be "managing up," alerting school leadership about such children immediately. "What's the deliverable there?" she asks Albert Barabas, who responds that 85 percent of the time, teachers should be able to de-escalate challenging behavior in the classroom on their own. "Not all the time," Vandlik elaborates, "but as often as possible." Next comes the "parent-investment deliverable" and "school culture goals" which are unusually precise: 97 percent of students present, 96 percent on time, 97 percent in uniform, 97 percent of homework completed, and 96 percent of reading logs completed. Vandlik reminds the teachers to collect summer homework and reading logs today "so that we can start holding our families accountable from the very first second." She reminds her staff of the "three pillars" of Success Academy's vision: "We cannot go wrong if we ask ourselves some questions around rigor, joy, and community," she says. "As we're pressing to meet that excellence bar, are we doing it in such a way that we're creating an environment that kids want to be in and that we feel good about being in?" She wraps up by reminding her staff to be ready to support one another. For struggling teachers, that means "asking for help in a way that's going to make you better as a grown-up." The kids are not the issue. "The kids are the wonderful, beautiful work that we do. We're the ones who need to grow and change."

She glances at the clock. The doors will open at 7:30 a.m. All staff must be in position by 7:25. Vandlik fires off last-minute reminders. "Don't forget to take attendance," she reminds them. "Don't forget to make phone calls." Every morning, teachers call the parents of students who aren't in school and whose absences weren't excused in advance. Amy Young and Kerrie Riley will be on duty on the second floor while children eat breakfast in their classrooms. Vandlik will be at the front door greeting children and parents with Jen Fuoco. Nick Carton draws uniform duty. Kids who aren't in uniform will be turned away. "We're starting with the accountability piece strong from the first moment," Vandlik explains. "We wouldn't feel good about doing it if our communication hadn't been so very, very, very clear about it. Everybody knows what's expected." If parents let the school know in advance they were having trouble getting uniforms or medical forms filled in, their children will be admitted. Otherwise, no excuses. "I just want you to be prepared for that," she cautions. It's possible a teacher might call a parent looking for their child, only to hear, "Ms. Fuoco or Ms. Vandlik told us we could not come in."

She makes sure everyone has a copy of their "critical path," a document with a minute-by-minute plan for the day. "You have your name tags? You have your charged cell phone? You have your keys?"

Fifteen minutes. She asks sports teacher Justin Wingard to "bring it in." A former basketball player who played professionally in Europe and the NBA's developmental G League, Wingard is a mountain of a man, and at least a head taller than everyone else in the room. The entire Bronx 1 staff crams in on a rug designed to hold thirty small children, hands raised and leaning into and on one another. "On three, we got 'Game time!'" Wingard calls. "One, two, three."

"Game time!" cheers the staff, who now take up their positions in hallways, stairwells, and classroom thresholds. As they head downstairs to the cafeteria, the kindergarten teachers exchange nervous smiles and words of encouragement.

"Ready?"

"As ready as I'm going to be."

"You look so bright and colorful and happy!"

Katie Kolenda, a special education teacher, and Carson Rocke-feller, a science teacher, grew up together in a small town in upstate New York. They peer through the bottom-hinged casement windows onto the South Bronx sidewalk that's a long way from home and start bantering with the kids and parents a few feet below. Vandlik joins them at the window and calls out to one, "Najee, where are your glasses?" Laura Belkin spots one of her former students and calls out, "There's Leanni, right on time!" Vandlik tells Belkin to be sure to congratulate the child's mom for her on-time arrival, which has been a struggle in the past. Vandlik directs Rockefeller to make himself a "human stanchion" at the top of the stairs, directing the flow of little bodies into the cafeteria. "You're going to have the best line of sight, and you're the most experienced person here." Her heels clack down the steps that lead down from the cafeteria to the double metal doors that open out onto Morris Avenue. She and Fuoco bang loudly to alert anyone who might be leaning against the door on the other side and then push on the bar. Harsh midsummer-morning light floods the stairwell, setting her Success Academy–orange dress ablaze. "Good morning!" Vandlik calls out cheerfully. "Nice to see you all! Happy first day of school!" Game time.

For the next twenty minutes, Vandlik is glued to her spot on the sidewalk by the cafeteria door, Bronx 1's de facto main entrance. She pops up and down like a catcher between pitches, alternately greeting students at their eye level and rising to shake parents' hands, while Fuoco answers parent questions—"Half day today!" and "Full days for kindergarten starting next week!"

"Good morning, Darren! C'mon in, Justin!" Vandlik discreetly steals a glance at the kids' name tags to greet the few, mostly kindergarteners, she doesn't already know, occasionally stumbling over an unfamiliar name. "Ramatoulaye? Can you say it for me? Good morning, Ramatoulaye, I'm Ms. Vandlik. Can you say 'Ms. Vandlik'?" Boys take off their hats as they approach the front of the line. Vandlik asks for eye contact and a greeting from those who don't reflexively offer one. A little boy named Franklin is very shy and on the verge of tears. "Good morning, Hosanatou. Good morning, Nyasia. C'mon in, Josiah. Yes, I remember your name! Do you remember mine?"

A pair of staffers from the Success Academy network office pull children from the line to take their pictures holding a sign featuring the hashtag #PathToPossible to post on social media. A massive New York City Department of Sanitation truck, the driver unconcerned with the throng clustered on the sidewalk, chooses this moment to lumber up noisily to a dumpster a few feet behind Vandlik in her catcher's squat. "Not a good look when you're bringing your kids to school," one dad mutters, shaking his head. Not a good smell either.

A mom with a neck tattoo of Mickey Mouse, which matches the one on her red T-shirt, is incredulous that her child has been turned away for wearing the wrong color socks. "I got an infraction," she huffs. Vandlik explains in a friendly but firm tone, "We're serious about this uniform stuff. So we have to be extra serious on day one." Another parent is unhappy that her child's shoes have been judged improper. "It's always something," she mutters. "I just bought her those shoes!"

In the cafeteria, one tiny scholar is having a full-on meltdown, loudly crying, "I wanna go home!" and resisting Kolenda's efforts to calm him down. Ms. Brudey takes charge of the boy, named José, and the situation. "After the first day, guess who's the first person you're going to see?" she asks the crying child. "Mama!" she answers her own question. "You want to call her? Let's go upstairs and call her." They disappear into the lobby and up the stairs. José never looks back.

—

In the kindergarten wing, the children have not yet finished breakfast, but Carolyn Syskowski has already put them to work, copying the numbers one through ten onto sheets of paper. Her classroom, in the farthest corner of the school, adjacent to Vandlik's office, is crowded with bodies large and small. First and second graders won't start school until Wednesday, so the periphery of Syskowski's classroom is lined with teachers whose students are not yet here, observing and helping out. Among the education shibboleths Eva Moskowitz dismisses is the benefit of small class sizes, which she insists matters less than teacher quality.

Tight classroom management allows teachers, once trained, to be more effective with larger classes, she argues, and for money to be spent elsewhere, from technology to support staff to relieve teachers of paperwork and other non-instructional tasks. "I don't think it is as important as art and music and sports and science five days a week and paying teachers more," Moskowitz says. Elementary school classrooms with thirty or more children are standard.

Students at Success spend very little time in front of screens until middle school, but every classroom is equipped with a digital "smartboard" and a document projector to display student work. While the kids work, a projected digital clock counts down to zero, triggering the sound of a ringing bell like on an old-fashioned windup alarm clock. "When you hear that bell, I want you to get in 'One, Get Ready'!" Syskowski begins. The children, who came to school for a few hours last week for a dress rehearsal, have already learned that "One, Get Ready" means sitting upright with their hands folded and their eyes on the teacher, waiting for instruction. Next comes "Two, Stand Up," followed by a third order to transition to whatever activity the teacher has planned.

Syskowski is "narrating the room," a signal feature of classroom management at Success Academy and similar schools: play-by-play, praising the behaviors she wants to see so that children will take the hint and follow suit. Her voice is big, and her tone and facial expressions theatrical. "Enrique put his hands locked on the table. Aleister put his hands locked on the table. Israel has his hands . . . locked! *On! The! Table!*" Syskowski exults, responding to each small act of compliance as if she were opening presents on Christmas morning. "Now, since your hands are locked and on the table, I should see *noooo* pencils in your hands. Let me check!" She adopts an exaggerated posture of searching, bent over at the waist with one hand across her forehead, scanning thirty faces arrayed before her. They stare back, cartoonishly erect, wide-eyed, and hyperattentive. "I don't see any pencils here! Whoa!" she gasps. "One hundred percent of you—that means *all* of you—don't have a pencil in your hand! I'm going to put one cube in the one-hundred-percent jar. And we'll talk more about that, because we get to have parties in school when the *whooooole* team works together!

"Now, when I say 'Go,' put your pencil in your seat sack. Raise your hand if you think you can do it!" Syskowski challenges. Every tiny hand rockets up, and the children grin, perhaps surprised at how easy school is turning out to be. "I notice that everyone at Fox in Socks put their pencils away and has their hands locked. I'm going to give you a table point! That means your team is working for a special snack! Fox in Socks, you're in the lead right now. Nice work!" In every Success Academy elementary school classroom, children have their own desks and seats, but they are grouped in pods christened with a name that reflects a theme chosen by the teachers, one of the few classroom features left to their discretion. Teachers use animals, sports teams, hometown landmarks, or mascots. Syskowski names her tables after Dr. Seuss books, and her classroom after the branch of City College where she earned her degree in elementary education and English language arts in 2010. "OK, Hunter College, now when I say 'Go,' you're going to put your paper in the middle of the table and lock your hands," she instructs. "Let's see which table gets a table point!" She pauses to ensure all eyes are on her.

"Go!"

A flurry of tiny hands push their papers to the center of their tables and race to resume their erect posture. "William put his paper in the middle of the table! Enrique put his paper in the middle." An audible gasp: "Hop on Pop, one hundred percent! Nice job, Aleister, helping out your team! Cat in the Hat, one hundred percent! Jocelyn, very focused; you go, girl! Jerome, kiss that brain! Nice work!" Syskowski prepares to transition her scholars to the rug, the central feature of every Success Academy elementary school classroom. "This is the place where we have a lot of fun and do a lot of learning!" she explains. Syskowski and her assistant teacher, Olivia Hanania, put every child's name on a piece of tape on one of the thirty large dots on the rug before last week's dress rehearsal. Syskowski already knows every child's name. "We're going to find our *own* rug spot and sit in Magic Five, like we did on Tuesday!"

With a finger over her lips, she instructs, "When I say 'One,' you're going to 'One, Get Ready.'" She pauses and smiles to create anticipation. "One!" she calls out. "Your hands are locked. Look at Adrian! Look at Bintu! Your teammates will always help you. Angelina, your eyes are on me the *whole* time." The child, a chubby-cheeked girl with a halo of dark hair, flashes an enormous grin at being singled out for positive attention. "Now, Precious, when I say 'Two,' you're going to stand up, with two hands you *sliiiiide* in your chair. Then hands are at your side." Syskowski interrupts herself. "I don't see everyone tracking me. Are you ready?"

"Tracking" is one of the first words that children learn at Success and similar charter schools. It means keeping your eyes on the person who is speaking, whether it's the teacher, another adult, or a classmate. Teaching children to track spread widely from the high-profile urban charter school network KIPP, which pioneered the technique in 1990s, teaching its students to SLANT: sit up, listen, ask questions, nod, and track the speaker. KIPP cofounder David Levin argued that Americans from more privileged backgrounds slant reflexively and use it to their advantage to take in information in school and elsewhere. Less-privileged children, he claimed, must be taught to do it. For every adherent convinced that tracking results in enhanced student attention, there is a critic who complains that aggressive policing of their behavior teaches children merely to be compliant and subservient. Some have even insisted it's a racist echo of colonial school systems and inappropriate.[11]

"William's eyes are on me. Joshua's eyes are on me," Syskowski continues. One child is looking all around the room and fidgeting in his seat. "Aleister, first warning. Keep your eyes here!" she corrects. Once every eye is on her, Syskowski calls out, "Two, Stand Up!" The kids comply, but the effect is noisy, not the crisp and brisk response she wants. She orders the class to sit down and get back into 'One, Get Ready' position. "During the transition, we want to get to the rug very quickly. We have a lot of fun things to do! But we cannot speak when we're going to transition. Deal?" No one replies. "Deal?" she asks a second time, louder. A smattering of voices say, "Deal."

"*Deal?!*" The kids get the message and yell back, "Deal!" Syskowski raises her arms and exults, "Wooooo!" A new or less confident teacher would likely be terrified to rev up the children like this, especially on the first day of school. Carolyn Syskowski is fearless.

"Let's try it again *suuuuuuper* silently!" she encourages. She places stickers on the hands and foreheads of her smiling, giggling kids as she circulates among them. "When I tap your shoulder, you're going to go to your rug spot and sit in Magic Five."

Every child she touches marches to the rug with the most serious face they can muster. "Bintu's going to her rug dot. Nadia's going to her rug dot." Syskowski continues her nonstop play-by-play. "Daniela . . . Precious . . . Christian . . . Alexander, right next to him, lovey. Adrian, you're right up front. Daniel, I know you weren't in dress rehearsal, but I want you to notice how Israel is sitting. See how his legs are crossed? Cross your legs." She points to his spot, a colored dot bordered by a black line, about eighteen inches square. "You stay in your body box, and you're safe." Syskowski threads between her little scholars and sits in the chair facing them, still scanning the room, wordlessly correcting placement and posture with winks, thumbs-ups, and body language. "Jerome, you're right here next to me, love bug," she motions, settling down one antsy boy.

It's taken some time, but finally the children are settled in place and attentive. Syskowski introduces Carson Rockefeller, who leads the class in a game designed to teach tracking and active listening. He tosses a ball to a child, who stands up and says her name and favorite food. Rockefeller asks a second child to repeat what she just said. Next, a first-grade teacher, Shanna Lewis, leads the children in a song to the tune of "Frère Jacques." She sings a line, and Syskowski's scholars echo her, call-and-response style.

> *Eyes are watching! (Eyes are watching!)*
> *Ears are listening! (Ears are listening!)*
> *Legs are crossed! (Legs are crossed!)*
> *Hands are still! (Hands are still!)*
> *[whispers] Mouth is very silent. (Mouth is very silent.)*
> *You should really try it. (You should really try it.)*
> *Magic Five. (Magic Five.)*

While Rockefeller and Lewis take the lead, Syskowski crawls among the children, monitoring and "noticing," quietly praising positive behaviors and putting more stickers on their heads and hands. She is also making mental notes about potential outlier scholars. One boy is noticeably out of sync. He's not disruptive, but he often doesn't do what the other children are doing. Another is distracted and consistently off task. A third rolls on the rug during a clapping game. Brudey takes him by the hand and quietly leads him outside, where Matthew Morales is once again practicing hallway routines, but this time with the kindergarteners in teacher Gisela Skinner's class. "Eyes on me," he instructs in his measured voice and then waits. "Line leaders, it's very important that you follow my directions, because everyone else is following you. You're going to walk at zero noise with your hands at your side. And you're going to stop under the clock." Another pause. "OK, show me." The children march forward looking resolute. "Audrey has hands glued to her side. Sekou has hands glued to his side. Fatimata has hands glued to her side." The children stop, as instructed, at the wall clock. Morales never changes his facial expression or his tone of voice. "For your first time, that was pretty good," he comments. True to his word while training his colleagues the other day, he never lapses into the up-speak so common to teachers of elementary-age children, the rising inflection that makes even simple sentences sound like questions. "But I think you're capable of doing this much better." They turn around to try it again.

In the fourth-grade wing, the tone is more grown-up. Constance Smith and Kerri Lynch, co-teachers in "Fordham-NYU," an integrated co-teaching, or ICT, classroom, which combines general and special education students in the same room with two teachers, are coaching their students on how to conduct a classroom conversation. "You need to be louder, and you need to say you can't hear. Otherwise 'active listening' goes out the window," Lynch is explaining. In the lower grades, scholars are taught to use hand signals to indicate when they cannot hear a classmate. Lynch and Smith want their students to simply ask their friends to speak up if they cannot hear them. Vandlik, who entered the room unnoticed a few moments ago, begins to speak, and thirty heads turn in her direction. "I like how your eyes came right to me when I started speaking," the principal says. Lynch seizes the moment. "See the natural adult scan?"

"You see me just looking at you to make sure I have everyone's attention?" says Vandlik, reinforcing the conversational norms Lynch and Smith are teaching. "As adults, do you think we sit around in our meetings and we're going like this to each other?" she asks, waving her hand next to her ear. "No. What do we say if I can't hear Ms. Smith or Ms. Lynch? 'Ms. Lynch, could you speak up? I can't hear you.' So, if you're going to do that as adults and in college, should we start doing that now?" she asks. Most of the fourth graders nod their heads; some take the hint and answer out loud, "Yes," experimenting with their newly conferred status as young adults with independent voices. "Great!" Vandlik says and smiles. She turns to leave, her team of junior leaders attached to her like remoras as they head off.

While teachers practice routines and take the measure of their new scholars, Vandlik and her assistant principals visit classrooms, as promised, to monitor the day's teaching deliverables. As they enter first-year teacher Steven Madan's third-grade classroom, named for Northern Arizona University, the smartboard countdown clock reaches zero and rings, and he prepares to transition his students to the rug. "Scholars, show Mr. Madan that we can get one hundred percent," he begins, referring to himself in the third person, as teachers have done since time immemorial. "One, get ready. Hands are locked, backs are straight, eyes are on me," he narrates in a soft but firm voice. Vandlik sidles up and whispers something into his ear. He nods and issues a warning to one distracted student. They do it again—"One, get ready"—and this time he gets 100 percent.

Madan assigns his third graders "carpet partners" for sharing ideas on the rug when they do a "turn and talk," another standard technique at Success Academy. Instead of calling on a single student to answer a question, teachers have students turn and talk to a neighbor, creating the opportunity for everyone to participate. Next, he might "cold-call" one child at random to summarize the conversation. This is meant to keep the entire class fully engaged and on their toes. "The best learning we get in the classroom comes from other scholars, because we learn from each other," Madan tells his students, a notion that Success drills into teachers during the network's summer Teacher School, or T School. The feedback new staffers hear most often is "too much teacher talk." The standard remedy is to "put the lift on the scholars": Don't do the work for the kids. Don't be afraid to let them struggle. That's how they learn.

Vandlik leads her team back into the hallway to compare notes. "What did you guys see?" she asks. Amy Young critiques Madan's low voice volume when he called kids to the rug; Nick Carton points out his lack of clear directions for handling papers when students sat down. Vandlik raises her hand. "We're going right to teacher moves. Just to train our brains, let's look at what student outcomes he was getting. Our goal was ninety-five percent on task." Carton looks at his notes, "Twenty out of twenty-one," he says. "Nineteen," Vandlik replies, without looking at hers. "What concerned us?" she asks.

"The kids weren't sure what to do."

"I also saw kids who were compliant but checked out."

"Are the adults clear on the purpose? Are they sharing the 'why' in the classrooms?" Vandlik asks, instructing, coaching, *lensing*. "When I whispered to him, I told him, 'Reset your expectations.' Jaden immediately got a warning. Unlike some of his colleagues, when he knows what he's looking for, he's not uncomfortable holding kids accountable."

"Let's go see kindergarten, shall we?" she adds brightly. "I haven't heard any screaming yet, so it must be OK."

An hour later, Bronx 1's leadership team reconvenes to review the results of the morning walk-through. "I'm trying to put people into two categories," Vandlik says. "Who do we think understands our excellence bar? And who needs an adjustment?" What follows is an unusually blunt assessment of what Vandlik calls "rooms of concern." One classroom is identified as "an outlier" and in need of "urgency and immediate changes." The lead teacher "isn't seeing the world the way we see the world," Vandlik insists. But she is even more concerned about two returning teachers. "They've been with us, and they're not sweating it on the first day," she says. Vandlik tells the junior leaders in charge of the rooms of concern that the priority for the next hour and a half is to "get back into those rooms, see if what you see is consistent with what we saw this morning, and find some time to follow up with these folks this afternoon." A third classroom, she says, is "definitely a priority for us" but then catches herself missing an opportunity to put the lift on her deputies. "Why are they a priority for us? What are we noticing?" Vandlik asks.

"Their directions are really clear," Kerrie Riley offers, "but they're not holding anybody accountable. They have a tone that doesn't command . . ." she searches for the right word, but Vandlik interjects. "That's a really important noticing," she says and coaches Riley on how to give feedback: "'I heard you be really clear. You should feel super comfortable that every kid knows what to do. So what's holding you back from expecting them to do it?'" Riley takes notes.

They turn to Mr. Madan's third-grade classroom, and once again the assistant principals seem eager to flex their supervisory muscles. "He needs to have a picture of what excellence looks like," says Young. Kellie Grant says, "He wasn't narrating consistently," and Riley piles on: "You can't narrate non-expectations." Vandlik calls a halt and rescues her new third-grade teacher. "He probably doesn't know what he wants and what it looks like," she says. "But you know what? For him on the first day, totally outside experience, I think he's doing OK. We can totally work with it."

To an outsider, the pointed assessment of each teacher is jarring and bloodless. But a certain pitiless transparency is stamped on the genetic code of Success Academy's adult culture. If it occurs to anyone to ask me to keep these first-impression evaluations off the record, or not to attach names to them, they do not ask. The teachers themselves will get the same honest-to-a-fault feedback and swiftly, via email by 7:00 p.m. tonight. "You can send it to me or just stick it under my nose for a quick approval," Vandlik instructs.

The teachers are not the only ones under the microscope. "I started identifying potential outlier kids," Vandlik tells the group. "Did you guys take any names?" They go over the kindergarten classes, naming students who seemed to have a problem focusing, following directions, or with some other behavior—at least three or four in every room. Young shares an anecdote about a kindergartener in Ms. Skinner's class who "is going to be an interesting one. He was like, 'I don't like tracking, and I don't like locking my hands!' I was like, 'OK, friend.'"

A network senior staffer, Kristin Jefferson, has been with the team all day. She is particularly concerned about one kindergartener who didn't come to dress rehearsal and was visibly struggling on his first day of school. She urges the team to bring the mother in after dismissal this afternoon. "The pressure needs to be on from day one that we are truly invested in helping him," she says. "If we don't communicate with her what we're seeing, and you're only communicating at the end of the week, it's not going to change." Business operations manager Jen Fuoco, who seems hardwired for sunny observations, notes that every classroom "has at least two to three kids you want your kids to be like. Even if you're new to Success, we know who those kids are, and we can help you leverage them" for classroom management.

Each assistant principal has parents of outlier scholars they need to call right away. "Is everyone clear on actions they need to take with teachers and families after this?" Vandlik asks. The junior leaders take out their phones and start dialing parents they want to meet with at dismissal, less than two hours from now.

⸺

The day ends where it began, in Elena Ortiz's classroom, with the faculty wedged into child-size chairs, on the rug, or leaning against the walls for a debrief. The giddiness of the morning has given way to a happy exhaustion, even though it's only been a half-day. Teachers and administrators go around the room offering shout-outs to colleagues who were on point or helpful in making the day go smoothly; they share kid stories, a standard icebreaker at Bronx 1 staff meetings. Garrett Block, a member of Fuoco's ops team, offers a shout-out to "everybody in this room." He was in the cafeteria when the children were leaving just moments ago. "Many of them are like, 'I don't want to go. I want to stay at school!' Especially the kinder-babies. They were just in love with this day. Good job, everyone."

Vandlik reviews the data. The schoolwide average was 85 percent of scholars on task, ranging from 74 percent in kindergarten to 94 percent in the fourth grade. "That's not terrible. We have room to grow and things to push for," she says. "Our fourth-grade team is almost there, so if you're curious to see how you get this done at a high level, you should go see fourth grade." There was full compliance on school uniforms, which she attributes to her staff making phone calls to parents all summer. "We have a lot of kids in black socks, but what a cool way to just set the standard for your maniacal level of noticing and addressing," she says. "They know it's supposed to be navy, but they don't expect you to actually check. Parents are getting an impression from us about how much we care about every little detail."

The issues facing inner-city children that directly impact their attendance, attention, and outcomes in school can be so daunting that, to an outside observer, this "maniacal level of noticing and addressing" can seem precisely that: maniacal. It's a safe bet that the majority of elementary school teachers would find it beneath their level of attention—and beneath their concern if they noticed. Black socks, navy blue, or green stripes with polka dots—does it really matter? At Success Academy, the answer is not just yes but emphatically so.

My own lensing in the weeks leading up to the first day of school meant getting used to Success Academy's unsparing and unapologetic view of the parents' role in their children's academic outcomes—and its aggressive efforts to get parents to accept, adopt, and enforce school "culture goals" at home. Even most charter school operators and education reformers would blanch at the degree to which Success Academy openly talks about holding parents accountable—for the socks, for getting their kids to school on time every day with homework checked, for reading to their children every night and religiously filling out reading logs. High expectations are not just for scholars, teachers, and staff but for every adult in a child's life. When things don't go as planned in a Success Academy classroom, the reflexive response is to look at adults' behavior, not kids', and that includes the children's parents.

Before dismissing the staff for professional development sessions, Vandlik, like a theater director giving notes at the end of rehearsal, has a list of fixes she wants to see for tomorrow. She praises the "all hands on deck" team spirit. She reminds the new assistant teachers that they should feel just as accountable as lead teachers for the outcomes in their rooms. Be on time for dismissal, she instructs. "We're so on our parents about being on time. We want to value their time as well," she insists. "Many of us are talking way too much," she adds, worried that too much teacher talk in the classroom becomes white noise. "And we need to stop using our bodies to fix kids," she says, meaning that teachers, particularly in kindergarten, are physically directing kids to where they need to be. "If we're constantly doing it for them, they're not going to learn what we expect."

As the meeting breaks up, I remind myself that this was only the first day of school. I wonder how long this level of intensity can be maintained.

CHAPTER 4

No Excuses

"WE'RE NOT A NO-EXCUSES SCHOOL. WE'RE JUST NOT. I DON'T REALLY know how to respond to that nomenclature," Eva Moskowitz bridled at her interviewer's suggestion in a 2017 *Atlantic* article that Success Academy schools are "harsh, 'no excuses' places where students are incessantly disciplined."[1]

"That doesn't mean you don't believe that high levels of learning can occur in chaos, and we do believe that students do need to say *please* and *thank you* to the lunch ladies. We do assign school uniforms to simplify things for parents . . . and really allow us to focus on learning [instead of clothes]," she elaborated. Moskowitz's visceral rejection of the term while simultaneously demanding academic results from students who have largely grown up in poverty, as well as her insistence that there is a proper way for children to conduct themselves in school, illustrates the complicated relationship that she—like leaders of many other high-performing charter networks—has with the no-excuses label.

It wasn't always this way. From the late 1990s into the era of No

Child Left Behind, urban charter schools proudly embraced the no-excuses label. It signaled an optimistic belief that the root cause of educational failure and black-white achievement gaps was adult and system failures—not poverty, not parenting, not children, and certainly not race. For a generation of education reformers and charter school leaders, "no excuses" became both a rallying cry and a brand, associated with certain standard features such as longer school days, data-driven instruction, testing and accountability, and classrooms named for colleges. Students scheduled to graduate from high school in 2026 are called the Class of 2030 as early as kindergarten, denoting the year they are expected to graduate from college, the holy grail of no-excuses schooling.

Expectations are everything. A well-off child has likely never known a day when it wasn't simply assumed she will go to college; the goal of no-excuses schools is to duplicate that unquestioned assumption among underrepresented segments of society. Every norm at a school run by high-profile charter networks is meant to signal the highest-possible expectations. The 2000 book *No Excuses: Lessons from 21 High-Performing, High-Poverty Schools*,[2] by Samuel Casey Carter of the Heritage Foundation, gave the movement and mindset its name.

Whether one wears the mantle willingly or not, Moskowitz's denial rings hollow. Success Academy is not merely a no-excuses school; it is the *most* no-excuses school. Her reluctance to embrace the label has more to do with how the term has evolved over the past two decades as well as criticisms of some widespread practices, particularly student discipline, at many such charter schools. "No excuses" has become a tainted brand, even as evidence accumulates that the approach has paid significant dividends. Stanford University's Center for Research on Educational Outcomes (CREDO) has found that in the aggregate, urban charter schools "provide significantly higher levels of annual growth in both math and reading compared to their traditional public school peers."[3] The strongest test score results among urban charter schools have been posted by charter management organizations (CMOs), which operate multiple schools. A 2017 CREDO report estimated that students in CMO-run schools received the equivalent of 97 additional days of school in math over traditional district-run schools and an extra 46 days of instruction in reading.[4] Although the sample size was quite small, Success Academy students gained the equivalent of 228 days in math and 120 days in reading instruction compared with their peers in traditional public schools—by far the most substantial gains among New York City charter schools. CMO-run schools posted similar gains, but not quite as dramatic when compared with so-called mom-and-pop charters, which operate a single school. Among the strongest CMO performers identified by CREDO were national and regional powerhouses like KIPP, Achievement First, Uncommon Schools, YES Prep, and others that share many of the same characteristics with Success Academy. To be sure, these schools are not monolithic; each has tinkered with its models and formulas over the years. But the general thesis—that a safe, well-run, and orderly school is a precondition to academic excellence—has not changed in a generation, regardless of whether its adherents embrace the name.

David Whitman, a social policy journalist who later became the chief speechwriter for Secretary of Education Arne Duncan, described the mindset common to no-excuses school leaders in his 2008 book, *Sweating the Small Stuff: Inner-City Schools and the New Paternalism,*[5] which profiles a number of schools that fall under that umbrella. "The founders of the new paternalistic schools believe that disorder, not violence or poverty per se, is the fatal undoing of urban schools in poor neighborhoods," Whitman wrote, describing schools that devote "inordinate attention" to ensuring students tuck in their shirts, track teachers with their eyes, and maintain a clean and orderly environment.

"A favorite slogan at Amistad Academy is 'We Sweat the Small Stuff'—just the opposite philosophy of most inner-city schools where teachers and administrators are advised to 'pick their battles.' This concentration on minimizing disorder also helps explain why these paternalistic schools are long on rituals, including school-affirming chants at assemblies, hallways of academic fame with photos of student honorees plastered on the wall, public recognition and awards for students who have done well scholastically, and activities that build a sense of teamwork and esprit de corps. Time and again, students say that one of the features of paternalistic schools that they most prize is that they feel 'safe' there," Whitman said. He may have been writing around the time that Success Academy was first beginning operations, but his words could apply to any of Moskowitz's schools today.

No single event, policy directive, or study marked the moment when "no excuses" went from a rallying cry to a curse, but over time a change in the weather became unmistakable. The broken-windows theory became closely associated with aggressive "stop and frisk" policing, leading to complaints about police misconduct and harassment aimed disproportionately at people of color in poor neighborhoods. Similarly, no-excuses schooling, which had signaled a laudable refusal to accept achievement gaps in schools or society, became conflated with thoughtlessly implemented zero-tolerance policies and harsh exclusionary-discipline practices, including complaints that children of color were being suspended from public and charter schools alike at disproportionate rates. In addition, no-excuses charters came under sustained attack from political progressives, teachers' unions, and anti-reform activists. Diane Ravitch, once a leading education reformer who famously repudiated her views and much of her lifetime of scholarship, evolving into something of a Joan of Arc figure to activists, politicians, and others opposed to charter schools, testing, and the education reform agenda, wrote a 2011 op-ed in the *New York Times* that captured the evolving mindset.[6] She derided "miracle schools," citing several examples of schools whose scores skyrocketed one year and crashed the next. "If every child arrived in school well-nourished, healthy and ready to learn, from a family with a stable home and a steady income, many of our educational problems would be solved," Ravitch wrote, "and that would be a miracle." Many no-excuses charter schools, however, continued to defy gravity, prompting activists and critics to sharpen their attacks. Rigid behavior standards and discipline practices became a natural extension of their overall critique.

Shifts in political winds further tainted the no-excuses brand. The 2001 No Child Left Behind Act, which made annual tests in reading and math from third through eighth grade federal law, was ushered in by the George W. Bush administration, which also had a narrow reading of civil rights laws by the US Department of Education's Office for Civil Rights (OCR). Starting in 2009, the Obama administration took a far more aggressive stance on school discipline, raising civil rights concerns. OCR officials in the Obama administration were civil rights activists who read studies by groups like the Civil Rights Project at UCLA, which had churned out a series of reports on the dangers of exclusionary discipline, recalled one Obama administration official. What had once been a concern of progressives slowly became a mainstream concern, particularly as the anti-testing movement grew, which itself fanned parental concerns about strict and over-directive schools.

Finally, education has a long history of sound policies and practices getting implemented haphazardly once they harden into orthodoxy. David Whitman noted that while most charters made relatively smart use of no-excuses discipline, many states and school systems overreached and failed when they tried adopting similar techniques. "One thing I consistently found was that no-excuses discipline failed if it was not combined with the sure knowledge on a student's part that teachers cared deeply about them and their education," Whitman told me. "There had to be a caring connection between teacher and student for strict discipline to work, or what I described as a kind of benign paternalism." When no-excuses discipline was applied statewide, as in Texas, he noted, it was mistakenly equated with zero-tolerance discipline. "The latter really did lead to abuses and racial disparities," Whitman said.

Today, it is hard to find a school leader who uses the term "no excuses" as anything other than an epithet, even if the model, the mindset, and many of the practices remain much the same. Indeed, significant irony is at work: Eva Moskowitz has arguably perfected no-excuses schooling at the precise moment the model, or at least the name, has fallen out of favor.

"I'm Jen, and I'm the bomb" is how Jennifer Fuoco introduces herself, before adding the punch line: "I'm not conceited. That's just my job title." She is Bronx 1's business operations manager, or BOM. It has become commonplace in K–12 education to say that a school principal should be an "instructional leader," focused exclusively on teaching and learning, rather than an all-purpose administrator overseeing everything from transportation and cafeteria staff to scheduling substitute teachers and ensuring that every student has a desk. The minute details of running a school can easily strip away every moment of the day. Success Academy has operationalized the principal's instructional leadership role to the maximum degree possible. If it does not directly pertain to teaching and learning, it's not her job; it falls to the BOM. Fuoco's name appears directly below Vandlik's on Bronx 1's organization chart, above the assistant principals' and education manager Kellie Grant's. Fuoco is part of every leadership meeting, accompanying Vandlik and her direct reports on instructional walk-throughs. When Fuoco comments on instruction and classroom culture, her words carry weight. But her primary role is to attend to every non-instructional matter that arises within school walls.

Each morning, no later than 6:45 a.m., Fuoco and her team arrive at Bronx 1 for a building walk-through. Working off a list that's hundreds of items long, they ensure that outdoor courtyards, shared lobby spaces, and stairwells are free of litter and graffiti, and that lightbulbs are working. Every classroom must be between 65 and 75 degrees Fahrenheit, a relatively easy task at Bronx 1, which is housed in a building erected as a stand-alone school in 1972 with air conditioners in every room. (Other Success Academies include windowless classrooms in buildings that have stood for more than a century.)

The level of detail is exhausting, from checking hallway bulletin boards for ripped papers and making sure classroom posters stay up to ensuring that the overnight custodians who vacuum classroom rugs remembered to replace the "baby plugs" that keep children's fingers out of wall sockets. As we speak, Fuoco notices one such plug missing in the hallway outside the fourth-grade classrooms and comments nonchalantly that Garrett Block, her ops coordinator, will "catch it in his nine a.m. walk-through and replace it." Walk-throughs are done nearly hourly by Fuoco or one of three staff members. While every Success Academy has an ops team and a BOM, the checklists are unique to the layout and physical condition of the building where each school is co-located. By September, the ops team no longer carries the checklist with them on their rounds; they know it by heart.

A friendly and agreeable woman, Fuoco is a utility infielder. She can talk chillers and blowers with the custodial staff, and classroom management and pedagogy with Bronx 1's teachers and leadership team. In a building owned and operated by the New York City Department of Education and staffed by custodians, cafeteria workers, and police officers who work for the city, not Success Academy, Fuoco's job requires a light, diplomatic touch. "When I first got here, it was rough," she admits. The building staff didn't much care for her predecessor. "We just have very different standards, and they're not used to it," she explains. "But if you come at them with, 'This is my standard, and this is how you need to do it,' they don't take it well." So Fuoco chooses her battles. She does not have keys to the toilet paper dispensers in the bathroom but keeps extra rolls on hand. Better to leave loose rolls perched on top of the dispensers than to pick fights over toilet paper. If the cafeteria staff is late in the morning, she knows where the keys to the refrigerators are kept and can fetch the students' breakfast herself; meals are not left to chance. "My kids will never not eat," she says. Her sunny demeanor and competence have made enough of a positive impression on building staff that the principal of the Bronx Academy of Letters, a DOE middle and high school located under the same roof, cobbled together discretionary funds to hire a BOM of his own. "Her name is Bianca," Fuoco says. "She's lovely. She started at the end of last year."

Fuoco goes out of her way to curry favor with the building employees who are not on Success Academy's payroll but on whom much depends. At holidays, she gets students to write thank-you notes to custodians and cafeteria staff. She frequently takes scholars who have earned "time-ins" for good behavior to visit the custodians' office. "They think it's amazing. Also, when you go to the custodian and you ask them to do something in front of a kid, they don't say no." She grins. The one time Fuoco noticeably bristles is when building staff refer to her school not as Success Academy or even Bronx 1, but merely as "charter." I encounter this nearly every day when I sign in at the front door with the uniformed school safety staff who are part of the New York City Police Department. Early in the school year, the officers would ask which school I was visiting. Before long, they would simply slide a clipboard and sign-in sheet across the desk and confirm, "Charter?" Just another non-DOE school.

Within Success Academy schools, the ops staff are the indispensable if unacknowledged culture keepers. Moskowitz tends to frame her focus on safety, order, and cleanliness in terms of aesthetics. "One thing that happens is that the buildings get dilapidated, and something gets broken and never gets fixed, and it's really hard for people to be invested in the maintenance as it deteriorates," she observed. When teachers return to their classrooms each year, they are freshly painted, the rugs have been cleaned, and the buildings look warm and welcoming. "Not only do we want a smoothly running and efficient school from arrival to dismissal to the lunch room . . . There's a very particular system if your [window] shade is broken or the lightbulb goes out, and you as the teacher should expect that fixed in twenty-four hours. When you create that kind of culture where you have very high expectations on the operational side, it's easier to maintain, as everybody's invested in the beauty and maintenance of the building," she said.

A standard piece of equipment in Success Academy schools is a broomstick with a tennis ball on the end, used for removing scuff marks left on the floor by students' shoes. Even Fuoco finds this level of detail over the top. "I very much believe in making it look like a world-class school, to raise the bar of the work that's done in this school," she says, but scuffs on the floor make the school look happily lived in. "Eva hates them," she whispers, as if Moskowitz might overhear the heretical utterance. Fuoco sometimes deputizes children with an abundance of energy for scuff-removal duty when they've earned a time-in and can choose to visit an old teacher, play "hall ball," or spend time with the ops team. "They love it. For certain kids, it's actually really good for them." She smiles. "They need to get energy out."

One of the longer-tenured members of the leadership team, Fuoco has a history with many students in the building and their families, and insights that equal or exceed those of most of her colleagues. She's no less concerned with lensing her staff than Vandlik is with hers. "We also all need to know what's going on," she notes as we sit outside Albert Barabas's fourth-grade classroom. "It's nice to be in the hallways and be like, 'Oh, I heard Mr. B doing this poem today.' It just gets us out of the little main-office comfort zone to know what's really going on in the school." It is not a coincidence that one of her staff, Lindsay Alexander, is transitioning this year from ops to teaching. She is a fourth-grade assistant teacher, or AT, dividing her time between Barabas's room and Brandon Richter's class across the hall.

Children regard her as having no less authority than their teachers or Vandlik herself. "Every kid that passes you with an untucked shirt, like one piece of shirt untucked, you have to tell every kid. Because if every adult tells them, 'Why are you different?' do you hold them to the same bar? You have to."

The "caring connection" Whitman described—school discipline

combined with authentic affection between teachers and students—
is abundantly in evidence at Bronx 1. On a fall afternoon following
dismissal, Fuoco, Vandlik, Barabas, and third-grade teacher Kaitlyn
Walsh are hanging out in the hallway. The elementary school
children have just left the building; now the middle schoolers are
streaming downstairs, pulling on coats and bantering with their
former teachers. When one boy brags that he hasn't had a single
detention all year, Vandlik whips out her phone and takes a con-
gratulatory selfie with him. Laura Belkin sidles up and says, "This
is the best part of the day!" as they watch the parade pass down the
hall. They tease their former elementary school students, some a
head taller than they were last year. "Are we really at the point
where we are changing in the bathroom before we leave?" Vandlik
jokes with one girl who changed out of her school uniform, teased
her hair, and put on lip gloss to make a grand exit. "Who are you
gonna run into outside?"

The last middle schooler passes, and I'm walking with Vandlik
toward her office when a father and son burst through the adjacent
door, the father angrily berating the child, who is covering his face
with his hands and crying. The man presses on several steps ahead,
turning his back on his son. Vandlik breaks off our conversation
and falls into step beside the boy. Placing her hand on his shoulder,
she slows his pace, turns his body to face her, wipes the kid's face
with her fingers, and whispers something in his ear. "Hurry up!"
she says and pats his shoulder. The boy runs down the hall to catch
up with his dad.

CHAPTER 5

~~~~~~~~~~

Whack-a-Mole

"Unbelievable," Nick Carton is fuming. "Just unbelievable."

"She is completely intolerant," Amy Young says, shaking her head. "And now she's putting that on her child."

"You're going to fight us on this? You can change schools. That's absolutely ridiculous," says Carton. He is a genial person with a round and friendly face, quick to smile at children and adults alike, but he's working himself into a lather. A short time ago, a student's mother showed up unannounced in the main office, complaining in front of other parents that her son's teacher is gay and demanding that he be put in a different class. "It's just a shame," says Kerrie Riley. The child "loves the class and loves the teacher."

Vandlik is speaking with the upset mother as the rest of the leadership team sits around the table in the conference room, agitated and waiting for her to return. "If parents come in angry, you don't have to meet with them," counsels Kellie Grant, the education manager and one of the more experienced members of the leadership team. "Actually, *don't* meet with them," she amends. "It's not going to be productive. Just say, 'I'm sorry but I'm really busy and don't have time to meet with you right now. I'm happy to set up a meeting with you later to discuss your concerns.'" If a parent refuses to leave, Grant advises her colleagues to call school safety; every public school building in the city is staffed by uniformed police officers.

It's been that kind of day. This morning when I arrived, Vandlik was in the main office talking to a parent who was upset over a uniform infraction. "He has to know how to use a belt?" the exasperated mother blurted out. "You have to teach him," Vandlik responded. Growing upset, the mom said that she didn't know how to use a belt either. I felt my eyebrows go up, but Vandlik's patient expression never changed. She put her hand on the woman's shoulder and steered her out of the office, down the hall, and through the double doors that open into the common space separating Bronx 1 from the Bronx Academy of Letters. Vandlik shot me a glance that I interpreted to mean, "Don't follow." A few moments later, through the windows in the double doors, I saw her hugging the mother, who was wiping tears from her eyes. She'd been drinking. It was eight o'clock in the morning.

Another parent has informed one of the teachers that her child will not be attending school on Wednesday—any Wednesday—because she's not available to pick her up at 12:30. Success Academy schools have half-days every Wednesday to allow teachers to attend professional development sessions; that's proving to be a deal-breaker for this mother, who is hard-pressed to make it to school in time for the regular 3:45 p.m. pickup.

Vandlik enters the conference room, fresh from the confrontation with the parent upset about her son's teacher. "You guys don't need to apologize," she starts. "You knew she was demanding to meet with you. My preference would be that it always happen on our terms, and that you guys not get pulled from the important things you're doing just because mom is demanding to see you," she says. There's a danger, too, in raising every parent concern to an urgent priority. "She thinks there's this big issue. We don't think so.

You don't want to accidentally communicate that this is worthy of a meeting," Vandlik says, shifting immediately to the transferable lessons of the uncomfortable encounter. Her advice echoes Kellie Grant's: set up a meeting at a time that works for you. "That gives you guys time to plan and it gives her time to . . ."

"Calm down?" interjects Grant.

"Step off the ledge she's on," Vandlik completes her thought.

When Vandlik found the mother, she was studying the staff pictures on the bulletin board outside the main office, commenting on the number of new faces this year. "Do you have questions? Or do you want his class changed?" she asked. The mother wanted his class changed. "Well, we won't do that," Vandlik answered. "I told her my concern is not the teacher. My concern is what [her son] is picking up from her. And that she needs to get her head on straight." The mother wasn't belligerent or angry, and she seemed to be listening and processing. Ultimately, she accepted Vandlik's decision. "She's probably lying through her teeth, but it's obviously a lot for her to deal with," Vandlik now says. "We have to find some empathy when we're having trouble." Young snorts derisively. "When you find it, you let me know," she says, drawing a laugh from her colleagues. But Vandlik continues to press her point. "It's like dealing with anything. If we don't find the way to change the mindset that's the root cause, then—right?—we'll just put a Band-Aid on it. We don't want to pretend that it's fixed when it's obviously not," Vandlik says, as always seeing a problem from many angles, anticipating the next fire while fighting the one in front of her.

There's always a next one. If a child misses ten consecutive days of school or twenty days in four months or less, New York City schools are required to look into it.[1] If there's no compelling explanation for the absence, they are obligated to call New York City's Administration for Children's Services (ACS), potentially triggering an investigation for evidence of educational neglect.[2] The mother who is refusing to bring her child to school on Wednesdays must be brought in before it gets that far. "That's a huge conversation,"

Carton says, and Vandlik agrees. "No phone conversation," she emphasizes. "She needs to come in and talk to you."

Vandlik embodies a kind of hard-nosed empathy that is emblematic of Success Academy's culture: understand the underlying issue, but move quickly and act decisively. There's not much room for sitting around and admiring a problem. Shifting from one crisis to the next, Vandlik brings up the mom who showed up drunk this morning. "She's been through a lot. I want to get preventive services involved before it becomes an ACS call," she says. Vandlik will set up a meeting with Britney Weinberg-Lynn, the principal of the Success Academy middle school one flight up, where the woman's older child attends; together they will come up with a plan. Then it's back to business—and data. Kindergarten has 98.9 percent attendance with 100 percent of students on time, Amy Young reports. Mr. Carnaghi's class, called Iona College, has 100 percent perfect attendance with every scholar in uniform. "What do you want to do for them?" Vandlik asks Young, who suggests throwing a class dance party.

"You can take them on a parade through the hallway," Vandlik counters.

"So cute!" Young gushes.

"We are bringing the joy today, people. Did you give them lots of coins?" Vandlik asks.

There is always some manner of incentive, raffle, or behavior-driven contest going on at Success Academy. At the moment, it's the Bronx Battle, a competition between classes to earn plastic gold coins, which are being given out for meeting culture goals, such as attendance, uniform compliance, completing homework and reading logs, or simply getting "caught being good." The class that collects the most will earn a field trip. "When you go in to announce the parade, bring a lot of coins," Vandlik says. "Make it rain coins!" Young laughs. The plan is set, and Vandlik steers the conversation to Bronx 1's attendance data.

Among South Bronx public schools, the average daily attendance is just over 86 percent, the second-lowest rate among New

York City's thirty-two school districts. At Bronx 1, attendance is 96.72 percent in the first grade, and kids who aren't in school have excused absences in advance. The attendance ticks lower as the grades get higher, but stays well above 90 percent. "Fourth grade is seriously slipping," Vandlik frets, even though Bronx 1's attendance data would be cause for celebration at any of the neighborhood's public schools. She reminds her team to make sure teachers are "owning it" on attendance and tardiness as the meeting breaks up.

On the way back to her office, Vandlik cruises into a third-grade classroom. "Excuse me, but I just walked in and saw 100 percent of kids tracking, focused, and looking so excited about what's about to begin." She gives the class two gold coins, which go into a clear plastic container on the wall by the door. "Kiss your brains!" she commands. "I know you're in third grade, but you're not too old for that." In Charita Stewart's second-grade classroom, called Michigan State, Vandlik banters with a child she spied correcting papers on the rug. "Did we hire a new teacher? Am I paying you for this?" Another gold coin. In Mandisa Brudey's first-grade classroom, Manhattanville, Vandlik throws gold coins in the air to reward the class for a crisp "One, Get Ready." The children seem nonplussed, perhaps unsure how they are supposed to respond when the principal comes in the room and throws something. "You can act excited when something good happens!" Vandlik says before turning and exiting.

The calendar has not yet turned to September; New York City public school students won't have their first day of class until the Wednesday after Labor Day, two weeks from now. Carolyn Syskowski is still spending much of her time building classroom community, establishing and enforcing behavioral norms, and encouraging her kindergarteners to regard one another as friends and teammates. Scholars turn and talk, facing each other knee to knee on the rug, when

Syskowski asks a question. She seems to spend most of her day on the rug with them to monitor conversations and behavior.

I perch at the edge of the rug to eavesdrop on the children, and Syskowski invites the kids to "story-tell." The vast majority of her students are pre-readers. But she has been exposing them to picture books, asking them to "read" to one another, and now to me, based on what's happening in the pictures. The idea is to begin to build a love of reading and a familiarity with "print concepts"—how to locate the front and back of a book, for example, and turn pages and follow a text from left to right.

While the children are sitting "knee to knee and eye to eye" excitedly storytelling, Syskowski takes out her phone and calls a parent. If I hadn't been looking at her, I might not have noticed; the phone call lasts just a few seconds. Within minutes, a dad in a Yankees cap and basketball shorts appears in the doorway. "Remember what I said about sitting on the rug?" he asks his son. His voice is soft, but the boy is rattled by the sight of his father. Syskowski gives a nonverbal signal and the father and son leave the classroom. If the other children notice any of this, they give no indication. A few minutes later, the man comes back in, leading his son by the hand; the little boy returns to his spot on the rug while his dad retreats to the back of the room. He settles on the floor, an earbud in his right ear, draws up his knees, and melts into the wall.

His son is not the only kindergartener struggling to adapt to classroom life. Another throws his body around the floor and seems incapable of sitting still. He breaks from the rug frequently to hug Olivia Hanania, Syskowski's first-year AT. Things have been at loose ends since kindergarten went to full days after the first week, but that's not unexpected. A school day that lasts from 7:30 a.m. to 3:45 p.m. is a long one for a five-year-old. Most of Syskowski's effort in the first weeks of school seems aimed at simply maintaining order, establishing routines, and turning her classroom into a warm and cohesive community where children help and praise one another. When a little boy struggles during a lesson, she asks the class to "send some love to Joseph so he feels loved and supported." They respond by aiming a wiggly-fingered hand gesture in the boy's direction. When another child speaks up clearly and confidently, Syskowski pantomimes squeezing a spray bottle and wiping motion and the kids take the cue, praising their classmate in unison: "Shhh, shhh, shhh! Fan-TASTIC!"

She works every angle to keep the kids engaged and attentive. Praises. Corrections. Narration. Lowering her voice to a near whisper to make students strain to listen. When the volume of voices gets too loud, she calls out a singsong, "Hun-ter!" The children respond in kind, "Coll-ege!" "Sit! Down!" she sharply commands a boy who seems oblivious to the other children waiting for their teacher to resume a math lesson. At that moment, Mr. Carnaghi appears in the door, brandishing a single gold coin. "Ms. Syskowski, I really want to give this gold coin to your scholars. But I'm looking for a perfect Magic Five."

"I'm really glad you said that, Mr. Carnaghi, because when a teacher comes in here, they have to *catch us* doing the right thing." Syskowski turns to her class. "If the teacher needs to tell you, 'I'm looking for Magic Five,' does that mean you're doing it? Did Mr. Carnaghi *catch you* sitting in Magic Five? Yes or no? So, did we *earn* a gold coin?" She makes her disappointed face and shakes her head, lips pursed. Carnaghi takes the hint from his veteran colleague; his face drops and his shoulders sag. "I'm going to come back, and when I do, I hope I see a perfect Magic Five," he says and turns to leave, still pressing the precious coin between his thumb and forefinger.

———

In the second grade, Adama is spending too much time out of the classroom because of misbehavior. The transition from half days to full days has been difficult, but at least there's been no physical aggression aimed at other children. When I arrive in Elena Ortiz's classroom, Adama is not in the room, but another boy, Jayden, has just been given a ten-minute time-out. He is agitated and holding a large plastic hourglass. Every Success Academy school classroom has a bin of them in various colors, indicating the length of an in-class time-out. "After those ten minutes, I expect you to join us on the rug," Ortiz tells him as I settle in at the back of the room.

"I'm still not going to join," the boy mutters within my earshot but out of Ortiz's, taking a measure of his defiance but not seeming fully committed to it. "If you're not able to do that, that's not OK. We're going to have a little bit of a problem," Ortiz continues. "You're missing learning time." Her tone is flat and factual, not angry or aggressive, as she tries to lower the temperature in the room. "I don't need learning time," the child protests under his breath, with his back to the class and his teacher. He stalks to a far corner of the room, avoiding eye contact with everyone.

"You have ten minutes to calm yourself," Ortiz instructs. "You can use breathing techniques. You can talk to yourself. You can write down your feelings." I missed the incident that has him fussed, but Ortiz attempts to bring the episode to a close, instructing the class to apologize to the boy. In unison, his classmates offer a singsong "Sorry, Jayden," and Ortiz returns to her lesson. "That's it. It's over. Hunter College, get ready for some grammar and vocab." She returns her attention to her class; the boy remains alone in the back of the room, sullen, pouting, and defiant.

Things are ragged and rough in Ortiz's classroom, noticeably so compared with the others I've seen. She struggles to keep her students focused and engaged, and unlike in nearly every other classroom, there is no full-time assistant teacher in the room to help her maintain order. When she sends the children to their desks to get pencils and whiteboards to lean on while they complete a worksheet on capital letters and punctuation, they don't move with the crispness and purpose of the other classrooms. They dawdle, vibrate, and bounce off one another, oblivious to Ortiz's narration and small corrections. One girl gets a demerit for talking. "Every transition we do is silent," Ortiz tells the class. But it takes several un-silent minutes before the class is settled back on the rug with whiteboards in their laps and pencils resting on the black lines bordering each square, as their teacher has instructed, with name and date on their papers. "Ten more seconds for name and date, then I expect you to have your hands locked on your whiteboard and your eyes on me." Those ten seconds drift well past a minute, even as Ortiz continues to narrate, praising compliance, giving out occasional warnings and marks and growing frustrated. "Whoever is tapping their whiteboard needs to *stop!*" she says curtly before finally launching her lesson. "Each of these sentences has a problem," she begins. "You guys are writing detectives. You're going to tell me what's wrong with each of these sentences."

While she's explaining the assignment, Nick Carton comes in to help settle down Jayden. Three different adults—Ortiz, Carton, and Casey King, a new assistant chess teacher who is frequently in the room as a part-time AT—all make attempts before he is finally ready to rejoin his classmates on the rug. The boy crosses the room and, from a foot or two away, lobs the plastic hourglass into its bin with a flick of his wrist, a deft finger-roll shot and one small final act of defiance. Ortiz tells him to "do it again nicely," and I hold my breath, thinking she should have pretended not to notice and just moved on. I brace myself for an outburst, but it doesn't come. Whether mollified by the attention of three different adults, not wishing to press his luck, or just wanting to rejoin his classmates, Jayden retrieves the hourglass, places it gently in the bin, and quietly takes his place on the rug among his classmates, who are fixing sentences with simple capitalization and punctuation mistakes.

Ortiz calls the children's attention to the first sentence—"what did you bring to school"—and instructs the kids to look closely. "Emir just noticed the sentence doesn't begin with a capital letter," she says. "Francesca, is he right?" Caught not paying attention, Francesca fumbles for the answer. Ortiz calls on Royale, who says that a sentence always begins with a capital letter. "With your pencil, fix that *W*. Is there anything else wrong with that sentence?" None of the children notice that the sentence is missing a question mark. Ortiz gives up trying to coax the correction from her students. She gives them the answer. "It's a question. So it needs a question mark."

At the back of the rug, a girl is silently crying because she doesn't have a paper. Again, the lesson grinds to a halt. "If there's something wrong, you guys need to use your words. We're not in kindergarten anymore," Ortiz says, an edge creeping into her voice. "If you're sitting here and you want me to get a message, and you're just crying, I'm not going to understand what it is that you want to say. Sometimes we've got to try to work through emotions and talk." She sends the child off to get a tissue.

The interruptions add up. Twenty minutes into the lesson, the class has made it through only five sentences of the grammar exercise.

By late morning, a new crisis demands the attention of the leadership team. A pair of New York Police Department officers arrive with a father who has several children at Bronx 1, both at the elementary school and the middle school one floor above it. The night before, he reportedly beat with a belt his oldest daughter, a teenager who is not a Success Academy student. She fled the apartment at two in the morning; neighbors called the cops. His younger children came to school distraught and told their teachers about what happened. As "mandated reporters," staff had no choice but to call ACS to report the suspected child abuse. The leadership team speculates that the children's father is mad at the school for blowing the whistle on him. His kids "weren't supposed to tell us," says Kellie Grant, "so I'm sure that's a big part of it."

Vandlik walks into the room thirty minutes late, speaking into her cell phone, briefing the network office. The police and ACS are handling it; they don't seem to want or need the school to be involved. The older sister is still missing. Vandlik ends the call and, without spending another moment on the presence of NYPD officers in the building, launches into her agenda. "OK, guys, we have limited time," she begins and passes around a handout she has prepared with deliverables, benchmarks, and goals for herself and each member of the leadership team, with data targets for personnel management, parent investment, behavior management, and other areas. "We have to know where we're headed," she tells her junior leaders. "Identify the gap between where we need to go and where we are right now, and make a purposeful plan to incrementally close those gaps."

The transition is jarring. At most other schools, the day might have descended into chaos. But Vandlik's focus never wavers. The chaotic day affords her another teachable moment. "We saw many things come up today. A parent shows up in the office intoxicated. A parent shows up demanding a meeting. The police are here. We didn't expect any of that," Vandlik says. "We could literally spend every moment of our day just playing whack-a-mole."

The NYPD may have failed to break up the leadership meeting, but Mr. Carnaghi's kindergarteners get the job done. There's a commotion in the hallway, and the group steps outside to watch and cheer as Carnaghi leads his children through the building chanting, "I-O-N-A," their class name and their teacher's alma mater—the promised parade to celebrate their perfect attendance record. Several of the children wave pom-poms. A boom box blares a Chipmunks-style version of "We Are the Champions." The students' faces reflect a mixture of excitement and bewilderment as they are greeted with cheers and congratulations from every adult they pass in the hallway. "About-face, scholars," commands Carnaghi, and the kids return to their classroom.

"Oh, those babies!" Amy Young grins. "They are so . . . *every-thing*!" The leadership team goes back to their meeting.

CHAPTER 6

"I Want to Slit My Wrists"

THE COVER OF EVA MOSKOWITZ'S 2017 MEMOIR, *THE EDUCATION OF Eva Moskowitz*, describes her as the "founder of Success Academy Charter Schools."[1] Actually, it was a New York hedge fund manager, John Petry, who wrote the application for what was originally called the Gotham Charter School. Petry and his business partner Joel Greenblatt hired Moskowitz to run it after submitting the application to the state education department in Albany but prior to getting a charter.[2] They remain members of the Success Academy network board of directors.[3]

Success Academy's origin story begins in 2002 with Greenblatt's involvement at a traditional New York City public school in Ozone Park, Queens. A legendary "value investor" focused on buying shares of blue-chip companies underappreciated by Wall Street, Greenblatt's Gotham Capital had been riding a nearly two-decade winning streak, averaging 40 percent annual returns. Starting with money belonging to junk bond king Michael Milken, Greenblatt grew his hedge fund from seven million dollars in assets to well over one billion dollars.[4]

Greenblatt had become fascinated with finding what he called "leveraged ways of giving back"—strategies that led to scalable, replicable, teach-a-man-to-fish philanthropic bets. "I'm a capitalist, and the system works as long as everyone has a fair chance," he told me in the conference room of his office above Madison Avenue in Manhattan. "Education is the most efficient way to give everyone a good shot in life. But education is the least fair thing." Greenblatt thought the answer might be a program called Success for All, a curriculum-driven, whole-school reform model developed by Robert Slavin, an education professor at Johns Hopkins University.[5] The program was in 1,700 schools at the time, which suggested it was both scalable and replicable. "I gave him a call and basically said, 'I've looked at your results, and you're getting forty or fifty percent of kids reading, but it's not 'success for all,'" Greenblatt recalled telling Slavin. "'I'm just a guy with money. Is it money?'"

Yes, Slavin replied; it's just money—if the money is spent in the right way. But it's difficult to maintain tight control in most public schools. The two agreed to try to find a school they could convince to put "Success for All on steroids," as Greenblatt put it. It proved difficult and frustrating to find a school willing to cash Greenblatt's checks, but eventually, at Slavin's suggestion, he ended up at PS 65, not far from John F. Kennedy International Airport. Greenblatt recalled telling principal Iris Nelson, "'I want to keep spending money until all the kids can read. Not because I'm an idiot. I just want to see how much it would take.'"

A February 2006 article in *New York* magazine tells the story of Greenblatt's $2.5 million "friendly takeover" of PS 65.[6] His investment equaled a thousand dollars per student for five years to cover the cost of Success for All's curriculum, a cadre of outside tutors, and an aggressive system of assessments and data collection—a standard feature of data-driven instruction by contemporary standards but somewhat novel circa 2002. "Success for All on steroids" led to the school's winning a state prize for improved school performance. Nearly every child who had been at the school for three years or more was reading and doing math on grade level—even special education students. At the end of the long magazine piece, the reporter mentions, almost in passing, that Greenblatt and Petry plan to open a charter school called Harlem Success Academy to implement Success for All and "the same sort of supplementary tutoring and data management" that drove PS 65's turnaround. "And the executive director of the charter school is Eva Moskowitz," the piece adds, "the former City Council member who chaired the education committee and often proved a tenacious foil to the mayor, the chancellor, and the teachers union."

Petry had become increasingly involved in supporting charter schools and was interested in starting one. Greenblatt phoned him over the Thanksgiving holiday in 2004. "'You want to open a charter school, and I want to replicate PS 65,'" Petry recalled Greenblatt pitching him. "'How about we start a charter school together to do that?'" Meanwhile, the financial journalist Andrew Tobias[7] had introduced Greenblatt to New York City schools chancellor Joel Klein.[8] "The first thing out of Joel Klein's mouth was 'You oughta do a charter school,'" Greenblatt said.

Greenblatt and Petry focused on creating a model that was replicable, a nonnegotiable conviction reinforced by visits to high-performing New York City charters like KIPP Infinity Middle School in Harlem. "We were watching this amazing English lesson. I elbowed the assistant teacher and said, 'Just for my interest, what's the background of that teacher?'" Greenblatt recalled. "'He wrote for [the television sitcom] *Frasier* for five years,'" she replied. The exchange reinforced Greenblatt's sense that a model based on attracting top teachers couldn't be duplicated at scale. "It would be wonderful if everyone could have that teacher, but everyone can't," he says.

The hallways of Success Academy schools reflect many of Greenblatt's concerns. When Greenblatt and Petry were doing their due diligence, it was standard practice for no-excuses charter school classrooms to be identified not by room numbers but named for colleges like Harvard, Princeton, or Tufts, with teachers from those elite schools—typically bright, polished Teach For America corps members—holding forth inside. At Success, children are more likely to sit in a classroom named for SUNY Oneonta, Brooklyn College, or Rutgers. Bronx 1 classrooms include Marist, Fordham, the University of North Carolina, the University of Massachusetts Amherst, and Iona. Carolyn Syskowski and Elena Ortiz each teach in a "Hunter College" classroom, their alma mater and one of the largest teachers' colleges in the state. One Bronx 1 kindergarten classroom is named "BMCC": Borough of Manhattan Community College. However Success Academy is achieving its results, it has little to do with luring the best and brightest with Ivy League pedigrees to inner-city classrooms.

Petry and Greenblatt also insisted on a model that could run on public dollars. "If we spend forty thousand dollars per kid, we're a private school," Petry said. "We wanted to do something that really could be done elsewhere." They were advised not to mention their grand plans for replicating and scaling up in their original charter application, but they privately decided on a "big, hairy audacious goal" of forty schools. "We thought if we could replicate it forty times, people could no longer say, 'Oh, it's just a one-off school,'" Greenblatt said.

Moskowitz entered the picture a few months later. Her husband, Eric Grannis,[9] an attorney who had been helping Petry and Greenblatt with their charter application, visited PS 65 to see the work on the ground. "He left the school, called Eva, and said, 'You have to see this school,'" Petry recalled. At the time, Moskowitz was running for Manhattan Borough president. "Fortunately for us, she came in second," Petry said. It is tempting to think of how the trajectory of education reform, charter schooling, and perhaps American education itself might have changed had New York City voters chosen Moskowitz over a state assemblyman named Scott Stringer,[10] who won the endorsement of the *New York Times*[11] and the election. "Eva Moskowitz, a former college professor, is smart and driven and an expert on education issues, although her style—often described by those who have worked with her as abrasive—would not be well suited to this office," opined the *Times*. "We endorse Scott Stringer."

Moskowitz needed a job and found herself talking to Greenblatt and Petry about leading Gotham Charter School, which was still awaiting approval from the New York State Education Department. "When she walked out of the room," Greenblatt recalls, "both John and I looked at each other and said, 'We need to get her to do this.'" They asked her to become the founding CEO of what would eventually be known as Success Academy. Moskowitz hesitated, telling the two she wasn't sure that a start-up school could pay the salary of $175,000 she was looking for in her first job out of politics. But Greenblatt, the value investor, had already determined with Petry what the position was worth.

"We don't usually negotiate this badly," he replied. "How about two fifty?'"

———

Moskowitz spends about a third of her time in schools every week, making both scheduled and unannounced visits. She directly supervises several principals. Her attention is drawn reflexively to the school's aesthetics, its look and feel. She notices foot traffic and watches how classes transition from place to place in the building, a tip-off, she assumes, to how well or poorly things are run. "Are we going to lose a kid because we're sloppy?" she asks herself.

One morning early in the school year, I shadow Moskowitz on a visit to Harlem 2 on 128th Street in East Harlem, across the street from a park and by the Harlem River Drive, a four-lane highway that cuts off the neighborhood from its waterfront. She introduces me to principal Lavinia Mackall, a Vassar grad and former opera singer who joined Teach For America and started teaching elementary school at Success Academy in 2011. Referring to me, Moskowitz tells her principal, "We're not going to pay him the slightest bit of attention. He's writing some book, and who the hell knows how it's going to come out." She asks to see Harlem 2's strongest classes and the ones Mackall is most concerned about.

From down the hall, I can hear the teacher in the first room we visit well before we enter, a shrill voice warning students that the timer is going to go off in twenty seconds and to be prepared. The children are hunched over their assignments; not a single one looks up as we enter. The smartboard timer rings, and the teacher instructs, "When I say 'Go,' you're gonna. Put! Your! Work! Into! Your! Yellow! *Folder!*" Each word is a hammer blow. My immediate impression is that she is nervous and on edge with her principal and Moskowitz in the room. She barks a few more instructions. After the children put away their work, she orders her students to take out materials for a math activity called number stories and then to "lock your hands and look at me."

"Do you think you can do it in"—she pauses to reset the countdown timer—"*under thirty seconds?*" She shouts the last three words and the children answer in kind, yelling, "YES!"

"Sit up! *Ready?* GO!"

She narrates the room and shouts, "Hustle, hustle, hustle!" The timer rings, but kids are still shuffling papers and supplies frenetically. She gives them ten more seconds and redoubles her volume, counting down, "TEN! NINE! EIGHT! . . ." The teacher's tone is not angry or harsh, but it is *loud,* and she seems to depend on that volume to hold her kids' attention. The effect, even after a few moments, is grating.

The same lesson is underway in the next room. And the same delivery. There's a lot of behavior management and "body checks" to ensure students are sitting up and tracking, but not a lot of math instruction. In the third classroom, there is still more high-volume call-and-response. The children in all three classrooms are calculating the number of volleyballs in a group where the total number of balls is known, as well as the number of balls that are *not* volleyballs. The teacher calls on a child named Dmitri to discuss his work.

"The total is thirty-two," he concludes.

"The total number of what?" she pushes.

"Um . . . of . . . the . . ."

"The total number of . . . ?" she loudly signals to the class to answer.

"Balls!" some but not all students call out.

"The total number OF!?" A shout.

"BALLS!" This time the whole class answers in unison, each child seeming determined to yell louder than the next.

She goes back to the child who hesitated. "So, these thirty-two, Dmitri, are the total number of . . ."

The whole class again answers for Dmitri. *"BALLS!"* they yell. It's deafening.

Moskowitz has seen enough and walks out. "You have an endemic problem with stupid shouting and call-and-response. Get them to a more intellectual place," she tells Mackall back in the hallway. "You've got to call time-out and lead a revolution around no yelling. They know what a ball is. They've known what a ball is since they were toddlers." Moskowitz is visibly irritated. "If that happened in an affluent neighborhood, people would pull their kids out," she says. "They need to understand that they're disadvantaging poor kids by doing that." Before we began visiting classes, Mackall was candid about what her boss was about to see: adult behaviors that indicate low expectations of students. "I was imagining a read-aloud where they weren't pressing the kids to get the biggest idea," Moskowitz says, "I wasn't imagining '*Balls!*'"

Calling out low expectations and holding principals' feet to the fire is one of the go-to moves in Moskowitz's playbook. "Eva held me accountable a number of times," recalled Jim Manly, the founding principal of Harlem 2. "Like, 'Why is that teacher still there? You told me two weeks ago that he was in trouble, and I don't understand why he's still in the classroom. You're hurting kids this way.'" School principals everywhere are reluctant to remove teachers from the classroom midyear. It is disruptive, creates logistical problems, and can damage staff morale. It's also human nature simply to worry about the teacher, and his feelings and job prospects. Eventually, Manly came around to Moskowitz's view: "Her point that I started to realize is that the teacher is going to land on their feet. They've got their college degree, and they're going to be OK. Those kids can't afford lousy teaching for another six weeks as I try and get this person to just be mediocre." The lesson stuck after Manly left Success to join KIPP, where he is now the superintendent of that network's New York City schools. "Charter schools must have a kids-first orientation to how we operate our schools, or we will never be able to break away from the fundamental tension that holds most traditional public schools back from getting results," he told me in an interview.[12]

Moskowitz wasn't looking for Mackall to change teachers, but it would be hard not to assume the clock was ticking on the ones whose rooms we just visited. "I wouldn't worry about the data for now. They're not seeing the big picture," she tells Mackall as they move on to the next grade. "It doesn't matter if the kids aren't paying attention. There's nothing worthwhile going on." Mackall takes in her boss's feedback nondefensively; she criticizes herself for giving the teachers too much feedback and invokes the same phrase, "playing whack-a-mole," that Vandlik used the other day. "Well, stop. Only give them one," Moskowitz agrees.

"I am worried about every single one of those classes," the principal says. "Their expectations are too low. A lot of excuses and pushback." The teachers mean well, she notes with a sigh, but they're consistently lowballing kids.

"That's why you're my kind of gal," Moskowitz reassures Mackall, and they continue down the hall.

There's an element of theater in school observations. As a public school teacher in the DOE, I remember what it was like in the days just before a scheduled visit by a city or district pooh-bah. Hallway bulletin boards were spruced up with fresh student work; some teachers even held back lessons and activities that would reliably generate attractive "bulletin board work." Classroom libraries and bins of instructional materials got tidied up, often uncovering wadded-up student papers if you were lucky; the remains of half-eaten snacks if you weren't. Walk-throughs meant the "aim and standard" of every lesson was clearly visible on the board in "child-friendly language"; lesson plan books were meticulously detailed and left lying in plain sight. With only a few moments to spend in any given classroom to make snap judgments, supervisors were trained to look for "visible indicators" of effective instruction. And teachers trained themselves to produce those indicators, not necessarily to produce effective instruction. Every classroom activity reflected the pedagogical flavor of the moment—group work, differentiated instruction, children working hands-on with materials. Sometimes this took on cartoonish dimensions. On the day before one walk-through, my special education supervisor came to inspect my room and asked me why I didn't have math manipulatives—brightly colored pattern blocks, fraction rods, and interconnecting cubes—out on each table within easy reach. "I'm doing ELA," I explained. "It doesn't matter," she replied curtly. "It's what they want to see."

I sidled up to Mackall and asked if having Moskowitz in the building causes a similar effect, putting teachers on edge or into show-pony mode, perhaps engaging in over-the-top displays of energetic classroom management on the assumption that this is what she wants to see. Mackall shook her head and noted that Moskowitz comes around frequently. "The problem is that they can't do any better than this."

Overhearing her, Moskowitz muttered, "And they don't realize that I want to slit my wrists."

<hr/>

If anyone in American education is indispensable to her organization, it's Eva Moskowitz. She is the creator, driver, and enforcer of Success Academy's culture, which reaches with remarkable consistency into the deepest corner of every classroom in the network's schools. A few weeks after the Harlem 2 school visit, on a Monday evening, Amy Young, Kerrie Riley, and Nick Carton are summoned to meet after work with Moskowitz at an informal session for new junior leaders at Success Academy's network office in Manhattan's financial district. Like the schools, the office is clean, bright, and well lit. With its contemporary feel and small army of employees scurrying about, it feels more like the offices of a design firm or a tech start-up than of a charter school management organization. Bronx 1's rookie administrators are joined by about a dozen other "leader residents" from Prospect Heights, Brooklyn; Springfield Gardens, Queens; Union Square in Manhattan; and other Success Academy outposts. Wine and snacks are on offer but go mostly untouched. Even when Moskowitz insists "like a Jewish grandmother" that her troops eat, the wine stays corked.

Moskowitz breaks the ice, asking each of her guests to introduce themselves and to describe the craziest thing that happened today at their schools. She's rewarded with stories of hallway runners, children scaling bathroom stalls, and assorted playground mishaps. One reports recording fourteen thousand steps on her Fitbit—about seven miles—without once setting foot outside her building. "Sounds like a very calm day," Moskowitz deadpans. The session with the CEO is not a formal professional development session, but it's not like Moskowitz to simply invite her leaders downtown for wine, crudités, and idle banter. "I thought it would be helpful to tell you how to excel at your job," she announces, preparing to launch into a Socratic seminar on leadership and the Success Academy way. "But before I share my thoughts," she challenges, "how do *you* think you could excel at your job? What does 'excelling' mean in *your* view?"

These leaders—most of whom appear to be in their twenties—offer up a litany of predictable answers: excelling means being reflective and collaborative, proactive not reactive, and solutions-oriented. Immediately, Moskowitz knocks them off balance, asking them to try to eliminate the word "like" from their responses. Success Academy pushes its students not to infuse their speech with such verbal tics, so network leaders have a particular responsibility not to model bad habits. She continues to go around the room; her young leaders shoveling up bromides, but her face never registers impatience. After each response—"accountability," "maintaining high expectations," "building teachers' capacity"—she records it without comment on a whiteboard. "OK, what else?" she presses. She wants something they are not offering. "This is a great list," she begins disingenuously, "but I think you are a little bit in danger of mixing up tactics with how we define 'excellence.'" The word she was hoping for—the one she starts with—is "ethics." "In my mind, you cannot excel unless you are ethical."

She cold-calls Carton. "Why do you think we're crazy about ethics?"

"It can undermine everything you can do. Like, if you aren't ethical, it undermines absolutely everything," he replies.

"Right!" Moskowitz exclaims, so pleased with the response that she doesn't correct the "like." "We're a values-driven organization," she says. "You can't be a great teacher if you are unethical." When she asks the group for examples of unethical behavior, the nearly universal response is cheating. That's an "obvious and rare" example, Moskowitz insists, pressing again for something they're not giving her. One woman suggests not pushing teachers or holding them accountable because "they might quit and we don't have a body for the classroom." Moskowitz seizes on the example. That's a very common problem, she tells them, especially among leaders who are not parents. "You've got to ask yourself, Would you have your child in that classroom? If you don't want your child in that classroom, why should someone else's children be in that classroom?" She echoes her caution the other day at Harlem 2. "That's an unethical decision."

Moskowitz frequently refers to "education crimes and misdemeanors." A misdemeanor might be when a teacher denies a child recess as a punishment. "I don't really believe in developmentally appropriate practice like everybody else does," she tells her disciples. "But I believe in recess with all my heart and soul. I just believe in it for, like, seventh graders as much as fourth graders." The list of misdemeanors is general, but crimes are particular, consisting mostly of offenses against Success Academy's model—teachers not doing a proper lesson wrap-up or not studying student work. "We have one design for all of the children, for all of the teachers, and all of the leaders, irrespective of race, socioeconomic status, gender identity, sexual identity." That doesn't mean teachers can't have their own style and personality, but the heart of the model is what Moskowitz calls a "no-nonsense nurturer" relationship between adults and children. "We all know it's hard to describe," she tells the group, "but there's a band. And you don't go outside the band."

Unprompted, Moskowitz brings up the video posted by the *New York Times*[13] showing Charlotte Dial, a first-grade teacher at Success Academy's Cobble Hill, Brooklyn, elementary school, ripping up a child's math work and exiling her from the classroom rug. "Go to the calm-down chair and sit!" Dial orders in the footage, secretly recorded by an assistant teacher. "There's nothing that infuriates me more than when you don't do what's on your paper," she scolds. Without protest, the child rises and leaves the frame; her face and those of her classmates were blurred by the *Times*. A caption posted with the video by the paper asks, "A momentary lapse or abusive teaching?" The video and article became a referendum on Success Academy itself. Dial was suspended. Taylor's story notes that Success Academy training materials "say that teachers should never yell at children, 'use a sarcastic, frustrated tone,' 'give consequences intended to shame children,' or 'speak to a child in a way they wouldn't in front of the child's parents.'" However, Taylor reports, "interviews with 20 current and former Success teachers suggest that while Ms. Dial's behavior might be extreme, much of it is not uncommon within the network." The piece went off like a bomb. Success Academy, which had enjoyed a halo effect for years, was shaken to its roots. They had lost the *Times*.

Moskowitz recapitulates none of this history now; everyone surely knows the details. "Charlotte Dial went outside the band. It was totally unacceptable, and we don't tolerate that. That doesn't mean that we always fire the teacher for doing so," she says, "because life is complicated." At the time the video went viral, Moskowitz faced considerable pressure to fire Dial, including from members of her board of directors. She refused. Whether out of conviction or stubbornness, Moskowitz often refuses to bend to outside pressure or to take advice, even from allies. Dial returned to her classroom less than two weeks later. Neither did Moskowitz dismiss Fort Greene principal Candido Brown over the revelation of his "Got to Go" list. "But everyone doesn't get to make up how they treat children," Moskowitz warns. There is "a sweet spot of level of sternness." Determining how much is too much requires knowing the teacher's relationship to her kids.

More than most charter school leaders of her stature, Moskowitz consistently sees and talks about schooling through a child's lens. Too much direct instruction—explaining the steps to solve a math problem, for example, rather than guiding kids as they struggle and strategize—sets her off. "If you see a teacher, 'Blah, blah, blah, blah,'" she says, pantomiming extreme boredom. Her tone has been restrained, her delivery pedantic, even when discussing charged topics like race, cheating, and the Charlotte Dial video. But now she grows animated, even agitated. "Who has seen a kid when their teacher keeps them on the rug for twenty-five minutes? *They're five, for God's sakes!* You try sitting on that rug for twenty-five minutes listening. *That is an educational crime!*"

She moves on to outcomes. If you don't get extraordinary student outcomes, you cannot excel as a leader at Success Academy. "Pretty obvious, no?" she asks, blandly. Her lieutenants nod eagerly, not anticipating the inevitable fillip: "It's a little buried in your list," Moskowitz notes. "Did you notice that? Did anyone *say* 'outcomes'?" She takes a step toward the whiteboard. The rhetorical question draws embarrassed silence and a few muttered nos. "That worries me a little bit; that it wasn't at the top of your list, right? Because you are thinking about inputs, not outputs," she says. "And you've got to keep outcomes top of mind."

The third guiding principal in Moskowitz's holy trinity is community. What she has in mind isn't the standard "It Takes a Village" homily, a shared commitment to student achievement among parents, teachers, and various "stakeholders." She means the Success Academy schools and network. "We're going for the greatest good for the greatest number, and we have a public-good mentality," she insists. "You would not be an excellent leader if you went around saying, 'You know, that damn network . . .'" Gesturing to Kerrie Riley and other junior leaders as she singles out their individual schools, Moskowitz says, "It's not about Bronx 1 or Washington Heights when you are thinking about the public good. It's totally different than *my* school, *my* teachers, *my* kids." When a student at Harlem 4 died the previous year, every school psychologist in the network spent a week counseling teachers and students. When the Union Square campus lost electricity, every student was taken care of at other Success Academy schools within twenty-four hours. "I don't mean this in a morally critical way," Moskowitz tells the group, "but having a sense of the public good, you're required to be less narcissistic. If you're asked to help a colleague and a school in need, and you say the commute's too long, that's not going to go over very well."

Had she given this speech publicly, Moskowitz would face gales of derision from her critics for claiming that Success Academy is an ethical, values-driven organization with a public-good mentality. The bill of particulars is long and includes charges of trigger-happy suspension policies, claims that Success systematically weeds out special education students and the hardest to teach and puts so much pressure on children to deliver top test scores that they routinely soil themselves in class. Large class sizes, high teacher turnover, and the refusal to admit new students after fourth grade are also among the criticisms. But it's impossible to dispute Success Academy's greatest observable achievement to date: The network has grown to more than forty schools without a single weak one. The network's poorest-performing school, Harlem 2, where Moskowitz grew exasperated with teachers' "stupid shouting and call-and-response," pushed 90 percent of its students to proficiency in math the previous year, a rate more than double the statewide average. Every one of nearly two dozen other Success Academy schools with children in testing grades scored higher; at three of them—Crown Heights and Fort Greene and Manhattan's Hell's Kitchen—every tested student was proficient or advanced. In English Language

Arts, Success Academy's "worst" school in 2016–17 was Williamsburg, Brooklyn, with 75 percent at or above proficiency.

Unlike other large US charter networks, Success Academy has no schools outside New York City. Moskowitz's ability to parachute in staff and resources from the network office or a stronger campus across town at a moment's notice, and the "drop everything" mindset when a sister school is in crisis, makes it unlikely that an outlier will suddenly emerge or would struggle for long. An aggressive regimen of network-administered reading and math "interim assessments" five times each year, with results reported to headquarters and disseminated throughout the organization, serves as an early-warning system. By the time students sit for state math and reading tests each spring, the network can reliably predict how every student will fare. There are no surprises.

"Ethics, outcomes, community—those are my three. Should we talk about how to get there?" Moskowitz asks the room. Building leaders cannot be effective if they are anxious, she asserts, and then, shifting directions, she makes a remarkable claim: "We have never fired a teacher over data. Ever. We've never fired a *leader* over data. All this anxiety—I don't know exactly where it's coming from." I feel my face register surprise, but the junior leaders sit poker-faced. The claim might be true in the narrowest sense, but senior staffers, past and present, agree there is immense pressure within the organization to deliver strong results on the interim assessments, practice tests, and state exams. One describes a culture of repeated "public shaming" over data that is acutely embarrassing for principals whose results are weak. "I have watched lots of folks walk away because they felt disrespected," a high-ranking former Success staffer told me.

There *are* things she wants leaders to stress about, such as the safety of children, Moskowitz insists. No subject gets her more wound up. Once, a teacher returned to school from a field trip to a farm and discovered a student had gone missing. Moskowitz's voice hits her agitated higher register. "I mean, we are responsible for the safety of the children, and *not losing them*!" she nearly shouts. No one should assume that the Administration for Children's Services, which the staff at Bronx 1 called on a parent the previous week, will do as good a job as Success itself can do in protecting its children. This us-against-them mentality seems imprinted on Moskowitz's mind. "We don't call ACS because we know that they will protect the child. We call ACS to check the box," she lectures. "But we don't check the box and then go to sleep at night. We make sure that ACS actually goes to the child's home and that the child is alive and well." Nights and weekends are no exception and no excuse. "We're not off duty on the weekend. Does everyone *understand that*?" she asks. "We are public figures in that sense. We're always on duty."

Recognizing that she has gone off on a tangent, Moskowitz returns to her main point: the need for the folks in the room to remain focused and calm. "If you are a ball of anxiety and stress, you can't make difficult judgments in real time. You wouldn't make really good firemen, would you? You have to make difficult decisions that affect the welfare of children, so you have the clarity of thought and judgment. If you are a stress ball, that is not going to work."

Moskowitz's advice seems to resonate with the three leaders from Bronx 1, especially Amy Young. "This seems like something I should have heard before," she says. "This is my missing piece." She confesses to the group that since the start of the school year, she has felt "like a chicken with my head cut off."

"It's hard to be mature when you're twenty-four," Moskowitz says. "But that's what the job requires." Her comment underscores one challenge Success Academy faces that's hiding in plain sight: It is a *very* young organization. None of the junior leaders in the room appears to be over the age of thirty. Many supervise teachers who are about the same age and with not much less experience. Someone notes that when leaders are immature, they often simply want to be liked by the teachers they supervise. The observation lights Moskowitz up. "Oh my goodness, you have hit the nail on the head! That drives me *crazy*. I call it 'leadership via BFF,'" she says. "This desire to be liked is very powerful, particularly among junior leaders who were just teachers. They're always seeing things from the teacher's point of view." Teaching is exhausting, frustrating, and physically demanding—and she wants the group to have empathy. "But you're here to do a job, not to be friends with everyone," she insists. The same is true of parents. You may like one parent more than another, "but both of their children are in your classroom, and you've got to get them to the same place."

The meeting winds down. Moskowitz invites everyone to linger, to eat and drink, or at least to take some food home. "It was fun to get to know some of you better. I really do wish you the best," Moskowitz concludes, but not before directing her final comment to Amy. "Don't be too self-critical, Ms. Young. I trust you. You're not going to succeed at first. We hired you for your potential." Then she adds, as everyone is packing up to go, "Does everyone understand that?"

CHAPTER 7

"Just Let This Latina Pass"

A ROBUST BODY OF RESEARCH SUPPORTS THE CONCLUSION THAT A parent's involvement in a child's education correlates strongly with academic outcomes.[1] Teachers have historically tended to define "parental engagement" narrowly, using as a proxy observable and measurable acts such as whether parents help children with their homework and attend parent-teacher conferences. Conditions at home are also weighed. Does a child have a designated place to do her homework? Are there firmly established household routines requiring that homework must be done before he can have screen time or go outside to play? Research suggests a more nuanced view of parental involvement that has less to do with observable behavior and more to do with what William Jeynes, a professor of education at California State University, Long Beach, calls "subtle social variables," including a parent's expectations of her child's academic performance, the quality of parent-child communication, and parental style. Jeynes, who has conducted several meta-analyses on studies of parental involvement in education, notes that the key qualities of schools seeking to foster and enhance parental involvement are also subtle. "Whether teachers, principals, and school staff are loving, encouraging, and supportive to parents may be more important than the specific guidelines and tutelage they offer," he wrote in a 2011 summary in the *Teachers College Record*.

Many of Jeynes's insights are on display at Success Academy. Most obvious, high levels of involvement "are more easily achieved when parents have chosen a particular school for their child," he noted. This is common sense. The very act of choosing one school instead of another implies a significant level of parental awareness and discernment. A child does not end up at Success Academy by accident. A high level of buy-in is a prerequisite. Jeynes's meta-studies also indicate that parental involvement is more likely if a child comes from a two-parent home. This, too, is unsurprising: parental bandwidth is doubled. Additional benefits also accrue, Jeynes has found, among families with strong religious values.

Education reformers and charter school advocates are often loath to discuss these benefits for fear of stigmatizing children who come from single-parent homes or those with different values, but that does not negate the evidence. "Family factors are even more important than school factors in terms of determining achievement. That's just a reality," said Jeynes, who has published research demonstrating that in religious (mostly Christian) schools, the achievement gap "mostly goes away" among African American and Latino students "who are religious and from intact families."[2]

At the end of a late-summer school day, scores of Bronx 1 mothers and fathers labor up the stairs for the first whole-school parent meeting of the year. The streets of Mott Haven are oppressive with heat and humidity, and they're sweating profusely by the time they arrive at the DMZ between Success Academy and Bronx Academy of Letters. Nick Carton and Kerrie Riley greet them with smiles, handshakes, and an unbroken stream of "Welcome!" and "Nice to see ya!" They already know a substantial number of parents by name, even though both are still in their first weeks at Bronx 1. They direct traffic to a registration table draped in Success Academy's signature orange, where parents pick up a name tag with their child's name, grade, and classroom.

The auditorium is a jarring reminder of Bronx 1's status as a co-located school in a building owned and maintained by the DOE. Bronx 1's hallways and classrooms are clean, well lit, cheerfully decorated, and air-conditioned. The auditorium, which is not under Success Academy's control, is a time capsule of a large public high school circa 1974—a trip back to Kansas from Technicolor Oz. The cinder-block walls are painted an industrial sea-foam green. Rows of fluorescent lights span the ceiling, reflected by the lacquered concrete floor. The hard-backed wooden seats are identical to the ones I remember from the Long Island high school where I graduated nearly forty years ago. A large and forlorn clock built into the wall is frozen at 8:43, too far from the stage to be noticed, too high off the floor to be repaired.

By the time Liz Vandlik takes the mic, the seats are half filled with about two hundred parents. She bids the crowd good afternoon and gets a lethargic response. "We'll do it one more time," she responds, "and pretend that we are not hot and sweaty and tired in the auditorium. We'll fake the energy until we feel it. *Good afternoon!*" This time the parents respond with more gusto; Vandlik smiles appreciatively. She needs the crowd fired up. Today's meeting is about the other half of Success Academy's dual mission: converting tens of thousands of parents into foot soldiers to agitate for charter-friendly state laws, additional space in New York City school buildings, and more generous per-pupil funding. A month from now at Brooklyn's Prospect Park, there will be a massive rally of parents, teachers, and students bused in from every Success Academy and dozens of other charter schools citywide. The hip-hop artist Common will perform. There will be speeches from politicians, and TV news crews to record it all. These kinds of displays of political muscle and star power give fits to charter school opponents, who object to the expense; to students missing a day of school to be used as props; and to efforts to push, prod, and cajole parents, most of them low-income, to miss a day of work for a political rally. Advocates insist these rallies are not political at all but a demonstration of the demand for quality education among low-income families and those most likely to be stuck in low-performing schools in the absence of choice. As Vandlik frames it tonight, activism is "education in itself. We're teaching our kids that they are powerful and they can advocate for themselves."

Vandlik's first priority is to reinforce the school's parental expectations and culture norms. Invoking a standard classroom practice, she asks parents to turn and talk to a neighbor about their hopes for their children for this year. The mother seated next to me says she is hoping to see her son, a kindergartener in Mr. Carnaghi's class, "improve with his speech." She has a sixth-grade daughter who has been at Bronx 1 since it opened in 2010; her youngest got in this year because of sibling preference in the lottery. She initially heard about Success through word of mouth and decided to apply even though her daughter had already started kindergarten at a public school on nearby Webster Avenue. "She wasn't learning anything," the mother adds, as Vandlik brings the turn-and-talk to a close and asks for a few parents to tell what they discussed. When there is no immediate response, she threatens to "do what I do to your children and cold-call you if no brave people stand up."

One by one, parents rise to share their hopes for their children. "For her to read more," says the first. "For me, it's that my daughter is able to write and be proficient in math," adds the next. A third mother wants her son to "continue to have a passion for learning." Vandlik nods. "We can teach many things," she says, "but if we can install a passion for learning, kids will want to teach themselves, and that will last forever." Scanning the audience for a final comment, her eye settles on Camille McKinnon, the mother of a fourth grader in Kerri Lynch's class. McKinnon rises to her feet and launches into a soliloquy about the high expectations that her daughter has been held to at Success Academy and the confidence she's developed by meeting them. When she notes that her daughter, Blessing, is almost ready to graduate from elementary school, McKinnon's voice starts to break and she grows flustered. "You can get weepy-eyed," Vandlik interjects. "This is big stuff!"

McKinnon's impromptu speech tees up an opportunity for Vandlik to segue into her main pitch: the rally in Prospect Park. "Success takes a lot of hard work," she begins. "Those of you who have been here for a while know this is a partnership; it's a marriage." Staffers frequently invoke this metaphor. The implication is less "till death do us part" than "for better or worse." "I'm going to work very hard, our staff is going to work very hard, and *you* are going to work very hard to make this happen," says Vandlik, who spends several minutes renewing their proverbial vows, reinforcing "culture goals"—the same ones she has been hammering into her staff for the past month. "If you do not give your child to me, we cannot teach them, right? I need you here every day on time," she says. Success Academy has moved its start time from 7:15 to 7:30 a.m. this year, shortening the arrival window before the doors close at 7:45. "I want you to understand what happens at seven-thirty," Vandlik explains. "Kids come in, grab breakfast, and the learning begins immediately." There is morning work, reteaching and tutoring, and "book shopping" in classroom libraries. "The instruction happens from the Very. First. Moment. So it's very important that you be here on time." There are only three reasons for children to be absent: a death in the family, a religious observance, or an illness with a doctor's note—minor sickness doesn't cut it. "This is an elementary school. We're sniffling all winter long," she explains. "We expect you to be here."

Behind her, projected on a large screen, is a network-prepared PowerPoint presentation titled "Recommendations for Parents." But Vandlik matter-of-factly says, "These are not 'recommendations.' If we're going to reach the success that we talked about, you *must* do these things." Her finger-wagging words do not sound harsh or condescending. Like nearly every senior staffer, Vandlik has mastered a style that wraps blunt demands for compliance in a warm and encouraging tone. Reading at home every night is "sacred." "You know we are maniacal about this," she reminds them. For the youngest Bronx 1 kids in kindergarten, first, and second grades, reading at home is a way to model a passion for reading and what fluent reading sounds like. By third and fourth grade, students are reading independently, but parents are still expected to monitor them, engage them in conversation, and probe for comprehension. "You are asking them questions about that book to hold them accountable and show them that you're interested and you care," Vandlik says. Reading is "not an independent task for our kids at any age." The list of demands grows longer. "You're responsible for making sure they know their spelling words. You're responsible for making sure they know their math facts," she reminds them. "Those are things you can do on your bus ride to school, your train ride to school, or your walk home. Very, very simple."

Reaching beyond the four walls of the school to shape families' home lives and routines is stamped on Success Academy's DNA. No one, staff or parents, gives any hint that they might view it as an intrusion or inappropriate. Putting the lift on parents to work with their children to build reading and math skills is seldom commented on by Moskowitz or other network officials, but it likely contributes, perhaps significantly, to student outcomes, particularly at the elementary school level. The guidance is specific, granular, and *deliverable*. Parents are expected to read six books aloud to their children every week through the end of second grade; they must monitor and log their children's independent reading and homework through high school, emulating the habits and structures associated with affluent families. Their commitment is codified in a contract they sign when they enroll their children, pledging "to abide by all of Success Academy's culture policies and values."[3] Classroom teachers collect data and monitor these "parent deliverables," which inform classroom teachers' conversations with parents, exchanges that can become adversarial, even confrontational. Such contracts are a common feature in no-excuses charters, but they are largely ceremonial documents intended to signal a school's aspirations and values, rarely enforced or even enforceable. Success Academy, however, aggressively signals to parents that it's serious about compliance. In her memoir, Moskowitz tells the story of one mother who repeatedly failed to read to her child. "I invited her to a meeting at which there was a surprise guest: her mother, whom I'd met one day when she was picking up her grandson from school and seemed to be more responsible than the mom." The grandmother was furious with her daughter and assured Moskowitz that it wouldn't happen again. In 2017, Success upped the ante, issuing "parent investment cards" grading how well parents are abiding by school policies and practices. It is no longer only students who find themselves "on red" but their parents as well. One Bronx 1 parent told me she felt "insulted" to receive what amounted to a parent report card; a handful of parents in Cobble Hill and on the Upper West Side, two of Success Academy's more economically mixed schools, confided they were similarly put off. But the move was remarkable not for how much pushback the network received from parents, but for how little.

Education is top-heavy with slogans and sermons. As teachers, we may nod in earnest agreement that every child must be held to high expectations and deserve to feel safe and respected, but our practices often reveal something less than a warm embrace of those lofty ideals. The disconnect between words and deeds—between ideals and deliverables—is perhaps most vividly on display in a school's relationship with parents generally, and low-income parents and parents of color most specifically. We may speak the language of "empowering parents" or "parents as partners" but schools, even most no-excuses charter schools, generally expect little from parents; it's a partnership in name only. Bring your children on time, check their backpack for notes from school, and stay out of the way. If there's a problem, we'll call you. Otherwise, we'll see you twice a year at parent-teacher conferences.

Among education reform advocates, there is a regrettable tendency to view urban communities through a lens of dysfunction, and to assume home support is unavailable or of little value. "Schools should not expect much from parents at all," the founder of one national charter school network told me. "We shouldn't build systems that assume we have leverage over parents when we don't." While that may be technically true, Success Academy's relationship with its parents suggests precisely the opposite view. The network makes significant demands of parents, assumes significant leverage, and makes no discernable negative assumptions about parents' ability to contribute materially to their children's education. Very little in the network's expectations, for good or for ill, suggests a view of low-income parents as any less capable and competent than affluent ones.

The more time you spend with families at Bronx 1 and other Success Academy schools, the more easily you can see that certain types of families are overrepresented, much along the lines predicted by William Jeynes' analyses: married, employed, deeply religious or spiritual, many recent immigrants. A mindset is also in evidence: All seem either supportive of, or at least willing to accept or abide by, the network's culture goals. Many are vocally and adamantly supportive. The most enthusiastic parents most often praise the very thing that Success Academy's critics most often deride: the perception that the schools are too strict, with little tolerance for misbehavior. I lost track of the number of parents who told me, "That's how I raise my child at home." A particular kind of family seems to be attracted to and to persist at Success Academy: those willing to have their behavior shaped and directed by the network's demands. And those demands are significant. "I will teach, model, and live by the Success Academy values every day," the parent contract states. "I will inspire my scholar to love learning and strive to be exemplary."

Unlike traditional public schools and many charter schools,

Success Academy does not offer school buses. This both limits the pool of applicants to parents who can attend to transportation logistics and allows for constant face-to-face contact, particularly in the elementary school years. Interactions between parents and staff are baked into drop-off and pick-up, in frequent "upstairs dismissals" that require parents to come into the classrooms and listen to the teachers or administrators before picking up their children, and in the frequent phone calls from teachers. There are no parent-teacher conference nights at Success Academy; it would be redundant.

For some parents, the constant contact, the ceaseless messaging and enforcement of school culture and academic goals, is refreshing and invigorating—in contrast with what they see as the indifference of neighborhood schools. For others, it's simply too much. In April 2015, the *New York Times* invited former and current Success Academy parents and students to write about their experiences.[4] "The dozens who did alternately described a learning environment that was a godsend for some children and a grind for others," the paper reported. One father, Evaristo Barrios, credited not his public education for his education and professional accomplishments, but his parents, who reinforced that school was important, excelling was mandatory, and that there were no limits to what he could accomplish if he worked hard. "I cannot understand the criticisms against Success Academy, which has consistently shown that discipline and effort results in academic excellence," wrote Barrios, whose son attended the network's Hell's Kitchen school at the time. "As adults, we are all expected to do our very best, and we expect the same of others. Why would we want our son to be taught in an environment that would expect any less from him?" But a Harlem 3 father, José M. Grajales, cautioned parents with special-needs children to be wary. "For those who try and try and can never get out of the 'red,' Success Academy is not for them," he wrote. "We are exploring other options for our children, and we are hoping for better options for the next school year." The testimonials, both supportive and critical, were notable for their evenhandedness. "We still believe that the basic philosophies behind Success Academy are admirable," wrote one mother, identified by the *Times* only as "Maren H.," even as she expressed disappointment with her school's handling of "children who might learn differently, or need a little extra patience and understanding." A Hell's Kitchen mother, Erin Felix, wrote, "For many of us, there isn't a better option than Success Academy," noting that while she disagreed with many of its ideologies, "unless you can afford to live in the Upper East Side or Upper West Side, the options for a decent education for your child are slim."

Back in the auditorium, Vandlik wraps up her speech about reading at home, monitoring homework, and bringing kids to school on time. "That's really all I care about within this building," Vandlik says, but there is one more item on her agenda. "When you decided to marry us—you decided to get yourself into this crazy, decade-long relationship with Success Academy—you agreed to commit to our dual mission." Bronx 1's parents, she says, wouldn't be sitting in this sweltering auditorium without the others who stood up and fought for it. "This school exists because parents in Harlem, who do not know you, marched across bridges, rallied in parks, wrote to their legislators, made phone calls, went to crazy divisive meetings where they were shouted at. They fought and said, 'No, this is important. Families in the Bronx need this school,'" Vandlik says. "And here we are. We're so lucky to be here. We need to pay it forward."

She cues up a video, sumptuously produced with a solo-piano soundtrack underneath heartfelt testimonials from parents describing their commitment to Success Academy and their resolution to fight for more space and funding for charter schools. The video neither mentions nor shows Moskowitz, but when it ends, Vandlik's pitch largely reprises her Liberty House talk about facilities, funding, and freedom. "We have children in seventh grade in this building. They do not have a high school," she says. When she says, "I hope you're here because you like the way we do schooling and you like what is going on here," she is interrupted by applause and cheers. "We have something special here," she concludes. "But we have that because we fought for it, not because anyone wanted to give it to us."

It's time to visit the classrooms. "Are you ready for some air-conditioning?" Vandlik asks. Parents, fanning themselves and mopping their foreheads, file out the doors and make for the climate-controlled aerie of Bronx 1, where the proselytizing—for early-childhood literacy and parental partnership, not "facilities, funding, and freedom"—continues. Carolyn Syskowski has been waiting with her kindergarten scholars. As parents find their way to her classroom, in the farthest corner of the building, Syskowski is handing out Dr. Seuss books to the children, who are sitting in Magic Five in their assigned places on the rug. "Welcome, Hunter College parents! How are ya!?" she booms as they filter in, welcoming them to their children's "second home." Once everyone is settled, balancing awkwardly on child-size chairs, she asks them to once again turn and talk about one thing they love about their child as Syskowski works the room.

Syskowski has been at Bronx 1 "quite a long time," she says, although that is true only by the standards of urban charter schools, where five years in a single school confers the status of a grizzled veteran. Continuing the family theme, she introduces her "significant other," Brian Hanser, who is lurking behind an easel in a corner. "I've been dating him as long as I've been here, so hopefully . . . ummm." She doesn't finish the sentence, but she holds up her left hand and gestures to her ring finger. Syskowski calls out over the parents' laughter, "All the kids will know. And you'll know!" Her boyfriend grins sheepishly.

Where Vandlik is measured and understated, Syskowski is expansive and effusive, but she is no less by the book. Her mission this afternoon is to build the community and stiffen spines for the rigors of the school year. "A lot of times in kindergarten, I will get a lot of pushback from parents saying, 'This is too hard for my kid. They're five. You're being ridiculous!'" But by June, she promises, these children will be reading, writing, and even doing fractions. "Right now it feels like, 'No way are they doing all that. They're still working on writing their name!' They do it and it literally brings me to tears," she says. "It's amazing what they can do at such a young age."

Kindergarten is the entry year for the vast majority of Success Academy students, which means that by the time they sit for state tests in third grade, most are nearing the end of their fourth year in its schools. When no-excuses charter schools began opening in significant numbers in the late 1990s and early 2000s, most focused on middle schools, the point at which achievement gaps in reading and math widened and calcified. It became quickly evident, however, just how difficult it is for children who have already fallen years behind, particularly in reading, to catch up—even at the best-run schools. Fewer than one-third of students who have fallen behind academically by fourth or eighth grade catch up and graduate "college ready," according to a 2012 ACT study.[5] As a result of these hard-learned lessons, most major charter management organizations, including KIPP, now prefer to start students in elementary school.

Kindergarten has become an object of intense focus in American education, rapidly expanding in reach and intensity. As recently as the 1970s, full-day kindergarten was nearly unheard of in much of the United States, before demographic shifts such as the rise of two-paycheck families and single parenting helped spur full-day programs in public schools. It is now widely viewed as essential to closing black-white achievement gaps, though as of 2018, only thirteen states and the District of Columbia require schools to offer it.[6] Thirty-three states do not require children to attend kindergarten at all, but 86 percent of five-year-olds do, a figure that has remained virtually unchanged for twenty years.[7,8] In those states, the overwhelming majority of children—no less than 70 percent—attend full-day programs.[9]

Syskowski's students are still getting acclimated to spending eight hours a day in this strange place called school. Some attended pre-K, but most are still in the very first days of their formal education. "They're used to being able to do whatever they want to do," Syskowski reminds her parents. "They're not used to being told, 'That's not what we do. That's not how we behave.'" She warns parents to expect times when their children will get frustrated and upset. "When I'm upset, I crave Chinese food and I call my mom," she says, but small children don't have the ability to self-regulate or cope; it's up to Syskowski and assistant teacher Olivia Hanania to help them develop coping strategies instead of throwing temper tantrums.

Hanania reminds parents to keep reading logs filled out and to "practice, practice, practice" the spelling and sight words the teachers send home. Having graduated from SUNY Oneonta, an upstate public college with one of the New York's largest teacher education programs less than three months ago, Hanania clutches a clipboard and speaks from notes in her debut in front of parents. Syskowski speaks from experience. For the next twenty minutes, she leads an informal seminar on early-childhood literacy and math, coaching parents on how to read with their children in their laps. Parents can ask, "What's happening in the picture?" They can learn what a title is and how to follow a line of text from left to right. Nightly story time helps develop a fondness for books and reading. Pointing out books that she has arranged on each table, she asks parents to take a moment to examine a Level A book and a Level D one and look for differences between the two. Israel's dad points out that the higher-level books have more advanced vocabulary and sight words. Precious's mom notices that the lower-level books have one simple sentence per page. Several parents speak in Caribbean and West African–accented English. "Our challenge is to get them from a Level A to a Level D by the end of the year," Syskowski says. "But I like to go past that and to an E." Children who are assessed at Level D at the end of kindergarten often regress after a "summer slump," returning in the fall at Level B or C. "Are they readers yet? No. Are they going to get there?" Syskowski directs the question to the parents, but it's the children still gathered on the rug who answer, "Yes!" They have been hearing this from their teacher for weeks.

"If they move up a reading level, we go crazy, because that was a lot of hard work, and we really want to celebrate it," she says. Many parents have been conditioned to expect bad news when a teacher calls in the middle of the day. "You'll be like, 'Oh no! Is my child misbehaving?' No," Syskowski reassures them. "We don't want to scare you when you're at work. But we want to call you so they can tell you how proud they are of themselves." She points out Precious, who is wearing a paper crown she made to celebrate entering six books on her reading log by Thursday, one day early. "Read like crazy. That's going to have them just soar to college." Encouraging parents to follow her lead in motivating children to work hard at home, she hands out sheets of stickers. "Sticker 'em up at home! They work really hard for stickers." Success Academy, she notes, is "blessed to have a lot of resources. You need more stickers? Just ask! You need more cubes, tiles, index cards? Just ask, ask, ask. We're happy to give you anything you need to support your child at home."

Children tend to enjoy math more than reading, Syskowski says, shifting into an explanation of Success Academy's math curriculum, which emphasizes counting in kindergarten. "It's repetitive, and they get *crazy* good at it," she explains. Writing "27 + 14" on the classroom smartboard, she warns parents to expect "a totally different world of learning math. We all learned math this way," she says, doing the sum while narrating her work: "Seven plus four is eleven; put the one here and carry the one." She stops and turns back to the room. "What does 'carry the one' mean? I love that you're giggling, mom," she says to one parent. "Before I came here, I had no idea why I carried that one. I knew I couldn't put it *here*"—she writes "11" below the stacked "7" and "4." "I did a procedure. No one ever taught me the real reason."

Syskowski promises a series of literacy nights, math nights, and open classrooms to help parents help their children. For now, she begs parents not to teach their children "procedures." She reminds them one last time about the importance of their kids coming to school every day, on time, with "book baggies" of library books for independent reading, and homework folders. If these items are left at home, it's an automatic yellow on the behavior chart. The point, she explains, is "getting them out of that concept of 'Well, my mom didn't put it in my backpack.' We're teaching them responsibility now. That's the way we are molding them." But it's not all drudgery. "We love dances," she promises. "You will find out that Ms. Syskowski *looooooves* to party. And the only way we get to party is when we have worked hard. I have a very high bar, and they *will* meet it."

One morning before the start of the school day, a fourth grader named Jessica, a student at PS 49, a few blocks from Bronx 1, comes in with her mom. It is well into October, but the girl's name has bubbled up to the top of the waitlist, and she's been offered a seat— the fifth new student since the start of the school year. She is assured a seat at Bronx 1, but there is no guarantee it will be in the fourth grade. Success Academy independently assesses the "backfill" students who come off its waitlist after first grade to determine the grade in which they will be placed. This inevitably results in some parents declining the seat rather than seeing their sons or daughters repeat one or more grades.

The girl says goodbye to her mother, and Kellie Grant takes her for her assessment. As I watch them disappear down the hall, another mother sidles up to me and introduces herself. Her name is Evelyn Ortega, and she's curious about my role at Bronx 1. Having seen me frequently since the start of the school year, she assumed I was a Success Academy staffer of some variety. Her son, Eleazar, is in Kerri Lynch's fourth-grade class. We agree to meet for breakfast a few days later after drop-off at the coffee shop in the lobby of

Lincoln Hospital up the block. Our "quick breakfast" stretches into several hours.

Ortega grew up in Fremont, California, a solidly middle-class community about an hour from San Francisco, across the bay from Palo Alto. Apple's first Macintosh manufacturing plant opened there in 1984, the same year that Ortega, had she stuck around, would have graduated high school. But it didn't work out that way. "I supposedly went to good schools, but I kept getting passed and I didn't know shit," she tells me. "They were like, 'Just let this Latina pass.' They were passing kids back then. I got lost in the system," she says, pushing a fruit salad around on her plate. "And I refuse to let that happen to my son."

The name Silicon Valley was just gaining traction at the time, and Ortega's parents were a solid part of the region's burgeoning professional class. Her father worked for IBM, then Loral, a defense contractor that built satellites; her mother worked for Xerox. Things went awry early and not just with school. "I'm a recovering drug addict," she volunteers. Registering the surprised look on my face, she continues with a tight-lipped smile. "I was smoking weed in third grade, sweetheart," says Ortega, who has now been clean for more than twenty years. Her mother and stepfather split up while she was still in high school. She dropped out and moved with her mother back home to Vieques, an island off the coast of Puerto Rico, where she got her GED and worked in restaurants. The death of a close cousin led to even more drug use. Ortega ended up in San Juan, where she continued managing restaurants and opening new ones, but her habit got worse. "I was doing cocaine five times a week, but I was a 'responsible' drug addict," she says. "I was presentable. I paid my bills." It still took a toll. "I lived that crazy *la vida loca* lifestyle. The drugs. Horrible relationships. But I worked in a really nice restaurant. They really cared. I was a manager. I learned a lot about the restaurant business, but I was a drug addict. It was crazy; it was stopping me from doing so much."

When she decided to move to New York City in 2000, friends

advised against it. "People were like, 'Why are you moving to New York? There's so much drugs!'" But Ortega knew that she was ready to stop using and that she needed a change of surroundings to do it. She found a small studio apartment with a shared bathroom on 14th Street near Union Square. Three months later she found a job at Dallas BBQ, a chain of restaurants in Manhattan and the Bronx, where she met the man she would later marry, Eleazar's father. "He was the perfect person for me at the time because he was so anti-drug," she says. "I've been clean ever since." Eleazar, sitting a few blocks away in Ms. Lynch's fourth-grade classroom while Ortega tells me her story, knows none of his mother's history. "I'm going to tell him," she says. She's been telling her nieces who are old enough to know.

I ask Ortega what effect her upbringing, derailed education, and drug addiction have had on her parenting, and she starts to cry. "If he wasn't at Success, he'd be somewhere else. He would be in a Catholic school. I would be doing anything in my right mind," she says. After she gathers herself, she notes that, like most children his age, Eleazar doesn't think about education as a means to any particular end. "He's like, 'Mommy, I want to be a soccer player. I want to become a coach.'" She says she tells him, "'OK, that's fine, sweetie. That's wonderful. But you have to have a backup plan. You want to teach soccer? You want to become a teacher?'"

Ortega's face brightens when she replays the conversation with her son. But the clouds return. "I wish I had parents talking to me like that. And I did not." She grew up in a predominantly white community. Her neighborhood and family were well off, but she struggled with reading. "And now that I look back, I think, 'That was a good school. Why were they just passing me?' And that's what I like about Success. If they feel that you shouldn't move on, they keep you back." I lose track of the number of times Ortega says, "They were just passing me." Decades have gone by, but it still stings. She also knows how much further along she could be if not for the lost time and bad decisions. "All the money that I made in

Puerto Rico, I was partying every night. I mean, I could have bought so much property in Puerto Rico."

She and her husband own a house a few blocks from Bronx 1. "It's not my dream home. Not my dream neighborhood," she admits. "But it is what it is. We're still there, God bless." Ortega, who had just turned forty, didn't even consider the neighborhood's schools when she and her husband bought the place just before the real estate market tanked in 2008. "Obviously, I'm not going to get pregnant, so let me buy a house," she remembers thinking. "But God had a plan." Across the street from where we are sitting is PS 18, where I stood in front of fifth graders in a second-floor classroom for the first time in summer 2002. It would likely be Eleazar's zoned school if there were no charter schools, no Success Academy. Based on state test results of nearly 2,400 elementary schools in the state, PS 18 is in the bottom 15 percent. Bronx 1, just down the street, is ranked at number 11.[10]

Ortega has preached about her son's school with mixed results to friends and family members. "I see my family, and I'm like, 'Listen, this is a really good school. You need to get your kid in there. Try to apply.' They didn't want to do it. They didn't go out of their way. And now they see Eleazar, and they're like, 'Oh, wow—maybe I should have.'" One relative took her advice, and her daughter is "doing awesome. She's so grateful to me. She's like, 'Oh, Evelyn. Oh my God. I can't believe it.'" Another friend briefly enrolled her child, but it proved to be too much for her to handle. "Because you have to be involved. And they are strict," Ortega explains. "They're going to call you for 'your kid is not tying his shoe,' or 'your kid is not wearing their proper uniform.' And some parents don't want to hear that crap. They're like, 'Go teach. This is your job!'" But Ortega doesn't have a problem with any of it. "Your job as a parent is to have your kid look that way. Be presentable when he goes to school. And I get that. They're just teaching him for life." Neither does she agree with critics who find Success Academy harsh and militaristic. Her son looks forward to school and misses it over the summer. "He goes,

'Oh, I'm ready to go back. I want to see my friends.' And he loves his teachers."

It's been nearly three hours by the time I ask for the check. One last time Ortega goes back to her childhood. She accepts that much of the blame for her lack of education is hers alone, but contempt creeps into her voice when she thinks back on her school days. "I remember in testing, I was just doing whatever. I wasn't focusing," she recalls. "I was completely fucking stoned, and I would just be like 'A, B, C, D, whatever.' I'm telling you. They were just moving me along."

CHAPTER 8

Marriage Counseling

Albert Barabas is having a bad day. One of Bronx 1's most beloved teachers, he has been struggling since August to build the esprit de corps that's become his stock in trade in his six years in the classroom. His inability to get his fourth graders to transition from one activity to the next without bickering and sniping at one another has him shaking his head in frustration. He brings the class to a stop. "Raise your hand if you think you're holding yourself to a high standard in the last forty-five minutes," he says. The challenge brings a mix of raised hands and sideways glances. "I would agree with you, Alfredo. I would agree with *you*, Destiny. Put your hand down, Devante," Barabas says, scanning each face. "I know for a fact that many of you are more capable than what you're showing."

His open, expressive face is a mask of wounded exasperation. He takes this personally. "I promise I will not give up on you this entire year, just like I would expect that you not give up on me. I care far too much about your future and capabilities as people," he tells the thirty kids staring glumly back at him. Among Mr. Barabas's gifts is the ability to say things guilelessly that might cause adults, and even some edgier children, to roll their eyes cynically. A Fordham University graduate and Cleveland native who bonds with his students and colleagues alike over rap music and sports, he speaks with a disarming, wide-eyed facial expression, usually accompanied by a boyish grin, even in private conversation with adults. He is the kind of teacher children hate to disappoint.

"We can practice lining up a dozen times," he insists. "I need you all to hold yourself to the standard I know you're capable of." Practicing transitions, as these kids know and their teacher surely intends, is mastered early in the school year by kindergarteners. To suggest that fourth graders—Bronx 1's senior class and elementary school royalty—should have to practice it is an affront to the dignity of their ten-year-old souls. But Barabas has been unhappy with the class tone and behavior since the first day of school, more than a month ago. There have been incidents of teasing and name-calling, mild perhaps by the standards of neighborhood schools, but beyond the pale in Mr. B's classroom. Earlier in the day, he read his class the riot act when one of his students called another one "dumb." "If anyone says anything disparaging to any of you, find an appropriate time to tell me, and I will take care of it myself," he tells them. "There's a pervasive idea that it goes against the norms of your neighborhood that it's not cool or helpful to tell an authority figure if something wrong has happened to you." Another signature feature of Barabas's classroom: he peppers his classroom patter with SAT words like "disparaging" and "pervasive."

He is preaching now. "Let me be the first one to tell you that kind of thinking is counterproductive," he continues. A child starts to raise his hand, but Barabas intuits the question. "'Counterproductive' means doing something that's not positive," he explains and presses on. "If you ever feel threatened, emotionally, intellectually, physically, tell me, tell another adult, so that you can feel as positive and secure and safe as a person as you can." Some teachers might limit their classroom sermonizing to their students' emotional challenges and feel that empathy alone makes them effective, but

Barabas pivots to academics. "Last year a hundred percent of the kids in my class passed the math test, ninety percent passed the state ELA test. In the school down the block, those numbers are about five percent and ten percent. That's frightening, and it's not fair. You cannot subscribe to that mentality." Barabas is freelancing the numbers, but he's not far off. Among fourth graders at PS 18 down the block, a mere 22 percent test at or above grade level in reading; math results are somewhat stronger, with 40 percent testing at or above proficiency. Only about one in ten students earned a Level 4, the highest grade, last year. If Success Academy meets its stated goal for the year, only one in ten will *fail* to reach a Level 4.

The class is late for lunch. Barabas promises—perhaps threatens—to continue this later.

"One, get ready . . ."

———

"We're not going back on this now. I need you to show up at the meeting tomorrow." Vandlik is on the phone with a parent, insisting that she come to a meeting with the Committee on Special Education, the panel that decides whether a child is eligible to receive services. The woman's husband is refusing to attend and pressing his wife not to go either. "I promise I will call him," Vandlik says, "but I'm telling you this: you need to come to the meeting. Is that clear?" A pause. "He cannot tell you that you have to stay home from an important meeting about your child." A longer pause, then exasperation creeps into Vandlik's voice. "You're *Mom.* You need to be there." She stabs the cell phone with her thumb, disconnects, and without a moment's hesitation, kicks off a meeting to plan professional development for her teachers. It's less than two months into the school year and Vandlik and her leadership team find themselves needing to do some "marriage counseling"—smoothing out tensions that have been bubbling to the surface among Bronx 1's unseasoned staff and faculty.

The United States has more than three and a half million full-time school teachers. Three out of four are women; on average, they are forty-four years old with fourteen years on the job. Urban teachers skew slightly younger and less experienced, while charter school teachers bring the age and experience down further still: They are younger (thirty-seven), less experienced (with nine years on average), and with less time at their current schools (a mere three and a half years in their positions). Given that charter schools are still relative upstarts in American education, this is not a surprise. As of 2017, the United States had more than ninety thousand public elementary and secondary schools; despite their rapid growth since the first one opened in Minnesota in 1991, charters make up less than 10 percent of the total.

Success Academy teachers are even younger and less experienced—and they don't stay on the job for very long. Instead of "rookies" or "veterans," they're typically referred to as "new teachers" or "returners." The implication is that it's somewhat out of the ordinary when they come back. It might be. School report cards cited by the *New York Times* showed three Success Academy schools with teacher turnover rates above 50 percent. Insiders say the retention rate is 60 percent network-wide, which means in a given year, Moskowitz's team must replace 40 percent of teachers, plus the number needed to staff the four or five new schools she opens each year. Given her ambitions to grow to one hundred schools, teacher turnover is at the very least a human resources problem, if not an instructional one.

Success Academy has a single, universal model. But that model is most often implemented by a hastily assembled staff of relative strangers—nearly all of them young, many of them in their first adult jobs after college—who are asked to bear the burden of one of the stiffest challenges in American education: raising the educational outcomes for low-income children of color to levels that match or exceed those at the most affluent and deeply resourced schools in the nation. It is not surprising that nerves fray.

"Everyone's pussyfooting around things," Nick Carton reports to his colleagues. "People are talking behind closed doors." Vandlik is unsurprised; this happens every year. "We spend more time with each other than we do with our families," she observes. Kellie Grant chimes in, pointing out that the only experience many of the Bronx 1 staff have working with others is on group projects in college. "That doesn't actually teach you anything." Amy Young expresses concern about putting some of her staff off teaching altogether. "It's fine if Success isn't the place for you," she notes. "I don't want you to be turned off from education because you've had a bad experience with a team. It's not fair to you professionally as a teacher." Vandlik pushes the junior leaders planning the professional development "to make this not touchy-feely." Ideally teachers should see this as "a feedback session, versus a 'you just told me you didn't like me.' It's not personal. It's about what makes your classroom work well," she explains, and Carton agrees. "If it's a successful session, they'll be relieved that they got some things off their chest and that they understand how to work better with their co-teachers."

Something else is brewing, but it goes unnamed. Normally, in the meetings I've attended, Bronx 1's leadership team is unguarded, speaking without a filter about issues with specific teachers and teams. But today they are more circumspect; they seem to be speaking in code. At one point Carton, who supervises second-grade classrooms and science teachers, asks euphemistically, "What about our delicate people?" He mentions no one by name, but everyone seems to know whom he's referring to. There's a brief, awkward silence, which Kerrie Riley breaks.

"You think she's going to go over the edge?"

―

There's no letup in Mr. Barabas's bad day. At recess, he took a handful of his boys aside for a long talk about their attitude and effort, leaving some of the kids frustrated at losing out on playtime. Back upstairs after lunch, he stops class yet again to express his disappointment with the room's tone. "I'll be honest right now, because I'm always honest with you," he tells the class. "What's most disturbing to me now is not the lack of effort but the lack of caring," he implores. "The work is going to get done. But we're not going to be uncaring to each other. The silliness I'm seeing hurts my feelings, but more importantly, I feel bad because you're holding yourself back."

Good teachers know when they're turning into the Charlie Brown teacher, their words background noise. Barabas dismisses his kids from the rug, where they are gathered, and sends them back to their seats to work independently on a math problem. He begins to circulate, and as he passes me, he raises his eyebrows and shoots me a wide-eyed look. "I'm grasping at straws, man," he mutters. "I've never seen this before." He sidles over to a boy named Nasir, who feigns a sudden interest in his number stories as Barabas quietly tries to surface whatever has the boy fussed. Another boy slumps theatrically in his seat, practically sliding to the floor in boredom. Barabas erupts. "If the dude next to you is struggling and sees you laying like that, do you think it's inspiring him to try harder?" he sputters, no longer able to keep his exasperation in check. "C'mon, brother! Hold yourself to a high standard! Sit up straight! *You can do it!*"

There are days when nothing seems to work for even the most skilled teacher. Just before it's time to take the kids to science class, Mr. B pulls the last arrow out of his quiver and calls for his class cheer, one of many raps he has written and taught to his class. "I need a little positivity in my life right now," he says, brightening. "If you believe that we can push through and become legendary, then I want you to sing it loud and proud." He tells a student to start a YouTube video on the smartboard at the front of the classroom. "Raise it up, Violetta!" he calls out, the boyish grin returning to his face. "Let's do this!" The music swells and fills Fordham 4. "We're going to be together and work it out," he calls out. His sincerity is almost painful. At the drop, the kids all shout in unison, "*Working hard! Never stop!*" The kids and Barabas begin pumping their arms, smiling and rapping together, but the joy is short-lived. Things quickly spiral out of control with more horseplay, and Barabas stops the music cold. He takes a seat at the front of the room and slumps, glum and dejected. "This should be a moment of reflection for everybody," he says, "including me." The classroom is eerily quiet. From the back, the hum of the air conditioner, normally inaudible in the lively classroom, seems to grow louder with each passing second. A solid minute passes as Barabas and his students just stare at one another. No one speaks or moves. It's time for the class to go upstairs for science. The look of despair on Barabas's face is bottomless. He breaks the silence without so much as a "One, get ready." "Silently line up," he says, his voice barely above a whisper.

Without a sound, his kids give Mr. B exactly what he asks for.

CHAPTER 9

The Window and the Mirror

WHILE HIS CLASS IS AT SCIENCE, BARABAS GETS THE GROUND BACK under his feet. He and his fourth-grade colleague Kerri Lynch have been asked to conduct a "shared text" workshop for the second-grade teachers who have been struggling with this linchpin piece of the literacy curriculum: an activity where the teacher and students read an article, a story, or a poem repeatedly over several days, teasing out its main idea, structure, and subtleties. The intended effect is "a mini English-lit seminar" for even the youngest students.[1]

Barabas and Lynch "have been doing this for a long time," Nick Carton tells the teachers he has gathered in the hallway, though the two are veterans by the standards of urban charter schools only. They will start in Laura Belkin's room, modeling the lesson with her students while the others observe. Then they will debrief and move on to Ortiz's room, where she'll try it, and then finally to Stewart's room, discussing, critiquing, and comparing notes at each stop. While Carton sets the stage in the hallway, Vandlik, her voice grown hoarse less than two months into the school year, prepares the second-grade students. "Sit up nice, straight, and tall and silently track Mr. B and Ms. Lynch," she says, as half a dozen teachers and administrators enter and crowd into the back of the room. Barabas comments on their excellent posture and attention. It must be humbling, even a little irritating, for the second-grade teachers to see the instant compliance their rambunctious scholars offer these two relative strangers.

"My friends, track me," Lynch begins. "Track the chart paper." Twenty-eight heads swivel to attention. There are whiteboards and pencils in each child's lap. These tools "are a fourth-grade thing," she adds matter-of-factly. "Think you can handle it?" The kids nod, straight-backed and silent before this intense fourth-grade teacher with her flashing eyes and rapid-fire staccato delivery. She tells the students the purpose of the lesson is "to understand the main idea of this text."

Each child has a printout of a "The Art of Arch-ery," a magazine excerpt that the second graders are reading as part of their current "project-based lesson" unit on bridges. Lynch asks them to "preview the text together." The kids either know or intuit that this means they are to scan the passage quickly, looking for clues on what the article is about. "What is the big idea I'm going to learn in this text? What are you trying to figure out when you preview?" One child raises her hand to offer an answer. "When you are previewing the text," she says, stumbling briefly over the fourth-grade word "previewing," "you're just figuring out what this text is going to be about." Lynch and Barabas smile broadly. "Beautiful!" Lynch exults. "Big picture! What am I going to learn about." Lynch asks Barabas to reward the girl with raffle tickets for the latest class-incentive contest.

"So we're going to preview the text to get that big idea. And as you read, you're going to be thinking, 'What did I learn here? How does it connect to that big idea?'" She turns to her easel and prompts the second graders to echo her after each point she's written on it.

What did I learn here?
How does it connect to the Big Idea of the text?

She turns them loose for thirty seconds to puzzle out the main idea. "Eyes tracking, hands locked when you have it," she instructs. A boy at the far end of the rug suggests, "The main idea is bridges." Lynch asks the class to give a thumbs-up or a thumbs-down to indicate whether they agree or disagree; she spots a boy holding his thumb neither up nor down but parallel to the floor. "Track my man in the back with the glasses," she orders, pointing to the child whose name she doesn't know. "Why do you have a thumb in the middle?"

"It's not going to be about all the bridges," he answers. "It's going to be about one specific kind of bridge."

"Woo! *Specific!*" Barabas blurts out. "Nice vocabulary word!"

Lynch encourages the kids to build on the boy's observation. "Prove it to me!" she challenges. This implicit demand to keep reading instruction grounded in textual evidence is one of the core "instructional shifts" demanded under Common Core State Standards, adopted by all but a handful of US states, but it has long been a linchpin of Success Academy's curriculum and pedagogy. The class discussion is on in earnest. One child points out that there's only one kind of bridge in the title. "That makes me think we're going to learn about arch bridges," he offers. "Ding, ding, ding!" Lynch cheers. "What's the type of bridge we're going to learn about? Say it all together."

"Arch bridges!" the second graders answer mostly in unison.

An identical poster hangs in every Success Academy classroom titled "Genre and Thinking Jobs." It lists four "core genres"—fiction, nonfiction, folklore, and poetry—and prompts for each. For fiction, for example, the thinking jobs are "character," "problem," "solution," and "lesson learned." For nonfiction, the thinking jobs are "teach?" (meaning what is the author trying to teach the reader) and "point of view?" By second grade, students are accustomed to looking at reading through these lenses; Lynch reminds them to jot down the genre and thinking job in addition to the big idea. "When that's done, put your pencils down and lock your hands. I'll give you fifteen seconds," she instructs, but takes a pause before beginning the countdown. As she counts backward, Barabas narrates. "I see

Jayrule writing 'NF' to represent nonfiction," he says, prompting the second graders. "I also see him writing the thinking job. 'What is the author teaching me?' 'What is the author's point of view?'"

When it's time to turn to the text itself, Lynch begins to read aloud, paragraph by paragraph. Periodically, Barabas reminds kids to "make a mind movie," another mantra in the Success literacy pedagogy: students should visualize what is happening in the text as they read. Lynch performs frequent turn-and-talks, asking the second graders to tell each other what they learned from each paragraph as she methodically works her way through the piece.

There is no particular magic to shared text, which, like small-group guided reading and teacher-led read-aloud, is a standard feature of the "balanced literacy" programs in nearly every American elementary school.[2] There can be a paint-by-numbers quality to approaching every piece of reading with a "genre and thinking job," the constant prompting to "make mind movies," or the oft-repeated reminder that the "main idea is king." On the other hand, the highly structured approach sets a baseline for rich discussions, particularly with repeated readings of an article, story, or poem. Casual visitors to Success Academy schools are frequently put off or even upset by the unmistakable premium placed on classroom management, which has been a struggle for most of the second-grade team at Bronx 1 this year. It can seem overly structured, inflexible, even harsh—as if teachers are determined simply to exercise control and demonstrate their authority over children for its own sake. But to watch this demonstration—and most important, to witness Barabas's and Lynch's ability to hold and focus children's attention—is to begin to appreciate the why behind all the tracking, narrating, and corrections.

Lynch admits she didn't understand or appreciate the importance of classroom management until she came to Success Academy. Now she sees it as "such a huge part of our philosophy and success" and works to create the "constant expectation" that students must be listening and participating at all times. In her classroom, the most serious consequences she metes out are "for kids who can't

respond to another kid's thinking or can't contribute an idea because they're not paying attention to what's going on." Like many of
Success Academy's best teachers, Lynch invokes the connection between classroom management, student talk, and academic outcomes
unapologetically and with near religious zeal. "I imagine that in so
many classes across the country, there are millions of kids who just
don't pay attention," she observes, "even if there's excellent learning
going on that they *could* be benefiting from."

Enter the subway at 149th Street and Grand Concourse, a short
walk from Bronx 1, and board the 4 or 5 express train downtown;
get off two stops later at 86th Street on Manhattan's Upper East
Side. In the ten minutes on board, you went from the poorest con-
gressional district in America to one of the wealthiest. The median
household income in Mott Haven is $21,553;[3] on the Upper East
Side, it's more than five times greater. This disparity weighs heavily
on a child's educational prospects. But the language disparity is even
more determinative. It sets in motion a verbal inertia that is fantastically difficult for even the best schools serving low-income children
to overcome, and which conversely can give weak schools serving
affluent children a reputation for excellence that is undeserved.

In 1995, researchers Betty Hart and Todd Risley published the
results of a sobering study.[4] The pair had made monthly observations of forty-two infants starting when the children were just seven
months old and continuing until they reached age three; they spent
an hour each visit recording every utterance in their homes. The
families they studied included thirteen middle-class households, ten
professional families, ten working-class families, and six families on
public assistance. The differences were stark. On average, children
growing up in professional-class households heard more than 2,150
words an hour, while those in working-class families heard about
1,250. Children of families on public assistance heard only about
600. Extrapolating their data to a fourteen-hour day from birth to
age four, Hart and Risley calculated that the gap between the

children of affluent families and those on public assistance surpassed thirty million words heard by age four—before setting foot
in a school for the first time.

The differences were not merely volume, but how language was
employed. Hart and Risley calculated the number of "parent affirmatives" or encouraging words such as "Do you like that?" versus
prohibitions like "Stop that!" or "Put that down!" The children of
professional parents heard a ratio of six encouragements for every
one discouragement. Among working-class families, the ratio slipped
to twelve to seven. The children of families on public assistance
heard five affirmatives and eleven prohibitions per hour, a ratio of
fewer than one encouragement for every two discouragements—
nearly the reverse of the first category. "Extrapolated to the first four
years of life, the average child in a professional family would have
accumulated 560,000 more instances of encouraging feedback than
discouraging feedback, and an average child in a working class
family would have accumulated 100,000 more encouragements than
discouragements. But an average child in a welfare family would
have accumulated 100,000 more instances of prohibitions than encouragements," the pair wrote in a 2003 article in *American Educator*.[5] "Even if our estimates of children's experience are too high by
half, the differences between children by age 4 in amounts of cumulative experience are so great that even the best of intervention programs could only hope to keep the children in families on welfare
from falling still further behind the children in working class
families," they added.

Most ominously, Hart and Risley pronounced themselves "awe-
struck" at how well their measures of vocabulary and verbal accomplishment at age three predicted language skill at age nine and
ten. When critics of standardized tests claim they are better measures of socioeconomic status than educational quality,[6] this is what
they mean.[7]

The study is not without significant flaws,[8] principally its small
sample size, but it remains one of the most widely cited in education
research. It suggests that affluent children enjoy a prodigious verbal

head start from birth and hints at the academic dividends that accrue over time. If you traverse the Upper East Side's grocery stores, parks, and public transportation, listen to the chatter between parents and small children. "Reflexively, the affluent, ambitious parent is always talking, pointing out, explaining: Mommy is looking for her laptop; let's put on your rain boots; that's a pigeon, a sand dune, skyscraper, a pomegranate," wrote *New York Times* columnist Ginia Bellafante in 2012. The well-off child spends her toddler years not merely "in continuous receipt of dictation,"[9] as Bellafante put it, but also in a constant state of stimulation and enrichment—museum visits, arts and crafts, summer travel, ballet lessons, and organized play—the hallmarks of what sociologist Annette Lareau dubbed "concerted cultivation" in her 2003 book *Unequal Childhoods: Class, Race, and Family Life.*[10] Like Hart and Risley, Lareau noted vast differences in how language was employed among the families she studied. Negotiation, discussion, and a comfort level in challenging authority, including a "robust sense of entitlement" among parents, mark the concerted cultivation style favored by middle-class and affluent families. She contrasted this with "accomplishment of natural growth," which she observed more commonly among working-class and poor parents. "For them, the crucial responsibilities of parenthood do not lie in eliciting their children's feeling, opinions, and thoughts," Lareau wrote. "Parents tend to use directives: they tell their children what to do rather than persuading them with reasoning. Unlike their middle-class counterparts, who have a steady diet of adult organized activities, the working-class and poor children have more control over the character of their leisure activities."

Experience-driven gaps don't close for disadvantaged children when they enter school. They widen owing to the "Matthew effect," a phenomenon described by Keith Stanovich of the University of Toronto, which takes its name from a passage in the New Testament gospel of Matthew: "For unto every one that hath shall be given, and he shall have abundance: but from him that hath not shall be taken away even that which he hath." In plain language: the rich get richer while the poor get poorer. Children who come to school already rich in knowledge and vocabulary are poised to extend those advantages over children who grow up in comparatively language-poor homes with few opportunities for out-of-school enrichment and stimulation.

Literacy experts often describe vocabulary as consisting of three tiers. Tier 1 words are those that children typically come to school already knowing: "desk," "baby," "walk," and "bicycle," for example. Tier 3 words are specific to an academic field or knowledge domain, such as "circumference" or "isotope," that you might use when discussing math or science but rarely say in everyday conversation. The richness of language usage and comprehension lies in the command of high-frequency Tier 2 words that are commonly used by speakers and writers but which may have multiple meanings depending on the context. A child might know that a sidewalk is made of "concrete," for example, but may be confused by the phrase "concrete evidence." The word "objective" can refer to a goal to be achieved, or it might mean not being influenced by your personal opinion. You may remember memorizing long lists of vocabulary when studying for the SAT, but the vast majority of words you know and use were acquired by repeated exposure. Consider how a child might encounter, learn, and ultimately add the word "endure" to her vocabulary:

* The first settlers of Jamestown *endured* Powhatan attacks, starvation, and ineffective leadership.
* "I believe this Government cannot *endure* permanently half slave and half free," Lincoln said in his famous "House Divided" speech.
* Protective mechanisms such as feathers and fur enable warm-blooded birds and mammals to *endure* exposure to extreme heat or cold.
* Mozart's fame has *endured* for centuries.

In order for the unfamiliar word to become a natural part of a child's vocabulary, she must understand nearly everything else in these sentences, so that the new word "endure" makes sense in context. The child who is familiar with Mozart and Lincoln and the Powhatans, who understands what it means to be "ineffective" and "protective," who knows that a century is a long time, what a "mammal" is, and that such creatures are "warm-blooded," is better prepared to make sense of the new word and more likely to incorporate it into her vocabulary after repeated exposure. For the child who does not know these things, "endure" is merely one more unknown in sentences that are full of unfamiliar words and concepts. This is the Matthew effect in action. With each new bit of knowledge learned and word mastered—or not learned and not mastered—language gaps either shrink or grow wider. Unless schools directly address this, via a knowledge- and language-rich curriculum and classroom experience, the effect over time is devastating to low-income learners. The environments in which children live and go to school tend to push them into either a positive feedback loop or a negative one, which affects the relative ease or difficulty they face as they learn to read and grow verbally.

"Vocabulary doesn't just help children do well on verbal exams. Studies have solidly established the correlation between vocabulary and real-world ability," observes E.D. Hirsch Jr., who cites long-standing patterns of results on the Armed Forces Qualification Test, which dates back to the 1950s, to determine the enlistment eligibility and job placement of potential recruits. "The military has determined that the test predicts real-world job performance most accurately when you double the verbal score and add it to the math score," he writes, adding that much of the disparity in the black-white wage gap disappears when you take verbally weighted test scores into account. "Such correlations between vocabulary size and life chances are as firm as any correlations in educational research," Hirsch concludes.[11]

Few schools serving low-income children make sufficient allowances for the Matthew effect when they teach children to read. This owes much to fundamental misconceptions about the nature of reading itself. Most proficient readers think of their ability to read, if they think of it at all, much like the ability to ride a bicycle—it's something you learned and practiced at a very young age until you could do it independently. Every hour you spent on a bike as a child enhanced your comfort and confidence, and once you mastered it, you probably never gave it any further thought. You just . . . *ride*. To literate adults, reading feels much the same: learned once, never forgotten, and something you get better at with time and practice. More significant, we tend to think of both reading and riding a bike as *transferable* skills: Once you learn how to pedal, balance, and steer, you can ride any bike. And once you learn how to read, you can read virtually anything—a newspaper, a novel, a restaurant menu—with equal ease.

But this view of reading as transferable is deeply misleading. Reading has two distinct parts: The first is your ability to translate written language into sounds, words, and sentences, or "decoding." The second part is your ability to make meaning, or "comprehension." Decoding *is* a skill, and a transferable one. Every literate adult will agree on the pronunciation even of invented words like "pliff" or "plizzle," because we learned and mastered the written code of language. But the soul of reading is not decoding; it's the ability to understand the words we decode. Reading comprehension is fantastically nuanced, much harder to influence or teach, and not a skill at all. Once again, the deck is stacked in favor of children who grow up in affluent homes and who bring their large and growing vocabularies and knowledge base to school.

Reading comprehension, like critical thinking and problem solving, is "domain specific." You need to be able to decode the words and know what nearly all the words mean. But it also helps if you know something about the topic. You can test this yourself by reading something arcane and technical such as a college textbook on a subject you never studied, or instructions for installing an operating system on your computer if you're not technically minded. You'll probably notice your reading rate slows down. You may read and reread as you sense your grasp over meaning loosening. You might even follow along with your finger, read out loud, or feel your lips moving—things you don't normally do. You didn't suddenly lose the ability to read; you're merely reading out of your depth.

A landmark study by Donna Recht and Lauren Leslie looked at a group of junior high students who were considered either "good" or "poor" readers based on standardized test scores.[12] In both groups, some students knew a lot about baseball and others knew little. All the kids were tested on their understanding of a passage that described a half inning of a baseball game. Ostensibly poor readers who had more prior knowledge of baseball easily outperformed good readers who knew little about the game. In other words, knowing a lot about the subject appeared to transform poor readers into good ones. If reading comprehension were a skill that could be taught, practiced, and mastered in the abstract—which is how most schools teach and test it today—then the good readers should have had no trouble outperforming the poor readers. "The wellspring of [reading] comprehension is prior knowledge—the stuff readers already know that enables them to create understanding as they read," notes Daniel Willingham, a cognitive scientist at the University of Virginia, who pointed out in his 2017 book, *The Reading Mind*, the "very robust correlations" between students who score well on standardized reading tests and those who also score well on tests of general knowledge and other barometers of "cultural literacy."[13] The solid, all-around reader is not the person who has practiced and mastered the skill of reading; it's the person with the broadest range of general knowledge—whether that knowledge accrues from home, school, personal reading, or life experience.

One of my most poignant moments as a fifth-grade teacher was spending a lunch hour in my classroom with a particularly bright and motivated child who was thumbing through a book I used as a resource for readings and homework assignments. The book was *What Your Second Grader Needs to Know*, one of the Core Knowledge series edited by Hirsch. She was troubled that virtually everything in the book was unknown to her, and she was universally regarded as the smartest kid in the school, the best student in every room since kindergarten. I could tell she was upset. How could she not know what second graders are supposed to know? "It's not your fault," I told her, and thought to myself, "But it *is* your problem." It's a problem imposed on low-income children when we deny them the rich curriculum in literature, science, history, and the arts that affluent children either get in school or accrue from after-school enrichment and experiences.

Systematically building background knowledge is not an explicit aim of Success Academy's English Language Arts curriculum. I had long assumed that its ELA curriculum played a significant role, even a dominant one, in the network's standardized test results. But when the network made its curriculum available for free online in 2017, the response among experts who emphasize the importance of knowledge-rich curriculum was muted. "Kindergarteners spend all but one of their seven units supposedly developing skills—like the 'skill' of reading nonfiction—and those at higher grade levels get only one or two more units per year that are content-based," observed education journalist Natalie Wexler, who noted that the lessons posted on the website "sound very similar to the fruitless exercises that are found in classrooms across the country. Teachers jump from one topic to another, using content merely as a delivery mechanism for skills, and then students are sent off to 'practice' the skills on books they choose themselves."[14]

Wexler is not mistaken. The ELA lessons are indeed skills-heavy and do not seem appreciably different from what countless other schools serving low-income children offer. Chief academic officer Michelle Caracappa argues that Success Academy puts "an enormous amount of effort and energy into text selections" to ensure that novels and texts used for shared reading are rich and convey meaningful ideas. "We're not just taking the Scholastic guided readings right off the shelf and saying, 'Well, here's our book selection.' We are really, purposefully choosing each text." In many balanced literacy programs, Caracappa says, even whole novels are quickly reduced to skill- and strategy-based lessons. Fourth graders are assigned *Because of Winn-Dixie*, for example, not to learn about the state of the human condition, but rather to do "character-development work, and setting, and compare and contrast." At Success Academy, however, the role of an established curriculum, versus each teacher deciding on the fly what children should read, is critical. When every teacher on a grade is teaching the same "shared text" or novel across dozens of schools, lesson planning has the opportunity to go further, inviting the kind of discussion and dissection Caracappa suggests. Questioning is deeper, student conversation richer. The teachers' own level of understanding grows, leading them to push, probe, and to surface connections that drive student engagement and comprehension.

Caracappa also insists that building background knowledge is indeed emphasized in Success Academy's core curriculum and school model. Students get science every day. They take art, music, dance, and chess. Moskowitz boasts often about their multiweek "project-based learning" units on subjects such as bridges, Eastern Woodland Indians, westward expansion, the American Revolution, and how different cultures around the world make and eat bread. Vocabulary growth has been shown to accelerate when students spend extended periods on a specific "knowledge domain," thus these units likely pay dividends in language development. The sheer volume of reading demanded, monitored, and enforced also contributes. The language of children's books is more sophisticated than even the spoken conversation of college graduates, with a greater number of rare and unique words.[15] So while it is true that Success Academy's ELA curriculum is less than optimally coherent and sequential, its knowledge-building elements seem significant, particularly in shared-text readings. Moreover, the overall student experience at Success Academy appears to be knowledge-rich and verbally demanding. Even the network's approach to math stresses the need for students to conceive and explain their problem-solving strategies and solutions to one another. This impulse also insinuates itself aggressively into the home, with the school's demands for twenty to thirty minutes of reading a night, documented, logged, and monitored aggressively for *parent* compliance.

Neither can the cognitive benefits of student attention and time on task be discounted. "We don't invest in behavior management because we want a culture of compliance," Caracappa explains, echoing Lynch. "We invest in strong management and discipline so that we can really cultivate this learning community where we can truly focus on learning. Where the teacher can pull a group of six kids and the other twenty-four can be working productively back at their seats and learning. That just doesn't happen in many other places."

Much of this stands in sharp contrast to the literacy and curriculum orthodoxy in many schools serving low-income children. There's a belief reflected in teacher training and practice that students will come to love reading and learning more broadly if their education is "child centered" and reflects the interests, aspirations, and cultural background of each individual student. In many American elementary and middle schools—perhaps most—efforts are made to choose texts and novels and to engage children in "authentic" writing tasks that are relevant to a child's personal experience. Similar arguments are often made in opposing more broadly any set curriculum whatsoever; a teacher's job is to discover what interests and engages students and plan lessons accordingly. This approach and mindset are almost entirely absent from the curriculum and pedagogy of Success Academy. The job of a teacher is to bring the curriculum to life for kids, rather than guide them to ideas and material they're already interested in. "Our philosophy is that your role as a teacher is really to be engaged in the subject matter," Caracappa says. "That's a little bit on you."

A few years after leaving my South Bronx elementary school, I was startled one morning by a familiar voice emanating from my car radio, which was broadcasting a story about the struggles low-income children face with standardized testing. The principal of my former school was lamenting the difficultly of raising scores on reading tests. "We see kids engaged. We see kids doing some—honestly—some really extraordinarily deep thinking and talking," she told the reporter. "However, it's not transferring over to standardized tests."[16]

Not only is this unsurprising; it is entirely predictable. The knowledge demands to read even simple texts with sophistication and subtlety are daunting. Once children can decode a piece of text fluently, a reading test is hardly a reading test at all; it is functionally a test of background knowledge.[17] "Deep thinking" is not a muscle that you can apply to any body of knowledge, the way you can train your body to deadlift weights in the gym. It doesn't transfer from one knowledge domain to another. The fatal mistake my former principal was making, and lamenting on NPR, was to assume that you build readers exclusively through student engagement—a steady diet of high-interest reading and writing that reflects back to a student his or her familiar experiences. To be sure, we want children to enjoy reading and spend as much time reading as possible. But to worship at the altar of "just read" fails to see reading for what it actually is: a complex and nuanced interplay of decoding, vocabulary, subject matter, and contextual knowledge. Well-intended but misguided teachers and administrators have imposed a kind of illiteracy on low-income children of color by focusing their attention relentlessly in the mirror, instead of out the window. Reading comprehension is not a skill you teach but a condition you create.

CHAPTER 10

Outliers

By October, the boys of Bronx 1 seem to be holding a competition to see who can loosen his tie the most at morning arrival without being nailed for a uniform infraction. Several slip through the door at morning arrival with visible daylight between their orange topknots and the collar buttons of their blue oxford shirts. Vandlik shouts down Morris Avenue to stragglers who are just coming into view at the far end of the block. "It's seven forty-five, elementary school! Keep running!" she calls. Several children, trailing backpacks and parents, break into a sprint. An older girl named Michelle, who most mornings is the first in line for Bronx 1's middle school arrival, which starts once the last elementary kid is safely inside, says to no one in particular, "She does that every morning."

Word came last week that Bronx 1 and another Success Academy campus, Harlem 4, are among three hundred schools nationwide that have been designated a National Blue Ribbon School by the US Department of Education. Since 1982, about 8,500 schools nationwide, public and private, have earned the title, either for academic excellence or for strides in closing racial achievement gaps. For many principals, it would be a career-making affirmation. Vandlik shrugs and says, "I told my parents, and they were like, 'Everyone gets a blue ribbon.'" Vandlik's own parents may be blasé, but Bronx 1 parents were not. No school in Mott Haven has ever earned the accolade. When word came from Washington, Moskowitz sent an email congratulating the staff, and the network's social media people put the news on Bronx 1's Facebook page. The next morning parents were lined up to congratulate the staff. Jen Fuoco promises a flag-raising ceremony once the banner arrives from Washington.

Vandlik is showing the strain of the school year, now nearly two months old. Nursing a low-grade cold and sipping tea, she makes rounds this morning with Kellie Grant and Diana Rawson, the school psychologist, to observe children they refer to alternately as their "special friends" or "the kids we love the most"—they are the "outlier" students with health or behavioral issues they identified from the very first hours of the school year. By the often-chaotic standards of Mott Haven's neighborhood schools, Bronx 1 is tightly run. But a significant number of children are challenging, some particularly so. This morning's walk-through is specifically aimed at seeing whether the behavior-incentive plans are having an effect or if additional services, or different placements, are needed.

The first stop is "Boston University," Laura Belkin's second-grade classroom. Nick Carton joins the group observing Tyrone, who is wearing an impassive expression and holding a thick stack of realistic-looking dollar bills, play money that Belkin and assistant teacher Alex Gottlieb distribute to the boy as positive reinforcement. "He's on task, doing well, counting his money, and working," Vandlik notes. "This is where it's key to find out what works for a kid, because he's motivated by nothing except money and sneakers, and we obviously can't be giving him sneakers every day." Tyrone prefers singles so he can add to the fat stack of cash that has become a permanent fixture in his fist. "Laura is like, 'This is my life now.' He's just very motivated by the cash," Vandlik muses and reminds her team to order more play money. Someone suggests running some off on the school copier, but Vandlik shakes her head. "Oh no. He'd know the difference." Tyrone's behavior plan isn't solving all the boy's issues; it's a struggle to keep him engaged and on task, but Vandlik is optimistic.

Across the hall in Hunter College, the group looks in on Adama, who is sitting toward the back of the rug and seems to be having a good day. His taciturn paraprofessional, Mr. Dorsett, sits just over his shoulder, expressionless and looking disengaged. A common sight in schools with a large number of special education students, "paras" are often assigned to support individual students with serious challenges related to executive functioning, emotional self-regulation, and other behavior issues. Paras are neither hired nor approved by Success Academy; they are New York City DOE employees. Back in the hallway, Grant observes that Adama "is doing OK, but he can easily go in a different direction real fast." She told Dorsett to sit closer to the boy to make sure he's on task and doing what he needs to do "so that he doesn't become, you know, escalated."

There is noticeable tension between the paras and Success Academy staff. Dorsett's lack of initiative with Adama clearly rankles the group. In science the previous day, Vandlik saw the para but not the one and only child he is paid to monitor. "Where's Adama?" she asked him. Dorsett replied, "He's back behind the bookcase." Vandlik asked him to keep the child in his sights. "I don't need you to pull him out, but I need you to be close enough to see what he's doing," she insisted. When she found him, the boy had a pair of adult scissors in his hands, potentially making things unsafe for himself and his classmates. On another occasion, I observed Adama crawling under desks and making animal noises while his classmates were on the rug. Dorsett made no visible attempt to intervene, refocus, or engage the child. Before they move on, Vandlik tells Grant and Rawson to schedule time to meet with Dorsett as soon as possible.

The "special friends tour" moves to the first grade and Towson University, Shanna Lewis's classroom, to check on one particular girl. They emerge satisfied that Lewis, a relatively experienced teacher who runs a tight classroom, is keeping the child engaged. But Vandlik is worried. "There are several kids in there who are not huge behavior issues, but they are," she pauses, "cranky." One boy has been "kind of mischievous lately, which I was shocked by," she says. "I still give him hugs, but then he's coming up here and tearing it up." In Marist-Clemson, a third-grade and integrated co-teaching class with both special-ed and general-ed students, Kaitlyn Walsh is launching a unit on the Iroquois and Lenape Native Americans, setting the historical scene with video taken from the elevator of the Freedom Tower in lower Manhattan. As the elevator climbs, a time-lapse animation shows how Manhattan and the city's skyline have changed from 1500 to the present. The children seem captivated by the video, including Habib, the focus of the visit, who has just returned to school from a suspension. "Definitely engaged," says Grant, and the team moves on.

Things are not going as well in UNC-UMass, where one of the special friends is at the classroom door, swinging it angrily between his hands as the group enters. Teacher Anna Luker is trying to re-direct the boy back to the rug, where her co-teacher, Joey Patterson, is doing exactly the same lesson launch as the other third-grade rooms. The boy starts crawling under desks, attempting to evade Luker. But Patterson's lesson never stops, and his classmates seem to pay no attention to the drama with Jabran, whom Grant finally takes charge of and leads out of the room. "You probably feel very frazzled inside," Vandlik tells Luker out in the hallway once calm is restored. "Feel however you feel, but I can't tell. The kids definitely can't tell." This is one of Vandlik's stock pieces of advice to her newer teachers: fake it till you make it. But none of this is helping the boy they have come to see in UNC-UMass. He is not learning.

In the kindergarten wing, Tyrone is lingering in the hallway near Vandlik's office, refusing to go upstairs to science. The boy, with his omnipresent wad of dollar bills, is swiftly incorporated into the tour, which makes one last stop in Carolyn Syskowski's classroom to check on two boys who will need to be evaluated for services, including one with autism spectrum disorder. Vandlik asks Tyrone to help identify "scholars who are ready to learn."

On the way back to her office, something catches Vandlik's eye. She peers through the window into one of the kindergarten classrooms and smiles. "Give Mr. Carnaghi two years and he's going to be amazing," she says.

There is no such thing as an elementary school without children who are hard to handle or who bring challenges born of a stressful upbringing to school. Bronx 1 has a surprisingly large number of children who have the potential to be profoundly disruptive. Adama was identified as the highest priority at the start of the year, but behavior management is a constant struggle throughout the school and in most classrooms, particularly in the lower grades.

A few weeks after the walk-through, on my way to Bronx 1, a mother and son wearing a Success Academy uniform sit next to me on the uptown 4 train. Given the great lengths to which motivated parents are willing to travel for good schools, such families have become a common sight on New York City subways and buses in the hour before arrival and after dismissal. It's become my habit to introduce myself to these parents and ask them about their experience. The mother tells me they're on their way to Harlem 2. She'd been trying to get her son into Success for three years; he finally got accepted this year, but the school is trying to get her to transfer him to District 75, the city school district for special education students. I think about the walk-through I witnessed and wonder if her son was a special friend at his school. His mother takes my business card as she exits at 125th Street and promises to send me her contact information. I never hear from her again.

CHAPTER 11

The Math Lesson

ON A BRISK THURSDAY MORNING, THE ENTIRE SECOND GRADE AT Bronx 1 prepares to march off to sketch pictures of the Madison Avenue Bridge, a nondescript hundred-year-old swing bridge connecting the Bronx to Manhattan across the Harlem River at 138th Street. They have been reading and writing about bridges and conducting experiments with different designs and models in science class. Now they will begin rambling around the city to see and sketch them. Mahelia Mighty, the school's community relations manager, gives each teacher a medical bag with an asthma inhaler, an EpiPen, and other supplies for the ten-minute walk.

More than their public school peers, Success Academy scholars spend a good deal of time out of the classroom on "field studies." In the fall, they visit farms, ride ferryboats, and pick pumpkins—standard childhood experiences for many, but exotic excursions for some and perhaps most low-income and immigrant South Bronx kids. As the second graders pull on their coats, I catch a glimpse of Vandlik in the special education office having what appears to be a difficult conversation with an older woman who is wearing a hijab and a scowl. It's not unusual for parents to be in the school during the day. Like every Success Academy school, Bronx 1 maintains an "open door" policy; parents are welcome, even encouraged, to visit their kids' classrooms virtually anytime. But this meeting looks planned and purposeful—maybe an intervention. Perhaps this woman is a parent or grandparent of one of the "special friends" we observed the other day.

In the fourth-grade wing, Kerri Lynch is teaching fractions. Because of its test scores, it is commonly assumed that math lessons at Success Academy resemble a Chinese cram school's, with instruction focused exclusively on "drill and kill" to prepare kids for high-stakes tests. However, Moskowitz, the daughter of a mathematician, is a proponent of a conceptual approach; she derides "direct instruction" and other standard explanatory pedagogies, where kids learn and practice algorithms and formulas, as "math by card tricks." While most schools have a sense that reading should be pleasurable, the same mindset seldom extends to math. "Kids should fall in love with math," Moskowitz says. "Particularly poor kids. They have much more access to math." For low-income children of color, non-native speakers, and other disadvantaged subgroups, it has proved much harder for even the best schools to move the needle in reading than in math, given the myriad factors outside a school's control. But math is largely a school-based subject and therefore "more democratic," in Moskowitz's view. It is where Success Academy's curriculum and teaching are seen to best effect, both in the verbally rich "talk it out" approach the network ostensibly prefers and its results on statewide math tests, which its students routinely make a mockery of—at least at the third- through eighth-grade levels.[1]

The math curriculum is cobbled together from different sources: an off-the-shelf curriculum called TERC;[2] Contexts for Learning,[3] a "conceptual math" approach pioneered by Catherine Fosnot, an education professor at City College of New York; and "a variety of things we found on the Internet," according to Stacey Gershkovich, who oversees math at Success. EdReports.org, an independent nonprofit that reviews curricula, has rated TERC poorly, reporting that it "does not meet expectations" for alignment to Common Core standards or for classroom usability. Gershkovich is unconcerned. "We kind of scrap it for its parts," she explained to me. While the curriculum is home-brewed, it is subject to endless tinkering and is consistent across all the network's schools in keeping with Moskowitz's insistence that everything Success Academy does must be "scalable." The curriculum, pedagogy, and classroom routines borrow and steal promiscuously from many other no-excuses schools, the cause of no small amount of grumbling among other major charter operators who privately complain that Moskowitz and Success should be more generous in acknowledging the foundations of their model. But Success also tinkers endlessly with what it takes from the others. This is particularly true in the network's approach to math.

For decades, an undeclared math war in K–12 education has pitted those who favor more traditional methods, such as teaching kids step-by-step procedures and processes, versus those who put a premium on understanding math concepts first and mastery of algorithms second. It is not enough to know why 4 x 6 = 24, conceptualists argue; if you cannot model the problem, explain it, or solve it in more than one way, then you might know the answer, but you don't know math. Success Academy is wedded to conceptual math but is not blithe about "automaticity," the instant recall of addition, subtraction, multiplication, and division math facts, and it fetishizes what it calls "no-hesitation math," a daily one-minute timed drill that starts in January of kindergarten when children begin adding and subtracting numbers from 0 to 5. First, the youngest children work on "plus zeroes and plus ones," adding 4 + 0 and 3 + 1, for example, and learning that every time they add a zero, the result is the same number. Children might then spend a month mastering doubles, then doubles plus one. The goal is not merely memorizing but building upon what children know to figure out what they don't know.

Lynch's students sit on assigned spots on the rug. "One thing we've worked on is to be able to compare fractions to landmark fractions, such as one half or one whole," she begins. "Today, when I put up the two fractions you're comparing, I don't want you to show any work. I only want you to write if it's less than, greater than, or equal to. Just the symbol." With those minimal instructions, Lynch writes 1/8 and 1/10 on the board and watches as her students bend silently over their whiteboards. "I'm seeing that some of us very quickly know it," she observes. "Go ahead and turn and talk with your partner. What knowledge of fractions did you apply to solve this question?" The chatter rises as Lynch circulates, asking questions, drawing students out, and listening to their explanations, making mental notes about which students she will ask to "share out" with the class.

"Back to me in three. Back to me in two. Back to me in one," she counts down, then instructs the students to "lock your hands and track Emmanuel." Lynch narrates constantly, praising and encouraging children who emulate the actions she is describing. "Wassa put his marker down . . . Jakai turned to track respectfully . . . Philip's marker is *going* down and his eyes are glued to Emmanuel." Behavior management is so deeply ingrained in her teaching that after several years in the classroom, Lynch probably isn't even aware she's doing it. She waits for "one hundred percent," meaning that every student has turned to face Emmanuel. "What fraction knowledge did you use to try to compare the two fractions?"

Emmanuel begins slowly and haltingly. "The fraction knowledge I used is . . ." There's an uncomfortably long pause during which neither Lynch nor her co-teacher, Constance Smith, nor any of the child's classmates speak. "The smaller the denominator is"— stumbling over "denominator"—"the bigger the pieces are. And if they both have one piece, eight is less than ten, so eight—so one-eighth—is bigger, has bigger pieces than the ten. Than one-tenth." Lynch makes no attempt to "round up,"[4] explaining or filling in details in Emmanuel's answer, or to restate it in clearer words. She pushes her class for more. "Why did he bring up the piece about 'they both have one'? Why does that matter?" She cold-calls Carlos.

"It matters because if the *numinator* was not the same, he

couldn't have done it. Because if, like, if the one-eighth was actually nine-eighths, I mean seven-eighths, and the one-tenth was nine-tenths, you couldn't do the smaller, because you could only look at the denominator is smaller than that. The *numinator* is the same." Carlos is tilting toward understanding, but his teacher still offers no comment, correction, or clarification. The discussion moves on. "Who can add on?" she asks. She calls on Matthew Casildo, a serious-looking boy who is concentrating so intently that his face appears scrunched up in a scowl.

"I want to add on that the smaller the denominator, like Emmanuel said, the bigger the piece. The bigger the denominator, the smaller the piece. I think the 'one' matters because . . ." A cascade of stops and starts follows as Matthew struggles to form a clear, concise explanation. "The more the 'one' gets closer to the denominator, it's gonna equal to one"—he struggles to point out that as the numerator approaches the denominator, the fraction increases in size. "Eight over eight is one whole," he concludes. "If it goes over eight, it's higher than one whole."

As the discussion goes on, the explanations gradually grow more economical and precise. When Lynch asks the kids to compare 2/8 and 2/10, Evelyn Ortega's son, Eleazar, is clear on the answer, if not the vocabulary: "I knew two-eighths is bigger than two-tenths because the *numinators* were the same," he answers, building on his classmates' conversation. Lynch raises the rigor. She writes 3/4 and 7/8 on the board. With no common denominator or *numinator*, the answer is less obvious, but she offers a hint: "Matthew, what you said about 'closer to one whole' might be helpful. Turn and talk with your partner." The room breaks into passionate arguments:

"They're equal!"

"Seven-eighths is more!"

"Only one piece is left to get it to one whole!"

"No, they *are* equal! They're both only one piece to a whole!"

"But this one's a smaller piece to a whole!"

Lynch's ears perk up. "What did you just say? They're both one away from a whole? How much further away from a whole? I want you to share that," she says to Matthew. The countdown timer rings, but Lynch lets the spirited debate go on for another minute before bringing it to a close. "Back to me in three. Back to me in two. Back to me in one. Silently track me."

She calls on Christine. "What me and Elyse said is that seven-eighths is bigger than three-fourths because the seven-eighths are smaller pieces to make it to a whole, and three-fourths are bigger pieces to make it to a whole," says Christine. "Do we agree or disagree with that?" Lynch asks. "Track Casildo," orders Lynch, who habitually refers to many of her students by their last names.

Trial lawyers learn never to ask a question on cross-examination to which they don't already know the answer. Lynch does the same thing. She knows whom to call on to surface the point she wants students to learn, not leading the conversation but conducting it. From listening to the conversations on the rug a few minutes ago and pushing her students' thinking, she knows that Matthew Casildo is ready for the pitch over the plate. "I agree with Chris," he answers confidently. "Seven-eighths needs one more eighth to get to one whole, and three-fourths needs *one-fourth* to get to one whole. And one eighth is *smaller*, so that means seven-eighths is closer to one." "Say that one more time. And I want everyone who disagreed with Chris to listen. Track Casildo," Lynch commands. "This is *very* clear thinking."

Fifteen minutes have gone by with almost no explicit teaching of fractions on Lynch's part. What started as an unfocused conversation has become progressively more precise and illuminating. Success Academy wants all its teachers to conduct lessons this way; Lynch, in her fifth year at Success, is particularly skilled at it. She wraps up by adding new ideas to a large sheet of chart paper—a "fraction toolbox" of student-generated strategies—and releases them to work on an "exit ticket," another fraction problem that she and Smith will use later to gauge their abilities. Once more, Lynch lapses into play-by-play.

"Christine is silently working. Matthew is silently working . . ."

While there is no hard evidence to back it up, it is nearly certain that the default mode for teaching math at all levels in American schools is "I do, we do, you do." It's probably how you learned math, whether last year or fifty years ago: The teacher explains a sample problem and solves it while the class watches and learns. Next, the whole class solves a problem together. Finally, students open their textbooks and do practice problems, working independently or in small groups, while the teacher circulates, checking work, troubleshooting, and looking for kids who need help and encouragement. Lynch's math lesson, with its push to get students, not teachers, to do the thinking, and its almost complete lack of direct instruction, bears the hallmark of Success Academy's approach and a focus—nearly an obsession—of its teacher training.

Nothing is scripted or rote about this style of teaching, but that is a mixed blessing. Not every teacher has the flexibility or confidence to adapt successfully to the improvisational style of teaching that Lynch has mastered. Lessons can veer off in unexpected but productive directions. During the discussion comparing 3/4 and 7/8, one child told how she turned 3/4 into the equivalent fraction 6/8, which has one less piece than 7/8. "I didn't expect that to come out today," Lynch tells me after class. "I didn't push for it, but once it did come out, I'll just put it up there [in the fraction toolbox] and continue to get at it," she says, noting that the actual fourth-grade fraction unit doesn't even begin until December. Today's activity is a one-off, an acknowledgement of children's struggle with fractions. "We don't want it to be like, 'You haven't seen a fraction since last May,'" Lynch says. "So once a week we do one little routine like that. This is just building their knowledge and skill set so when we get to the unit, they're already comfortable in that knowledge."

As impressive as this style of teaching can be when successful and done well, observing it often left me feeling that I'd be hard-pressed to make the leap of faith it requires. It takes more patience and perseverance than I typically possess to allow kids to grope and fumble without intervening; the impulse just to explain and demonstrate can be too hard to resist. During my first year teaching fifth grade, I spent several frustrating days watching my students struggle and fail with a unit on "partial quotient" division, a cumbersome, multistep strategy aimed at developing a child's "number sense" and ability to estimate. When asked how many times 12 goes into 280, for example, the method teaches children to whittle down the dividend into manageable chunks: take ten 12s out to make 120; ten more 12s to get to 240; then single 12s, and so on—repeatedly tallying the total until there's not enough left to take out any more 12s. The sheer number of steps led to mistakes and aggravation. Eventually, I did what so many teachers do: I shut my door and taught my students the standard method of long division. If I were to run into one of my former students on 149th Street even now and ask them, "Do you know how to divide?" I suspect they'd answer, "Does McDonald's sell cheeseburgers?" a mnemonic device I taught them to recall the steps: Divide. Multiply. Subtract. Compare. Bring down the remainder. Teachers tend to become set in their ways and wedded to their philosophies, methods, and practices. I was no different. Math by card tricks.

Perhaps I could I have taught this way had I been trained in it. Moskowitz and her colleagues talk often about education crimes and misdemeanors. Direct instruction, teaching kids the formula, is high on the list. When too many kids get the same answer to a math problem, it's viewed with suspicion by school administrators, evidence that direct instruction is occurring. Even when students know the algorithms, they're discouraged from using them. "Never. That's procedural," says Lynch's fourth-grade colleague Albert Barabas. "There are two kids who transferred here this year that use it, and I'm trying to get 'em off it." It's better, he insists, for students to be able to "break numbers up flexibly. It's cool."

———

Success Academy's curriculum, not just in math but also in ELA, science, social studies, the arts, and even chess, almost certainly contributes to its results. But the nuts and bolts of the curriculum may matter less than the fact that Success has a set curriculum in the first place. American education tends to defer broadly to "teacher autonomy," often giving even the least experienced teachers enormous latitude in deciding what to teach and how. It is not uncommon for children in the same grade in a given district to be learning different things at any moment, not just in different schools across town but across the hall in the same school. There is a surface plausibility to this "mass differentiation." In theory, a child's teacher is in the best position to know what every student needs. But it's an idea that can easily be followed off a cliff. Is it possible that José needs to learn photosynthesis and the three branches of government, while Maria needs to learn about ancient Egypt and how a magnet works? Not if a lack of shared knowledge is one of the factors that inhibits language growth, particularly among disadvantaged children. It is also common to ask, "Well, what do children *want* to learn?" The assumption among "child-centered" teachers and schools is that student engagement and motivation, not any particular body of knowledge, are the keys to achievement. Both approaches emphasize skills such as critical thinking, problem solving, cooperative work, and communication, eliding the fact that all these cognitive processes are largely domain specific. You cannot, for example, teach children to become all-purpose critical thinkers and problem solvers; just as with reading comprehension, those cognitive skills can be applied only to a specific body of knowledge you know well.

An unintended and largely unrecognized consequence of the lack of an established curriculum in this country is the profound effect it has on how teachers spend their time. American classroom teachers spend a prodigious amount of time cobbling together lessons from scratch. A 2016 study by the RAND Corporation revealed that virtually every ELA teacher in America—99 percent of elementary teachers and 96 percent of secondary school teachers—draws on "materials they created or selected themselves." Among elementary school teachers, 94 percent report turning to Google to find ELA lesson plans and instructional materials; 87 percent search Pinterest. The numbers are virtually the same for math. The default curriculum in American education, at least in elementary and middle school, is simply stuff teachers find on the Internet.

The deleterious effects of this grab-bag approach cannot be overstated. Time spent creating lessons from scratch or culling them from disparate websites is time *not* spent analyzing student work, offering feedback, building strong relationships with parents, and other higher-yield activities. The mere existence of a curriculum changes the job of a teacher from instructional designer to instructional deliverer. While many educators argue, often strenuously, that their autonomy is sacrosanct, allowing teachers to build a curriculum around their students' interests or customize their lessons to maximize their engagement, an even stronger argument can be made that the mere existence of a curriculum allows the teacher to build expertise herself, leading to richer conversation and thoughtful questions, with deeper student thinking as a direct result. Subject mastery makes it easier for a teacher to anticipate and clear up misconceptions and to prevent students from stumbling down blind alleys. For new teachers who don't have previous years' lesson plans to sharpen or fall back on, the benefits are particularly pronounced. There is every likelihood that the presence of an established curriculum—even a mediocre curriculum—creates teacher *capacity*, refocusing effort on effective delivery and enabling teachers to be diagnosticians and evaluators of their students' thinking and work. The uniformity of Success Academy's model can seem stultifying, but its merits reveal themselves gradually, maximizing the value of the one resource that cannot be expanded: a teacher's time.

Success Academy is not the only school or charter network to have discovered the power of an established curriculum. No one else has equaled its results. The formula, if one exists at all, has multiple ingredients, not all of which are replicable or even desirable, in other schools and settings. However, Success Academy's approach exemplifies Moskowitz's hard-core belief in "making one model great." Walk into a Success Academy anywhere in New York and you will see the same rugs and furniture, the same posters on the wall. "There's a team at the network that decides what are the best color crayon holders ever," quips Gershkovich. But the joke underlies a serious point. If you are the principal of a Success Academy school, the expectation is that you will be focused entirely on instruction, student data, and outcomes. The ops team can handle budgets, inventory, and contracts. Someone else can pick out the rugs, the desks, and the crayon holders.

Success Academies do not merely look the same; they *sound* the same. The constant narration of student behavior that Lynch has so deeply internalized is a standard feature. Children read in "2-2-2" (two feet on the floor, two hands on the book, two eyes on the page). Teachers don't discuss; they "discourse." They set the level of classroom conversations at "zero noise" or "restaurant level." After giving instructions, teachers frequently check for understanding, asking in Italian, "Capisce?" Thirty-odd children invariably respond in unison, and *not* in Italian, "Caposh." The curriculum, culture, routines, and pedagogy are so consistent that if a student attended a different campus every day of the week, she might not miss a beat.

———

A few days later, the second grade is off again, preparing to ride the subway to lower Manhattan for another field study. This time it's a ferry trip under the Brooklyn Bridge and around the Statue of Liberty. Ortiz breaks her class into groups and sets her expectations for behavior; Adama is named a line leader. Her long-winded instructions boil down to "stay with the teachers and chaperones and have fun." The class has been blessed with a perfect warm and sunny early-fall day. For some of the children, it will be their first time on a boat.

It's also the first day the second graders are changing classrooms for guided reading, a teaching technique where students of similar abilities work with the teacher in small groups, focusing on particular reading skills. Before the trip, the children practice transitioning to other rooms for their reading groups, a light challenge since the second-grade classrooms are clustered closely together. Still, second graders generally don't move from classroom to classroom on their own; they're used to being marched from place to place by their teachers. When other students enter, Ortiz reminds them to sit in 2-2-2. Adama, who had left the room for a brief time-in, comes back waving a blue swim noodle. He sits down at his desk, but not before repeatedly tossing his book in the air. "I love the effort I'm seeing right now," Ortiz narrates, praising students by name and trying to cue Adama to settle down. She places red raffle tickets on the desk of students who are following directions. "Don't focus on it," she reminds them. "Stay focused on your books."

Adama opens his book and begins to read, so Ortiz puts a raffle ticket on his desk. Ignoring her directions, he picks it up and begins to examine it, turning it over and over between his fingers. When Ortiz taps his shoulder—his para has done nothing to refocus him—Adama returns momentarily to his book, *The Year of Billy Miller* by Kevin Henkes. It's a challenging read for early in second grade and far above Adama's reading level; he appears to be pretending to follow along, and not convincingly. He gets up to get a tissue, and as he passes another student, he flicks his fingers inches from a classmates' eyes to make him flinch and smiles mischievously.

After several minutes, it's time for the class to return to their homerooms and get ready for their trip. Ortiz lets the kids talk at their seats for a few moments while she distributes clipboards and name tags. Madison's mother has made Halloween-themed bookmarks for the class. The students are bringing clipboards and pencils with them to sketch the Brooklyn Bridge, just as they did the previous week when they walked a few blocks from school to the Madison Avenue Bridge. Nick Carton comes in and reminds them to make sure their drawings are neat, since they'll be using them for the rest of their unit. "Why do our drawings need to be really neat?" he asks. "What class did you learn that you need to be precise with your data collection and super neat with all our observations?"

"Art?" one boy replies.

"C'mon, guys," Ortiz prompts, incredulity creeping into her voice. "*Data collection?*"

"Observations. Data. Really neat," Carton tries again, larding on the hints. "On the count of three, we're all gonna say it, 'cause it's gonna be crazy if you don't know it. One, two, three!"

"Science!" the class yells back.

"I hope you guys have a lot of fun." Nick smiles and then notices Adama, who has his hand up.

"You have to draw labels," the boy says.

"Interesting. You might want to label your drawing," Nick repeats Adama's suggestion. "That's really interesting, actually," he says to himself.

As the second graders gather in the courtyard in front of the school, older students from Bronx Letters taunt them from the windows above. The little kids avoid eye contact, but they're noticeably cowed by the big kids from the co-located school. The mood lightens as they hit the sidewalk. The first train to rumble into the subway station is packed, and Ortiz waves her class off, reminding them, "When you're on the platform, you're at zero noise." On the train, they settle into their seats; Ortiz takes up a position in the middle of the car and drapes her arm around one of the students as girls pair off to play hand games. One girl reaches up to rearrange a strand of Ortiz's hair. There is excited talk among the kids about favorite rides at Six Flags amusement park in New Jersey and an upcoming field trip to a pumpkin patch. Few things will empty a subway car of cranky commuters more quickly than rambunctious school groups. But their fellow riders seem either indifferent or charmed by the well-behaved second graders.

Several parents are chaperoning the trip, including a number of fathers. In my five years at PS 277, I can't recall having a single father on a class trip; they were uncommon even on parent-teacher conference nights. Ortiz calls out in Spanish to one of the dads as we leave the subway. One of the chaperones, Jacquin's dad, who used to work security in a nearby office building, swipes a stranded rider in with his MetroCard, setting himself back $2.50. "Hopefully that's good karma," he says, as his son and his classmates emerge into the sunny morning. "Oooh, look! The Empire State Building!" one girl shouts, catching a glimpse of the Freedom Tower, the 104-story building on the site of the former World Trade Center. I fall in step with Chloe's dad for the walk to the South Street Seaport. He's wearing a paint-splattered Nike sweatshirt with a matching gray Roc Nation ball cap turned backward and a neck tattoo. Another father drops back from the group. A few minutes later, I catch a glimpse of him furtively puffing on a cigarette. Chloe's dad split from her mom, who lives with their daughter in the Bronx, but both parents are very high on Success Academy. His daughter was a strong reader by first grade; so much so that his coworkers were skeptical that she could really read, since their children were struggling. "Everyone in that school can read," he says, as we cross the street to the dock.

"The Brooklyn Bridge is right over there!" a girl shouts. There's a long wait before we board the ferryboat. Ortiz's student Ady and several of his classmates become fascinated by a duck paddling a few feet off the pier, and soon a few dozen kids gather to watch the bird, before Ortiz and the other teachers settle them down. They sit in small groups, talking and sketching the Brooklyn Bridge, several hundred yards offshore. Some boys are trying to impress Ibrahim's dad, Solomon, a Nigerian immigrant, with everything they have learned about Washington Roebling, the chief engineer of the bridge. "He got ill and died," one says. A social worker with a master's degree from Yeshiva University, Solomon learned about Success Academy from friends. Showing good teaching instincts, he pushes the boys for more. "How do you know that's not the Queensboro Bridge?" he demands. "Tell me how you know." The boys point out that it's a suspension bridge but seem at a loss to "prove" that the suspension bridge in front of them is Roebling's masterpiece. They just know.

It's a gorgeous day on the water. The academic lift on the students is modest; most of the children did their sketches while sitting on the pier waiting to board the boat, which is filled with tourists. On board, it's a holiday mood; the children hug the rail as it heads up the East River, passes briefly under the Brooklyn Bridge, and then steams across the harbor for a close view of the Statue of Liberty. Two Chinese nuns are standing with their backs to the rail, posing for a picture with Miss Liberty behind them as two of the second graders wander past. The nuns reach out for them and pull them into the frame. The four of them, united by nothing more than the beautiful fall day and their exuberance at being in the shadow of one of the world's iconic sights, smile for the camera. Ortiz watches the scene unfold with a bemused expression. "What was that all about?" she chuckles. Someone responds, "America."

As the boat pulls into the dock, and Bronx 1's students and teachers assemble themselves to head back to school, I exchange phone numbers with several of the dads. On the way to the Bronx, the express train stops at Union Square, a few blocks from my apartment. I try to catch Ortiz's eye to wave goodbye, but she is engrossed in a conversation with a few of her scholars and doesn't look up. The doors close and the train pulls away, rumbling uptown.

It's the last time I see Elena Ortiz.

CHAPTER 12

"Catholic School on the Outside, Bank Street on the Inside"

A FEW MONTHS INTO THE YEAR, I HEAR FROM A COLLEAGUE AT another charter network about a pair of two-day Success Academy professional development sessions—one on the network's approach to math instruction, another on its middle school model. The meetings are free for any educator who is willing to come to New York City at their own expense, first come, first served. I sign up for both. Attendees descend on a midtown Manhattan hotel from all across the country, including a large delegation from a school in Memphis, Tennessee, and a handful of educators from England. The highlight for most is the chance to hear from Moskowitz herself, who stops by at the end of each workshop for a brief talk and to take questions.

Moskowitz, who can be prickly and impatient, is discernably at ease talking to fellow educators who come to learn from Success, not to challenge its policies and practices, or even its right to exist. She smiles, jokes, and banters freely. She remains unapologetic on her convictions around Success Academy's design and the standards to which it holds students, parents, and particularly staff members. When one of the attendees asks what she looks for in hiring, she answers, "Not crazy." The line gets a laugh. I've heard Liz Vandlik give the same reply. At odds with her public persona, Moskowitz is often self-effacing, even humble in such gatherings, candidly acknowledging the limits of her model. Asked what she would do if she were put in charge of a district high school and had ninth graders who couldn't count or do fractions, she responds "that would be a very different undertaking" from what Success does. "I don't claim to know how to do that."

Moskowitz also admits to "sleepless nights" over her aspiration to send every graduate to a selective college. "In seven or eight years, we'll have three thousand high school seniors," she explains to the middle school group, which includes school leaders from across the country, including some from competing CMOs, such as Uncommon Schools and Rocketship Education. "And my model assumes none of your kids get in." The same problem she obsesses over in her own schools, keeping students in lousy classrooms with ineffective teachers, will be out of her control in a few short years. "There are crappy colleges," she says. "Who wants to send their kid to a college where 70 percent of the minority students drop out? We educated the hell out of them and then deliberately send them to a place that has . . ." Moskowitz throws up her hands in exasperation. "That's my cold sweat. I don't have an answer for that." If it has occurred to her that not every Success Academy student will or even should go to a selective college, she gives no hint. That's not her model.

Moskowitz describes that model as "Catholic school on the outside, Bank Street on the inside," a label that encompasses the old-school uniforms, routines, and strict classroom management that makes possible the kind of teaching championed by the Bank Street School for Children, a one-hundred-year-old citadel of progressive education. No one challenges Moskowitz's description, but like so many other terms in contemporary education thought and practice, the term "progressive education" is promiscuously used, impressionistically defined, and subject to interpretation. No credentialing body certifies a school as progressive the way the United States Department of Agriculture might certify whether an apple can be sold as "organic." Nor is the phrase related to the political use of the word. If John Dewey, the intellectual father of the progressive education movement, were to set foot in Bronx 1, he might run screaming into the street and across the Third Avenue Bridge, not breaking stride until he was safely back at Columbia University, a few miles and a world away. Success Academy's curriculum and pedagogy is simply not "progressive" in the way that most educators understand and use the term.

David Steiner, the executive director of the Johns Hopkins Institute for Education Policy and New York's former education commissioner, defines progressive education as "a movement that champions child-based, experiential learning, and enlists schools as agents of building a democratic society characterized by public intelligence based on the free-flow of knowledge across all social sectors."[1] Child-based or student-centered education suggests a view of schooling that treats children not as passive receivers of information but as active participants in constructing their own understanding and knowledge of the world through experiences and reflections on those experiences. Success Academy's approach to math instruction is easily the most "constructivist" aspect of its curriculum; at least at the elementary level, very little direct instruction in math is in evidence, although instant command of the facts is stressed and expected: the children know their times tables. The network's daily hands-on science instruction and project-based learning sound like progressive education staples, but in execution they are less so.

Project-based learning is revered, nearly fetishized, in progressive education circles. Again, there is no single agreed-on definition, but most teachers who swear by it would likely agree that it entails identifying a real-world problem and encouraging children, typically working in cooperative groups, to develop a solution with minimal direct teaching and advice.[2] Because of its unpredictable nature, project-based learning can be difficult to plan and challenging for all but the most talented teachers to implement effectively—a heavy lift for elementary schools, which are more likely to adopt the name but not the practices. At Success Academy, project-based learning is much closer to what most teachers would consider a "cross-curricular unit." Children read about bridges in language arts, build models in science, and sketch them in art class. Such an approach can build knowledge and vocabulary and help students to see connections across subject areas.

Most significant for would-be progressive educators, Dewey and his philosophical heirs hold that learning is a natural process. Echoes of this belief and mindset can be heard in the clichéd and unhelpful advice to teachers to be "the guide on the side, not the sage on the stage." The progressive educator sees herself as a gardener, not a lecturer, concerned with creating the optimal conductions to encourage natural growth. However, in her memoir, Moskowitz dismissed the impulse to "idealize children" or to imagine that the world is the way we'd like it to be. "As Freud observed, human beings didn't evolve to live in civilized society. Neither did they evolve to attend school," she wrote. "If you start with the idea that children will naturally behave the way you want them to, that it's just like planting a seed and watching it grow, you will likely be disappointed and less successful at teaching them. You are more likely to succeed if you accept the fact that schooling often requires getting children to act contrary to their natural inclinations."[3] This is as far from Dewey as one can conceive.

The oft-heard refrain at Success to "put the lift on students" and to socialize learning, encouraging children to work collectively in pairs or small groups, is the kind of teaching one would expect to see at Bank Street, Saint Ann's, or any of the progressive private schools beloved by affluent New Yorkers. However, it is nearly inconceivable that parents at those elite private schools would abide their children being made to sit in Magic Five or issued a correction if they failed to track the speaker; ditto on the behavior charts and "data walls" that leave no mystery as to where students stand at a given moment, behaviorally and academically. Moskowitz has adopted the language of progressive education more than its practices. The Catholic-school half of her analogy is more apt. Success Academy is closer to the tradition, at least in New York City, of the inner-city Catholic schools that educated the children of working-class parents, and assimilated generations of immigrants. In this way, Success Academy serves politically progressive ends such as closing black-white achievement gaps but employs largely traditional means to accomplish it.

Moskowitz ran and served on the New York City Council as a Democrat and likes to remind people that she is a political liberal. Her obsession with closing achievement gaps and ushering a generation of low-income children into college and lives of upward mobility would make her a liberal icon were it not for the fact that political progressives are generally more likely to support traditional public schools and to view most charter schools as despoilers of geographically zoned public schools. She concedes once having more faith in government than she does now. "I am from an F.D.R. liberal Democratic family," she said in an interview with the Philanthropy Roundtable. "With proximity to government, I have become more libertarian." All this makes Moskowitz something of an orphan, politically and educationally. Equally certain is that none of this matters to the parents of children Success Academy serves nor, by all outward appearances, to Moskowitz herself.

Wrapping up her talk in the midtown hotel conference room, she apologizes for not having more time to spare. When someone asks her to describe the constant personal investment of time she makes to keep Success Academy running smoothly, Moskowitz seems eager to disabuse her questioner of the notion. "It doesn't always go so well. Every kid is a struggle. Every grade is a struggle. Every school is a struggle. It's hard," she says. "It's really hard." In the few minutes she's been speaking, her cell phone has rung six times. She wonders out loud if some terrible thing has happened to a child. "It's part emergency room work and part education. I don't want to glorify it." She thanks the group and exits with her assistant Jocelyn Galvez. Before she is even out the door, her cell phone is pressed to her ear.

———

The air of invincibility attached to Success Academy, its students' testing prowess, and Moskowitz's ostensible commitment to "Bank Street on the inside" teaching suffered a considerable blow when its first scholars left middle school. In fall 2014, the network welcomed thirty-two members of its future Class of 2018 to the Success Academy High School of the Liberal Arts, the network's first high school, located on the third and fourth floors of a Park Avenue office tower two blocks from the Empire State Building.

The man hired to launch the school was an unconventional choice. Almost without exception, Moskowitz promotes principals from within the ranks. There is a discernable type: young, driven, female more often than not, and with a fierce commitment to the network's model and a demonstrated record of success within it. Marc Meyer was not the type. Sixty-three years old and working as the director of education and special initiatives for the actress Goldie Hawn's education foundation, Meyer had been recommended to Moskowitz by Gardner Dunnan, the longtime head of Dalton, one of Manhattan's most elite and expensive private prep schools, and a founder of Avenues: The World School, a private school that charges fifty thousand dollars per year in tuition—and where Moskowitz's oldest son, Culver, was a student. Not wanting to turn her scholars over to New York City's public schools after eighth grade, Moskowitz told Dunnan she wanted to start a high school. Meyer was a respected veteran of elite private schools who specialized in designing independent schools.

Like Moskowitz, Meyer has a PhD in history. His résumé includes stints at the Ross School in East Hampton; the School at Columbia University, which he and Dunnan founded; and Brown School in Schenectady, New York. He's also consulted with many schools around the United States and conducted scores of teacher-training workshops in social-emotional learning around the world. "I absolutely loved working with Eva," he noted. "I like her energy. She's super smart." Meyer spent eighteen months drafting a plan for the high school, which included a core curriculum in mathematics, science, computer science, history, humanities, composition and rhetoric, sports and fitness, fine arts, speech and debate, and journalism. Core courses would focus on questions "meant to invite and provoke classroom discussions and deep, independent thought, while simultaneously covering the depth and breadth of subjects that are at the heart of the liberal arts tradition," according to the school prospectus that Meyer wrote. "She said, 'Give me an Avenues for Success Academy. Make it the most magical school in the US.' It was the best design work I've ever done," Meyer said. The physical space was meant to evoke an Exeter-ish feel, with heavy wooden tables and chairs. "Rooms were designed as college-seminar rooms with a lot of dark oak and bookshelves, yet with a lighter, tech-savvy layer above it," he recalled. "It combined a traditional liberal arts ambience with a twenty-first-century emphasis on blended learning."

The high school was a disaster. Encouraged by Moskowitz, Meyer hired teachers almost exclusively from the private school world, including Deerfield and Hotchkiss. But his handpicked staff was sobered to discover Success Academy's inaugural class of students "were not prepared to do what I had expected they were capable of doing. They didn't know how to study independently without teachers hovering near them," Meyer told me over breakfast at a diner near Albany, where he now lives. "Not unless somebody was sitting as close as I am to you." Worse still, student behavior was off the hook, something Meyer's teachers were unequipped to handle. "Marc had this idea that there weren't going to be that many rules or boundaries," recalls one teacher. "You're going to call teachers by their first name. It was the private-school mindset."

Success Academy's reputation and test scores had led Meyer and his staff to assume the eighth and ninth graders who would attend the school would be up to the challenge of seminar classes, dual enrollment in high school and college, and an "Honors Academy" to develop their intellectual and leadership potential. "We underwent two weeks of training assuming these students had been groomed for this type of education," recalls one of the first-year core academic teachers. "Then the kids show up, and it's just a fucking disaster. It was a nightmare." Freed from the tight classroom management and routines they'd grown accustomed to, and in the throes of adolescence, they ran wild. "You can imagine, right? You're a kid. As soon as you take away those rules, 'You mean, I can just walk over there to get a drink without even asking?' It's like, 'Fuck that. I'm going to go to the tenth floor because that's where the gym is,'" said one teacher. "'I'm going to go play ball and just do whatever I want to do.'" The teachers had no formal training in dealing with those types of behaviors; very few had any experience whatsoever outside of independent and boarding schools. "So it reverted to, 'I'm going to get what I want by yelling at you.'" By Thanksgiving, at least half the students were failing their classes. Moskowitz "just kind of freaked out, thinking this wasn't going to work, especially for the eighth graders who had to take state tests," the teacher said. "She got really nervous and basically brought in all her Success Academy people to do test prep" for the eighth graders, who made up more than half of the student body.

By January, the most magical high school in the United States was being run like a Success Academy middle school. Meyer's private-school veterans were relegated to tracking student behavior on clipboards and watching experienced Success Academy teachers run their classrooms. Of the core academic faculty Meyer recruited, not one returned the following year. "I couldn't protect them from the onslaught of 'We've got to get these test scores,'" said Meyer, who resigned and was brought back to the network office. He was replaced with Andrew Malone, who had started with Success Academy as a fourth-grade teacher in 2011 before becoming the principal of the Harlem Central middle school. He remained the principal until the first cohort of Success Academy students—only sixteen remaining—graduated in 2018.

Meyer still praises Moskowitz. "I kick myself a lot for it," he said. "I kind of bought into the myth that the high test scores obtained by Success Academy students were indicative of disciplined, well-educated, and self-motivated students. I didn't anticipate as well as I should have that the kids wouldn't be able to handle it." His only complaint "is that Eva really doesn't give things a chance to settle before making changes. I know she doesn't cook," he said with a rueful smile, "but I suspect she would make a really bad spaghetti sauce from scratch." A good school, like a good sauce, needs time to simmer.

The first class of students to have spent their entire school careers as Success Academy students faced an intense level of scrutiny from critics determined to prove that there is less to Success Academy than meets the eye. In June 2014, while Marc Meyer was weeks away from launching the high school, Diane Ravitch, the longtime ed reform antagonist and fierce Moskowitz critic, wrote an article in the *Nation* pointing out that of the initial class of thirty-two Success Academy eighth graders, twenty-seven took the competitive exam that determines admission to one of New York City's selective high schools. "Despite their excellent scores on the state test, not one of these students gained admission to a specialized school like Stuyvesant or Bronx Science," Ravitch wrote.[4] The test, New York City's Specialized High School Admissions Test, has long been criticized for the low number of black and Hispanic students who make the cut each year. (In a small-world coincidence, Meyer taught Ravitch's son Michael many years ago when he was a student at Dalton.) "Still," echoed *Daily News* columnist Juan Gonzalez, "if Harlem Success students had matched even the 12% admission rate for black and Latino students who take the test, you'd expect at least three of the Moskowitz students to have been admitted."[5]

In the spring of their eleventh-grade year, Daniel Loeb, the chairman of Success Academy's board of directors, announced the SAT scores of the Class of 2018 at the network's annual fund-raising dinner at Cipriani, across the street from Grand Central. The average score was a 1230 composite—610 verbal and 620 math. Only eighteen students sat for the exam, but 1230 is 84th percentile for SAT test takers nationally; 94th percentile for black and Latino students. The lowest score was 1000, the highest 1440 (another student earned a 1430). By comparison, the average SAT score for students of color in New York City is 831; it's 1026 for white test-takers. Ann Powell, executive vice president of public affairs and communications, pointed out to reporters that Success Academy students outperformed New York State seniors with annual household incomes above $200,000, who had an average total score of 1164, or the 76th percentile nationally.

The network's track record at getting students into selective high schools has also somewhat improved. The second cohort, like the first, failed to qualify a single student, but in 2016, six made the cut.[6] The following year thirteen more won admission to one of the city's eight specialized high schools, including LaGuardia High School of Music and Performing Arts, which admits students by audition. While only about one-fourth of its students sit for the exam, to date there have still been no Success Academy scholars accepted to the two most competitive of New York's specialized high schools, Bronx Science and Eva Moskowitz's own alma mater, Stuyvesant.

The first students to be educated from end to end at Success Academy graduated in 2018. Of the inaugural class of seventy-three elementary school students, only sixteen remained to walk across the stage at New York City's Alice Tully Hall to receive their diplomas.[7] From there it was on to several elite colleges and universities, including the Massachusetts Institute of Technology, Tufts University, Emory, and Barnard College. It will be decades before we can say with authority whether Success Academy and other no-excuses charter schools have what it takes to close the ultimate achievement gap in American life, putting low-income children of color on a trajectory to equal or even exceed the life outcomes of their more advantaged peers, either in educational attainment, lifetime earnings, civic engagement, or other critical measures of opportunity. It should never be forgotten that these—not test scores—are the ultimate aim of education itself. Short-term indicators like test scores are suggestive, but cannot be conclusive.

It may be illustrative to consider students who have attended KIPP, the nation's largest network of urban college-prep charter schools. As of the 2017–18 school year, KIPP had served more than 87,000 students, from pre-K to high school. No urban charter network has more students that have gone on to college, with 11,000 enrolled and 2,000 graduated. Around the corner from Bronx 1 is KIPP NYC College High School, which serves 1,200 students. On the first floor is the office of Jane Martinez Dowling, the executive director of KIPP Through College, who oversees efforts aimed at keeping more than a thousand KIPP graduates in college and persisting once they leave high school. Dowling's parents emigrated from the Dominican Republic to New York in the early 1960s. She graduated from Loyola School, a Catholic school on the Upper East Side; majored in government and psychology at Georgetown; and was among the first selected to be a Teach For America corps member shortly after Wendy Kopp founded the organization in 1989. She ended up teaching bilingual kindergarten and first grade at a public school in Washington Heights, not far from where she grew up.

With more than two hundred schools in twenty states and Washington, DC, KIPP casts a long shadow over urban education, charter schools, and education reform. Founded in 1994 in Houston, Texas, by two former Teach For America corps members, Michael Feinberg and Dave Levin, the Knowledge Is Power Program created or popularized the no-excuses model, whose techniques and mindset have been adopted or adapted by a generation of education reformers, including Moskowitz.

KIPP's oldest college graduates are now in their thirties. Their experience might offer a glimpse of the challenges Success Academy students will face in college and beyond, once significant numbers leave the network over the next decade. In 2011, KIPP released a remarkable self-examination of its own effectiveness, delivering a mixed verdict: 33 percent of the earliest classes of KIPP middle school students had graduated from four-year colleges within six years of finishing high school. KIPP calculated its graduation rate not beginning with the freshman year of college but with the beginning of ninth grade, thus accounting for attrition in high school. By comparison, 31 percent of all US students, and a mere 8 percent of low-income students in their late twenties, had earned a college degree. KIPP was slightly exceeding the national average and four times better among low-income students. "The problem was that the graduation rate fell far short of what high-achieving charters like KIPP thought they could accomplish (and predicted they would achieve), which is closer to 75 percent," noted veteran education reporter Richard Whitmire.[8] For well over a decade, a halo effect had attached itself to urban charter schools, and none more than KIPP, which, like its peers, had routinely won glowing praise for their college admission rates, often 100 percent of graduates. KIPP's study set a new standard for judging the effectiveness of ostensibly high-performing charter schools—college *completion*, not admission. To his credit, Richard Barth, KIPP's executive director, observed that it was untenable to tell two different stories, "a blunt story for internal consumption and a cheery one for the general public."[9]

KIPP's candor drove a sobering appreciation for just how difficult it is for children from low-income families to make it *through* college, even with the most energetic efforts of schools expressly designed to prepare them for that goal. Since 2011, KIPP has managed to raise its college completion rate to 38 percent nationally and 47 percent in New York City. The main thrust is on matching students to the right college, not necessarily selective or elite ones. "The thing we're now baking in is to look at how schools are doing with students who match our profile," Dowling says. That typically means students of color from low- or modest-income homes who are usually the first in their family to go to higher ed. Students should be applying to the schools that have the best chance for their "academic band," she says, referring to a student's GPA and standardized test scores, and that have a demonstrated track record of success with first-generation students.

Refocusing on college completion, not acceptance, also led KIPP to reevaluate some of its practices. "The very first year that our kids went to college, they came back and said to us, 'We didn't know how to sit in a seminar class where you don't get homework every day but at the end of the seminar you have to hand in a paper,'" Dowling explains. As with Success Academy, the limitations of KIPP's pedagogical model became clear at the high school level. Many KIPP high schools have increased Advanced Placement offerings and taken other steps to increase academic rigor. "One of the things we learned over time is that we need to simulate as much as possible a college environment. We need to build critical thinking skills, habits of mind, and academic behaviors," she says. "Independent schools do this all the time," she adds, echoing Marc Meyer and his aborted design for the Success Academy Liberal Arts High School.

Former KIPP students who struggled in college reported wishing they'd had more discussion-based classes and opportunities to earn college credits in high school—more features of Success Academy's original high school. "We were also told by our students, 'Don't help us with our papers as much as you have,'" Dowling noted. "We have retaught our college advisers to teach our students how to fish, if you will, versus doing it for them." Perhaps most critically, KIPP launched an extensive effort to ensure its alumni on college campuses continued to pursue their degrees instead of dropping out. The KIPP Through College initiative starts with college placement advice but also includes financial literacy, mentorships, college and career counseling, and ongoing support from full-time network staff aimed at keeping its alumni on track past graduation.

At present, Success Academy has no plans to create a similar program.

CHAPTER 13

Survival Mode

A COLD, DRIVING RAIN SOAKS MOTT HAVEN ON A TUESDAY morning the week before Thanksgiving. Carolyn Syskowski's kindergarteners do a morning math exercise as the latecomers straggle in and throw off their sodden coats. Syskowski announces the word of the day is "wet" and calls her class to the rug. The children break the word into its component sounds in a well-rehearsed phonics routine. "Wuh," they say, making a hand motion like a gentle karate chop to the opposite shoulder. Next, they touch their elbows while making an "eh" sound, then a hard "t" as they touch their wrists. Finally, they run their hands in a single smooth motion down the opposite arm while blending the sounds together—*Wwwwettttt*— while settling themselves into their spots. The children are wet. A few have wet coughs. A gray and gloomy blanket has settled over the South Bronx. The old furniture warehouse across Rider Avenue is only dimly visible through the fog. The word of the day is well chosen.

Syskowski is teaching a lesson on active listening and being assertive, leading a song with a hand puppet named Puppy, when something catches her attention. One of the children appears to have some discoloration on her face, perhaps a black eye. She hands the lesson over to Ms. Hanania and pulls the child aside. Quietly summoned, Jen Fuoco appears in the doorway, and the three of them leave the room to investigate the cause of the little girl's bruise.

The morning wears on. Cold and snow do not keep the kids indoors for recess, but rain does. When there's no letup by late morning, the ops team lets the teachers know officially what they'd already assumed: recess will be held in classrooms today. In third-grade teacher Alyssa DiGirolamo's classroom, half a dozen girls dance along to "YMCA" and Pitbull's "Timber," mirroring the moves of a video tutorial that plays on the smartboard, while a group of boys busy themselves with a set of connecting blocks. Another child, one of the "special friends" who was the focus of the leadership walk-through in September, is in the closet, kicking and hitting the wall while muttering curse words. Amy Young, alerted by DiGirolamo, appears and leads him out.

A few days after the Brooklyn Bridge trip, there was an incident that no one seems willing to talk about, even privately. Adama's parents were scheduled to come in for a meeting about their son's progress; the school had been recommending that he be placed in a more restrictive "12:1:1" special ed class, composed of no more than twelve students, a trained special education teacher, and a paraprofessional. Every Success Academy has special ed staff and services, and there are seventeen 12:1:1 classrooms across the network, but none at Bronx 1.[1] During a prep meeting with the leadership team prior to the sit-down with Adama's parents, Ortiz freaked out. Whether it was over Adama, the cumulative stress of leading a classroom with a large number of challenging students, the lack of a second teacher in the room, or some other factor, no one is able or willing to say. By all accounts, however, Ortiz went back to her classroom, grabbed her belongings, and stormed out. She never came back.

Nick Carton has been pressed into service teaching second grade; a full-time assistant teacher, Brandon Whitaker, has arrived from the network. Adama has a new para. Mr. Dorsett has been reassigned to one of the first graders.

Ortiz's flameout elevated the struggles facing Bronx 1's second-grade team from a concern to a crisis. Every year, Success Academy conducts a series of five annual interim assessments, or IAs, in reading and math, at the end of September, November, December, March, and May. Fewer than half the second graders passed their November reading IA. When Moskowitz met with the junior leaders from Bronx 1 and other Success Academy outposts at the start of the year, she described the network's "drop everything and help" culture when one of the schools is in trouble. The cavalry now arrives in the person of Kaitlin McDermott. Her role is not unlike the Wolf, the character played by Harvey Keitel in the movie *Pulp Fiction*: she appears when there's a mess to be cleaned up and the clock is ticking. A calm but authoritative presence, she started her five-year Success Academy career as a junior leader at Bronx 1 before becoming the principal of Harlem 2, and then moving up to the network level as director of instructional training.

"We want to make a plan for how you're going to change *your* practice in order to better support your kiddos," she tells the second-grade team, which has gathered in the conference room to review their data from the November IA. Teachers have a tendency to identify struggling students and pull together ad hoc groups for tutoring and remediation to fix those kids. "A much more simple answer in most cases is, 'What do I have to fix about my own teaching, my own practice?'" McDermott says, a move right out of the Success Academy playbook: The kids aren't the problem. It's the adults.

She and Vandlik spent the previous day observing in each of Bronx 1's three second-grade classrooms. The November interim assessment showed 47 percent of the grade "on yellow" in reading, including the majority of children in Michigan State and Hunter

College, the room Ortiz abandoned and that Carton is now leading. Yellow means kids can all "read" but not with the level of sophistication or ability to make inferences independently that they want to see. Even the kids who passed the reading IA aren't killing it, Vandlik observes. They answer questions by retelling details they remember from a given text, but they're hard-pressed to synthesize information in their own words or draw conclusions that are implied but not stated in a passage.

"When you guys are planning for shared text, what's the process? How does that work?" McDermott asks the team, drawing an awkward silence. "Well," Belkin says, "it's been a little bit of a hot mess." At times, the teachers sit and plan together; at other times, Belkin, as the most experienced member of the group, has "owned" it and shared her strategies with them. The second-grade team has gotten out of the habit of planning lessons together, they all admit. When the meeting breaks up, Vandlik and McDermott ask Belkin to stay behind. Her data is stronger than the rest of the team's; they enlist her to take the lead in grade-level planning and improve her colleagues' practice. At the same time, they assure her that they want to support her continued growth as a teacher, not just put the onus on her to get her colleagues up to snuff. After she leaves, McDermott commiserates with Vandlik. The second-grade team "doesn't seem like they're on the same page at all. It's like they don't even know each other." A few moments later the kindergarten team comes in for a planning meeting with McDermott that catches fire on the launch pad: half the teachers show up without having read the assigned "pre-work." McDermott and assistant principal Noreen Cooke-Coleman ("Ms. CeeCee") send them back to their classrooms. Things are falling into a tailspin.

An oft-heard expression in teaching is "meet the children where they are." It's an acknowledgment that children come to school with a broad range of skills and knowledge and that it's up to the teacher to find a starting line for each. But with the grade-level teams in very different places, it's becoming obvious that it's not just students who need to be met where they are, but their teachers. Vandlik always maintains her game face, but this is proving to be the most difficult year of her career. Every school in the Success Academy network takes the same IAs with the results shared transparently among building leaders. As long as Vandlik has been in charge, Bronx 1 has been a standout. On the most recent round, it's near the bottom. This is not entirely a surprise. Vandlik knew that she would be directing a largely new and inexperienced cast of characters, but it's proving to be far more difficult than she expected. It's visibly wearing her down.

The deepening November gloom is punctured by a moment of joy, which everyone seems to be in on except second-grade teacher Charita Stewart. One afternoon, about a half dozen of her friends, wearing T-shirts bearing the logo of Stewart's beloved Michigan State Spartans, set up an amplifier in the hallway adjacent to her classroom. Every staffer who is not in front of children gathers as the troupe strikes up a dance routine to the Ashanti song "Helpless," luring Stewart out of her classroom. As she looks on, perplexed, the dancers form a circle around her, clapping and waving their arms in the air as the song changes to Bruno Mars's "Marry You." The dancers pull out handmade signs to spell out a message. Stewart's students have spilled out of the classroom to watch the scene unfold, and one puts the words together and blurts out, "Will you marry me?" as Stewart's girlfriend emerges from the stairwell in a long green dress. Her voice breaking, she proposes. Stewart says yes, the dancers throw confetti, and Ms. CeeCee ushers the children back into their classroom as a dozen Bronx 1 teachers and staff look on, taking videos, laughing, and shedding tears.

———

Success Academy scholars get something their brothers and sisters in DOE schools do not: the entire week of Thanksgiving off. The teachers and staff come in on the Monday and Tuesday before the holiday for staff development and planning. The staff has been counting down the hours until they can go home to their families. Vandlik is heading to Chicago, where her parents will worry that she's not sleeping enough and that the stress of her job is making her skin break out. Gathered in the classroom that now belongs to Nick Carton, Vandlik tries to rally her troops. Hanging on until Thanksgiving is an accomplishment, she reminds the room, and encourages them, especially the new teachers, to give themselves a round of applause. "You made it," she says. "You're still here. This is the first big milestone of the year." There's a slide on the smartboard that she puts up every year at this time. It tracks the arc of a teacher's year, from anticipation in August, spiraling into survival mode throughout the fall, and bottoming out in disillusionment right around Thanksgiving, when winter approaches and teachers come to work and go home in the dark, and begin questioning their commitment. "This still applies to so many of us, even leaders, well beyond our first year of teaching," she says to a mix of nodding heads and tight-lipped smiles. "And we have more new people than we've ever had in my time at Bronx 1."

I'm nodding too. I spent a few years as an adjunct professor working with several first-year Teach For America corps members assigned to schools in this neighborhood. The first meeting of the year found them excited and determined to close the achievement gap single-handedly. As the fall wore on, they sagged noticeably. By Thanksgiving, most were miserable; usually one or two didn't come back after Christmas.

Before the teachers go home for their respite, there is planning to do. The four weeks between Thanksgiving and Christmas will be an intense "intervention" period. Grade-level teams will pore over the results of the November IA in math and literacy to identify "emergency scholars," who are well below where they need to be, and "cusp scholars," who are just below. Vandlik sets the expectations for some "down-and-dirty analysis" to make sure every teacher knows which kids they have to move up in scores. What are their goals, where do they need to be by January, and what's the plan to meet them? she asks. It goes unspoken, but it's well understood why cusp and emergency scholars need immediate and extra attention: when the calendar turns to January, the intensity will ratchet up considerably as state testing draws near and test-prep season gets under way.

CHAPTER 14

Releasing the Beast

In 2013, New York became one of the first states to align federally mandated tests to Common Core State Standards in ELA and math, which emphasize deep analysis and problem solving.[1] The results were devastating, particularly in New York City, where only one in four children in grades three through eight was deemed proficient in reading, and only 30 percent passed the new, harder math exam. At a stroke, the number of children perceived to be performing on grade level was cut in half. Among city charter schools, which had long boasted of test scores far outpacing those at traditional public schools, the results were particularly brutal—with one exception. "The flourishing Success Academies network of charter schools continued to post outstanding results on the new exams, especially in math," wrote *Politico*'s Stephanie Simon. Citing Bronx 1 specifically, she noted, "an astonishing 90 percent of third graders passed the math test, and 68 percent passed language arts. Both results far exceeded the citywide average of a 33 percent pass rate for math and 28 percent for language arts."[2]

Dacia Toll, the CEO and president of Achievement First, which operates thirty-four charter schools, including twenty in New York City, recalled getting the spreadsheet with the scores and thinking that there had to have been a mistake. "It was like an earthquake," she said. "It's like all of us are standing amidst rubble in the aftermath. Then you look around and there's this gorgeous skyscraper that appears to have suffered very little damage. We had to ask, 'Who the hell is the engineer?'" Toll and her co-CEO and superintendent Doug McCurry, who is a Success Academy parent, emailed Moskowitz the same day to ask how she had managed to hold the line on the new, more rigorous tests. It was the first day of what Toll calls "a two-year obsession" with understanding what Success Academy does and how they do it. "And more importantly, what we could learn from it to do right by our kids. Because we felt, appropriately, like we had really failed," she said.

Toll, McCurry, and a cadre of leaders from Achievement First visited Success campuses, reviewed materials, met with Moskowitz, and tried to unpack what was driving their results. They concluded there were two big areas where Success knew things they didn't. One was curriculum. "I remember just looking at the texts that were in front of kids. The poetry, the literature, the nonfiction," Toll said. "It was both high rigor and high engagement. She was Common Core before we knew about Common Core." Success also did science instruction "spectacularly well," Toll concluded. "Cared about it. Did it well. Started in kindergarten." Toll and McCurry's second takeaway concerned professional development for school leaders and teachers. "I thought we did a lot of it. [Moskowitz] did more than we did," Toll said. But the difference was not merely tonnage. Much of the professional development offered to teachers and administrators across American education tends to be broad and generic, with sessions on classroom management and general pedagogical skills such as questioning strategies, checking for student understanding, and giving precise directions. "Eva was like, 'No, that's not enough. If the teachers are going to be teaching this lesson on the central idea of this poem, then the leaders need to be getting together two weeks before, and doing the intellectual prep themselves,' even practice-teaching everything themselves so that they can then go lead that effectively with teachers,'" recalled Toll.

Once Achievement First shifted its focus to improving its curriculum and "intellectual preparation" during lesson planning, they began to see "wildly better results." "There was a period of time when we gave teachers daily lesson resources, and the results weren't as good. Because the resources were crappy," Toll concludes. "You can't teach at a high level with a low-rigor text."

To judge by test scores alone, there is no such thing as a bad Success Academy school. When New York State released the results of its annual tests in summer 2016, the lowest-performing Success Academy campus with students in testing grades—the very *worst* one—had 90 percent of its students at or above grade level in math. At three of those schools—Crown Heights, Fort Greene, and Hell's Kitchen—every single student scored at or above proficiency in math. Bronx 1 just missed it, with 99.3 percent of its third- and fourth-grade scholars earning Levels 3 and 4—at or above proficient, respectively. It is conceivable, at least in theory, to test-prep children to high scores on a standardized math test. Math is a hierarchical, largely school-based subject that arguably follows a sequence of instruction. Language proficiency, however, is neither hierarchical nor school-based; it is cumulative and profoundly influenced by factors outside school. This makes Success Academy's ELA results even more remarkable, even if they don't appear as robust. Among the network's eighteen schools that tested children in reading that year, the lowest scoring—again, the very "worst"—had 75 percent of its students at Level 3 or 4. By sharp and dispiriting contrast, in at least one-fourth of New York City's elementary schools, 90 percent or more of black and Hispanic children failed to reach proficiency.[3]

Test scores are not the full measure of a school's worth. Still, it is difficult to overstate the significance of Success Academy's accomplishment. Among the country's highest-profile and most-successful charter networks, none has managed to expand as rapidly without at least a few (and sometimes many) poorly performing schools. The vast majority of charter schools—of schools, period—are hard-pressed to post results as strong as the weakest Success Academy. Still, Moskowitz bristles when pressed about test scores. "There are eight hundred kids in our midst who failed these exams. I don't think it's necessary," she says. "We have failed those kids."[4]

Even school leaders whose students acquit themselves capably tend to have a complicated relationship with standardized testing, at once lamenting its outsize importance and effects on schools while reaping the reputational benefits of earning better scores than competing neighborhood schools. Testing has lent legitimacy and urgency to the education reform movement: providing political and public relations oxygen to operators of charter schools and other efforts to close achievement gaps. Still, few issues in American education burn hotter than testing, which, for the last few decades, has come to wield a vast influence on how we teach our children and evaluate schools.

Any discussion of the outsize role of test prep at charter schools or across the education landscape must begin by acknowledging that the aggressive effort to raise scores is precisely what we have demanded through decades of public policy at the federal and state levels. Moskowitz is an unabashed defender of standardized tests and dismisses the notion that they measure only superficial test-taking skills and rote learning. "I believe well-designed standardized tests measure real learning and understanding," she wrote in her 2017 memoir.[5] She shows no patience with the immune response to testing among teachers and parents. "If you're a teacher who doesn't like standardized tests, by all means advocate for your position. Petition Congress. Write to universities. Publish op-ed pieces," she wrote. "But please don't tell your students that tests don't matter because you're just selling them a bill of goods." Her belief that test scores are both valid and create opportunities for those who perform well are on full display in her schools. Her message could not be clearer: Tests matter enormously. It is disingenuous to claim otherwise. And a prodigious amount of time, energy, and resources is brought to bear to ensure students at Success Academy score every possible point.

—

The week after the winter holiday, assistant principal Kerrie Riley, who oversees third and fourth grades, leads a lab site in the art room on "Think Mastery." By any name, it is test prep for the state reading exam, a three-day test starting at the end of March. First-year associate teachers Varshini Srinivasan and Lindsay Alexander are joined by about a dozen ATs from other Success Academy elementary schools for their first training on testing. Riley distributes a handout enumerating the network's audacious achievement goals for the year: In English Language Arts, the network expects 85 percent of its six thousand scheduled test-takers in grades three through eighth to pass, with 30 percent earning a Level 4, the highest possible grade. In math, the goal is so aggressive it seems comical: 100 percent passing with nine out of ten children reaching Level 4. Fourth graders also sit for a statewide science exam. Many schools treat science as an afterthought and pay scant attention to the state test, which counts for little in terms of public measures of school accountability; ELA and math are the coin of the realm. But Success Academy prides itself in giving kids science every day. The goal is 100 percent reaching Level 4.

While critics frequently attribute Success Academy's results to systematically weeding out low-performing students,[6] it would be hard to get anywhere near these targets by third or fourth grade, even if you hand-selected each child. Success Academy outperforms New York City's gifted and talented schools, which actually do handpick their students, three-fourths of whom are white or Asian, and only 43 percent of whom are eligible for a free or reduced-price lunch.[7] A 2016 internal report shows that ten of New York City's top twenty-five schools on the state ELA test were Success Academy schools. Of the other fifteen, only three—PS 172, the Watson School, and All City Leadership Secondary—are Title I, which allocates funds to schools and school districts with a high percentage of students from low-income families; the rest were selective admission, gifted and talented schools, or schools located in affluent neighborhoods. In math, the network accounts for nineteen of the twenty-five highest-scoring schools in the city, including selective admission and gifted and talented schools. If just Title I schools are considered, Success accounted for twenty-four out of twenty-five of the highest-scoring schools in New York City. Put another way, if Success Academy were a school district, its proficiency scores in math and ELA—95 percent and 84 percent, respectively—would make it New York's top-performing district. The top five districts in the state—Jericho, East Williston, Syosset, Chappaqua, and Scarsdale, all in suburban Long Island or Westchester County—have far fewer students per classroom, fewer than 10 percent students of color, and average household incomes at least five times greater than Success's.

Riley's professional development session is mostly aimed at acculturating the new associate teachers into Success Academy's view of testing—what it means to families and how it's experienced by students. Riley shares a story about a student she taught at the network's Crown Heights campus—a boy named Miles, who came into second grade reading at a Level E, where Success Academy typically expects kids to be early in first grade. He made minimal progress, barely earning promotion to third grade, where his struggles only intensified. The boy was in her intensive guided-reading group, a morning tutoring group, and an after-school tutoring group. She sent him home each day with coaching prompts and questions for his mother to use during his independent reading at home. "When we got into small groups during Think Mastery, he was in my intensive group with only six kids," Riley says. None of the six were reading on grade level. They had not yet learned all their sight words or even mastered the letter sounds that most Success Academy students leave kindergarten knowing reflexively. "Every day, he would get a one, maybe a two" on his practice tests, Riley said. "And every day he would look at everybody else and look at his score and just take it in and keep going." Riley wouldn't be sharing this anecdote if it didn't have a happy ending. Eventually the child got a 3 on a practice test, and her whole class stood and cheered for him. "It didn't stop—they just spontaneously applauded," Riley says, tearing up. "It was the first time I've ever seen Miles's real smile, and it was amazing."

The boy's mother called over the summer to share the news that Miles earned a 4 on his fourth-grade math test, and a 3 on reading, passing both. "That's not a unique story," Riley tells the room. "It happens across the network all the time." To ensure her story lands the way she intends, Riley lays it out plainly for the associate teachers. The network's curriculum, partnership with parents, and whole-school efforts "work when implemented correctly." The mindset to be encouraged is "to feel like I could keep going when I'm getting a one and a two, rather than being defined by it."

Riley moves into the meat of her session. "So today we're here to introduce this thing called Think Mastery, to release the beast and to take it on full force," she says. No attempt is made to minimize the importance of tests or their central role in Success Academy's culture and narrative. They are the proof point, and no apologies are made for their pursuit. "We're competing against people across the city and across the state who can afford to send their kids to a private tutor, who can afford extra after-school lessons, who can afford to have test prep that our kids may not have access to." Channeling Moskowitz, Riley notes that students in the South Bronx take the same test as kids in Scarsdale. "It really does show that our model does work, our curriculum works, and that any kid, anywhere can achieve. That's a huge part of our model and our mission." The high scores also draw attention and funding from donors. "We live in a world where that matters a whole lot, it gets us noticed, and it gets people from across the nation coming to visit and donate," Riley explains.

The assistant teachers are silent, taking it all in. Riley pauses and reads the faces of her junior colleagues. "I see some expressions happening," she notes, and asks if there are any questions. "It's just stressful for me," one woman begins. "I'm a science AT, so . . ." She doesn't want to be the only science teacher at her school not to get every one of her students to Level 4 on the fourth-grade test. Another asks about the "seemingly large difference between the English and the math goals." It's an excellent question that Riley circles but doesn't quite land. She simply replies that Success Academy's bar is much higher in math than New York State's and tells the ATs that it's much easier to quickly grow in math versus reading, which is true. "We're still unlocking that." She moves on.

As ever, adult culture and practice is a primary concern, and Riley steers the session to teacher mindsets around testing, "because that's going to come into play a lot, especially as we get deep into the Think season, and the days are a little darker, and a little colder, and we're here a little bit longer. It's going to play out in our kids." She's being oblique and none of the ATs rises to the bait, so Riley lays it out plainly. "All we do is tests, right? It's just about the test. August to December, that was teaching. Now it's tests," she prompts. Still no one reacts, perhaps reluctant to challenge the school's orthodoxy, so Riley speculates on what they're thinking. "Testing takes precedence, right? Art's going to fall away. Science is going to fall away. No community circle. Oops, games day? That's gone! *Right?*"

Kaitlin McDermott, the senior network troubleshooter who has become a constant presence at Bronx 1 since the survival-mode days before Thanksgiving, has been sitting to the side, but now she speaks up. "How many of you actually think that? We've said right now, starting in January, we're entering Think season, right? How many of you feel like we're dropping everything and just doing test prep for the next couple of months?" A few of the staffers nod or raise a diffident hand. "OK, great. Thank you," McDermott replies. "I'm glad you're being honest." One associate teacher confesses that she thought so at first, "but then when it started, I thought, 'Oh, this is actually shared text; they're just applying it to a different kind of thing." Everybody assumes that, McDermott responds, "then having been in it, you're like, 'No, actually kids are learning a lot, and they're reading a ridiculous amount of stuff.'"

McDermott's point is valid but imprecise. If it's inaccurate to characterize Success Academy's Think season as "drop everything and test-prep," that's because there is an overtone of test prep to the curriculum throughout the entire year. It is a short distance to travel from beginning every reading lesson with the "genre and thinking job," previewing texts, and searching for the main idea, to test prep. Success Academy's approach to reading can feel like test prep all year-round, not just in the weeks leading up to state tests. The habits of mind students are encouraged to practice and develop lend themselves seamlessly to the kind of tasks they are asked to perform on state tests.

Success Academy's prowess, and the network's effort to habituate its staffers to its view of testing, comes at a time when anti-testing sentiment has been sharply rising. The backlash has been particularly strident in New York, one of the hotbeds of the testing "opt out" movement. In 2015 and 2016, approximately 20 percent of eligible students statewide refused to sit for mandated tests, prompting numerous changes from the state, including shortening tests and eliminating time limits on their administration.[8] Moskowitz has been unsparing in criticizing the opt-out movement, which she claims risks leaving students unprepared for more important tests later, such as college entrance exams.[9] At the same time, Success has been accused of pushing kids too hard to earn top scores. A 2015 report in the *New York Times* cited the reports of former staff members who "described students in third grade and above wetting themselves during practice tests, either because teachers did not allow them to go to the restroom . . . or because the students themselves felt so much pressure that they did not want to lose time on the test."[10] Much as Success Academy has perfected the no-excuses model at the moment it has fallen from favor, it similarly appears to have cracked the code on standardized testing just as that, too, has fallen into disrepute.

No such misgivings are in evidence today. "One of the most dangerous mindsets to my mind is, 'It's too much, you all are doing too much, it's too hard on them,'" McDermott tells the ATs. "Kids are so resilient, and they can handle so much more than we think they can, and so much more than their parents sometimes think they can too," she adds. "We need to be careful of those mindsets as well and guard against them in ourselves." This is a tidy summary of Moskowitz's views and yet another manifestation of the consistent culture and language across the Success Academy. No one at the Think Mastery lab site seems inclined to debate the merits of testing, at least not out loud. Of course, if a would-be teacher was stridently anti-testing, it's unlikely she would apply to work at Success Academy in the first place, or get very far in the application process. Some teachers have likely adopted the view articulated by Bronx 1's third-grade AT Srinivasan, who says that despite having "personal beliefs" about testing and whether it truly reflects a child's ability, what matters is the way the world views children of color. "You might not believe that this is truly a reflection of your kid's ability, but there are people that do," she explains.

Riley sees her comment and raises. "However you feel about testing, whether you think they should or shouldn't opt out, at the end of the day, these things will open doors for our kids, and that's our overarching view and what we all want for our kids. Sometimes that means putting personal feelings aside." What's best for our kids, she insists, "is for them to show their absolute best on this test and to excel, because it will open so many more doors for them."

No person in the room, Riley included, likely ever spent a day in school, as an administrator, a teacher, or even a student, that was not dominated by the imperatives of standardized testing. The No Child Left Behind Act, which made annual tests in reading and math from third through eighth grade federal law, was passed before Success Academy was founded, and while the teachers in the room were in elementary school. "You know how many tests you took to get your teacher license, or how many tests you took to get into college, right? For a lawyer, for a doctor, to get a real estate license, to be a CPA? In life, you're going to have to take tests; you're going to have to have those skills, and primarily that confidence and that grit to move forward and move through, and to push yourself. Those are all skills that, when done right, we develop in our kids."

———

Think Mastery season is only one of the major changes at Bronx 1 in the new calendar year. After two months of teaching in one of the second-grade classrooms he was hired to supervise, Nick Carton leaves Success Academy to become the director of culture at the Neighborhood Charter School of Harlem, a stand-alone mom-and-pop charter. Taking over Ortiz's classroom began as an exercise in making a virtue of necessity, honoring the all-hands-on-deck imperative that Moskowitz preached to the junior leaders in her "education crimes and misdemeanors" talk back in September. Vandlik thought it would benefit Carton, a newcomer to the network, to gain hands-on experience with curriculum, culture, and classroom management. But he had moved to New York from Florida to be an assistant principal and take the next step in his career, from teaching to school leadership. "We parted amicably," he told me months later. Amy Young is gone, too, off to nearby Success Academy Bronx 3 as an assistant principal.

It's rare to find an experienced lead teacher midway through the school year, but Carolyn Syskowski heard of a teacher who was "excessed" because of declining enrollment in her New York City public school, making her available to take over in January. Alanna Kowalski is still learning the culture and lingo. She calls children "boys and girls," not "scholars." When she summons them to the rug for reading and math, she asks them to sit "crisscross applesauce," instead of in Magic Five. But she is warm and energetic and excited to be at Success. Kowalski and co-lead teacher Brandon Whitaker, who arrived in November, have less than five months to bring stability to the classroom, and to get Adama and his classmates ready for third grade. It remains one of Bronx 1's biggest challenges. An integrated co-teaching classroom combining general education and special ed students, the classroom has observable issues with a significant number of children, perhaps in part because of the revolving cast of characters leading their class. There is no longer talk of "rooms of concern" as in the first days of the school year, but if such a list exists, the second-grade classroom formerly known as Hunter College, but which has been existing for months in a state of limbo, would be on top. It receives the most attention from the leadership team, even as Think Mastery season gets underway in the upper grades.

One afternoon, assistant principal Noreen Cooke-Coleman schedules a real-time coaching session for Kowalski and Whitaker, during which they will teach while wearing headphones, taking live, in-the-moment feedback from "Ms. CeeCee." Beforehand, CeeCee asked Kowalski which students she's struggling with the most. She names a girl who has a habit of peppering her with off-topic questions; she's having trouble discerning when the child is genuinely curious and when she's merely trying to get a rise out of her teacher. Another boy is argumentative and defiant. A third cries at every correction, making it difficult for her to gauge when to push him and when he needs a break. Still another is often zoned out. (Interestingly, the list of students with whom she's struggling does not include Adama.) Classroom management has been a struggle generally for Kowalski, who has sought advice from Jen Fuoco and Laura Belkin on how to implement the school's discipline hierarchy. "I've gotten a lot of tears. Yesterday five kids cried because they were on yellow," says Kowalski, who is trying to be more confident and authoritative. She already sees a difference between asking students to move "quietly" and "silently" when transitioning between activities. "I've been more confident giving directions. When I wasn't being specific and saying 'Sit down' instead of 'I want you to sit down,' I didn't come off as authoritative." One of her deliverables today is to more consistently narrate and praise the more difficult students.

Kowalski and Whitaker's headsets make them look more like they're working the drive-through window at McDonald's than teaching a shared text lesson. While Ms. CeeCee is coaching the two teachers, Karen Baptiste, a consultant with a teacher-training company called CT3, coaches Ms. CeeCee. From the back of the room, Cooke-Coleman whispers into her headset microphone, a mix of her own observations and those prompted by Baptiste.

"Whitaker, narrate Jacquin and Emir."

"Kowalski, stand and scan the room."

"Whitaker, economy of language," she says, a reminder to use fewer, clearer words when giving instructions. When Ms. CeeCee tells him to "narrate scholars who have three sentences" on their paper, Whitaker nods and says, "Jacquin is focused. He's already on his third line." The boy replies proudly, "I'm on my fourth!" Whitaker gives the kid a high five and flashes a knowing glance at the assistant principal.

Afterward, Whitaker is elated, particularly at how well students responded to positive reinforcement. "What did you notice about Jacquin after you gave him a high five?" Ms. CeeCee asks Whitaker. "Endorphins," answers Whitaker, a former college basketball player. "The smile. The perkiness in his posture. It was one hundred and eighty degrees. It went from 'No, I'm not doing this' to 'What else do you want me to do?' Those little things reassure him that, like, 'Oh, he's not a mean guy out to get me. He doesn't want me to get in trouble. He's actually trying to help.'"

"This feels good!" Whitaker says. He's beaming.

CHAPTER 15

Come to Jesus

I catch Carolyn Syskowski's eye, and she waves me in. Teachers and students at Success Academy are accustomed to a parade of unannounced observers and visitors in their classrooms, but even after six months it's still my habit to pause at the threshold and wait to be noticed rather than materialize in the back of the room. An orchestral version Frank Sinatra's "The Way You Look Tonight" is playing softly on the smartboard. Half of her class is at blocks with Ms. Hanania; the rest is working on book reviews—perhaps an aspirational term for the pencil sketches and nascent writing the children labor at, but Syskowski takes their work seriously. She sidles over to a boy who is staring off into space. "Your book review doesn't make sense," she says as she takes a seat next to him. I cannot hear the entire conversation, but she makes no attempt to mask her disappointment. She tells the child quietly, "So, tomorrow you can't go to blocks."

The boy doesn't complain or protest, but tears well up in his eyes. "You're not in trouble; you don't need to cry," Syskowski says.

Her face remains expressionless; she speaks in an even, matter-of-fact tone. "What were you doing when we did our book reviews? You just sat there." At no time does she break her direct gaze, which must be uncomfortable, even excruciating, for a five-year-old.

A good teacher can be engaging, nurturing, empathetic, and funny, but must know when it's time to be exacting and even inflexible. "It's not 'I care about you, but you still must serve the consequence for being late,'" explains Doug Lemov, who describes the technique as "warm/strict" in *Teach like a Champion*, a bible among teachers in urban charter schools, "but 'Because I care about you, you must serve the consequence for being late.'" Syskowski's demeanor is warm, but now her voice betrays no more emotion than if she were a postal worker selling stamps. Her expectations have not been met, and there must be a consequence. "It's OK," she says matter-of-factly. "You just can't go to blocks."

And that's that. She moves on to another table.

Later, I remark to Syskowski that I lack the capacity not to crumple at the sight of a five-year-old's tears. She expresses regret that the boy will miss blocks, which is "important for social and emotional learning," and because her class is learning three-dimensional shapes—she gestures to a poster she created that hangs on her classroom wall featuring prisms, cylinders, cones, cubes, and spheres—but she does not second-guess her decision. "I sat with you. I helped you. And you had one sentence that didn't make sense," Syskowski says. "You know the deal."

I observe that this is the first time I've seen a child cry in her room, and she flashes the enormous grin that she regularly beams at the students gathered around her on the rug during read-alouds and number stories. Like every other early-childhood teacher at Success Academy, Syskowski builds classroom culture and strong work habits through the use of rewards, including "effort parties," to recognize not grades but persistence. After the first effort party in Syskowski's classroom, which not every child earned the right to attend, "we had *no one crying*," she says. "I was telling Olivia [Hanania], 'This is weird. Usually we have kids crying!' But they said to me, 'I didn't do my best.' We really don't have a lot of crying in this class." Her students know the deal.

Still, not all is well in Hunter College. The unusually wide range of academic levels troubles Syskowski. Next to the smartboard is a vertical chart with the large block letters A through D. Clothespins with each child's name cling alongside each letter, indicating their individual reading level. Success Academy follows the "leveled reading" system developed by reading researchers Irene Fountas and Gay Su Pinnell, which starts at Level A early in kindergarten and reaches Level Z, usually by the end of eighth grade. It's the end of January, and the majority of her students are stuck on Level B. "I usually have way more Cs by this time," Syskowski says, frowning. There's a creeping concern that something is just "off" this year. Lateness is up and attendance is down in all three kindergarten classrooms. Parent engagement is not as focused or energetic as the other teachers would like and have grown accustomed to; parents haven't been taking advantage of the open-door policy either. "I'm used to parents calling me nonstop. I'm used to parents coming in and setting up meetings, and I've only had a handful this year," Syskowski says. The teachers have called a "Come to Jesus" meeting for all the kindergarten parents this afternoon.

At the end of the school day, Syskowski and Matt Carnaghi empty their classrooms of their kindergarten-size chairs and arrange them in three rows in the open area adjacent to Liz Vandlik's office. The children are held for dismissal, forcing parents to come upstairs and listen to the teachers before picking them up—a standard tactic when staff has something they want to say to parents, either individually or as a group. At 3:45 p.m. sharp, Syskowski launches in. "The reason we're having a meeting together is because there's a lot of work to be done. We need to come together as a Bronx 1 community and figure out what's going on and set goals." She scans the thirty adults seated before her in chairs meant for five-year-olds. "As you can see, right now we have a meeting for ninety children and this is the parent turnout. It's not good."

Syskowski walks them through the reading benchmarks for

kindergarten. "It's January. A number of our children are still Level A or pre-A, which means they don't know how to read." The kindergarteners will be tested again in February, by which time they're all expected to be at Level C. If the point is lost, Syskowski lays it out plainly. If their children are not at Level C by the end of February, they are unlikely to reach Level D by the end of the school year. "If they do not reach D, they do not go to first grade," she says, "Do not. Period." She pauses to let the message sink in, then repeats it. "They will not go to first grade if they're not a Level D. That has been said before, and I'm just restating it."

Now that she has the parents' full attention, Syskowski pivots from reading levels to school culture and expectations—for adults. "A lot of you are brand new to Success Academy. We know it's a new world," she tells them. "We *want* you to ask questions. We know what we teach here is a little different. It's different than the way you learned and the way we learned. We received a lot of training and we know this is the best way that children learn. If there are things that you need, you need to ask. So, this is us reaching out, having that parent meeting and saying, 'Here we are. This is our space. And we need to talk because we're not meeting benchmarks.'"

The benchmarks Syskowski is referring to are not only the reading-level chart in her classroom but achievement levels of the kindergarteners relative to dozens of other Success Academy schools. "Other schools within our network over in Brooklyn, in Manhattan and Queens, their children are reading at benchmarks," she says pointedly. "All of us in this room are not doing enough for our kids. The children in Brooklyn and Queens and Manhattan can do it, and our kids can't, even though we all have the same curriculum, we all have the same training."

There are no secrets in a Success Academy school. Classrooms and hallway "data walls" leave little to no doubt which children— by name—are at, above, or below academic standards. This can be off-putting to some parents and has been attacked by critics outside the network. On the other hand, it is the rare student in any school who isn't aware of who the standouts and strugglers are in class. Success Academy puts it on the wall for all to see. Syskowski begins to spin a sobering tale of the trajectory children can find themselves on in the absence of energetic efforts. "First grade is a *huuuuge* literacy year," she says. "If we don't set them up in kindergarten, they will drown." The parents sit silently. "We need to step it up."

Carnaghi has been standing alongside Syskowski, nodding stoically. He introduces himself as a "first-year LT," then adds almost apologetically, "I'm pretty resourceful and here for you guys." But it's Syskowski's intervention, and she's just getting started. Her tone is unfailingly warm and encouraging—she wants to win the parents over and make common cause, not alienate or antagonize them—but her words are unsparing. Standing behind the rows, I cannot see all the parents' faces, but most appear to be nodding along. If there's discontent with Syskowski's brand of tough love, there's no sign of it. "If your children are late or they're not here, we can't teach them," she says. "We really need you to get your children here by 7:45 if not 7:30." The first moments of each day, kindergarteners have breakfast with their class, and teachers do a "re-teach," working with individual children on skills in which they've fallen behind. "If they are not here on time or not here at all, we can't do that," she says. "We have some children in this grade who've already been absent eleven times. Anytime I'm sick, I come here. I can't afford to lose that day with your children. At the same time, your child cannot miss that day with any of us. We're here, we need to be here, we want to be here, and every second is really . . ."

A toddler starts crying loudly, drowning her out, and without breaking pace, Syskowski orders the toddler's sister, Rama B., one of her students with a serious, almost adult face, to take her into a nearby classroom. Syskowski is rolling now and doesn't want to lose her audience, which now fills all the chairs and spills down the hall. "You want your child to go to college. You sent them here to a college-bound school. Our philosophy is that every single child goes to college and it starts when they're five. I know that you want that for them, because that's why you brought them to Success Academy.

At the same time, it's a daily grind. You need to put that work in to get them there."

Syskowski asks for a show of hands. "Whose child is reading at a Level A right now?" A few hands go up. If the parents are aware of their child's reading level, many more hands should be in the air. Carnaghi scans the room and jumps in. "There's one," he points and calls out. "Two. Anyone else? There are plenty here." It is impossible to tell if the parents don't know, don't want to reveal that their child is below benchmarks, or are feeling called out and embarrassed. "We want to get it out there. You're not alone!" Syskowski implores, trying to encourage more parents to own up and join in.

"Level B?" More hands go up. "There's three, four, five," Carnaghi counts off. By the time she gets to Level D, only one hand is up. "So that means out of everyone here, we have one child who is ready for first grade," Syskowski says, growing quiet. "We're a community of parents. Use each other to help each other. I know you guys have daily struggles as parents. I'm not a parent, so I don't know that struggle. I know that struggle as a classroom teacher when I'm with your scholar and really pushing them, and they're like, 'Ms. Syskowski, this is hard,'" she says plaintively. "And yeah, it's hard."

Syskowski's urgency is not misplaced. By January, the children should be learning to read. Midway through kindergarten, they should recognize and be able to name and write upper- and lowercase letters. Five-year-olds are also developing phonological awareness, such as recognizing syllables, rhymes, and "phonemes," the forty-four units of sound that make up every word in the English language. An essential literacy building block at this age is beginning "sound-symbol relationships" and the ability to read consonant-vowel-consonant words like "cat" and "dog." Syskowski and her colleagues do not expect parents to be surrogate reading teachers or to have a nuanced understanding of these skills or progressions. But they nonetheless put a heavy lift on parents to read nightly with their children and to monitor and ensure that they are reading at home—something affluent parents tend to do reflexively, often without even knowing why.

"We're seeing two really big issues," Syskowski says. "Your reading logs still have your scholars' books on them. They can read those books by themselves. Those are not the books that go on the reading logs," she instructs. The reading logs are for books that parents read aloud. Very young children can understand even sophisticated texts when they are read aloud, which helps them develop as readers by exposing them to new vocabulary and allowing them to hear mature readers' fluent pronunciation and expression.[1] Kindergarteners should also spend twenty minutes reading independently at home each night. "That doesn't mean they read on their own, you go do laundry. It. Is. *Challenging*. I hear you. We need that patience and excitement to tell them, 'You know what? You *are* a great reader, and you can do this.'"

Carnaghi has been largely silent, but now it's his turn to take the lead. Reading logs must be completed 100 percent of the time. "If we look cross grade right now? Ninety percent. Ninety-two percent. Eighty-six percent," he says, indicating the compliance rate in each of the kindergarten classrooms. "It's not getting done." If any other elementary schools in the neighborhood asked parents to maintain reading logs, 90 percent compliance would be a cause for celebration. Here it's a crisis. "The reason we're so on you about these reading logs is because it sets up routines, right?" he continues. "These routines help build up memory skills, problem-solving skills. These are all cognitive skills. If you're not at home constantly building those, your child will not be successful." There is a long pause as Carnaghi and the parents stare at one another. "Really cold, hard fact. You really need to listen. You need to hear it. Like *hear* it."

This is one of the first times I've seen Carnaghi "on." While few restrictions have been placed on my observations, Vandlik asked early in the school year that I "give Mr. Carnaghi some room." As a new teacher who expected to be an associate, not lead, teacher, it seemed an undue burden to be under an outsider's microscope, unhelpful to him and a distraction to his students. As a result, I've barely set foot in his classroom. Like so many of his colleagues, he radiates earnestness, even as he tries to play bad cop to Syskowski's good. "One in six children in our community who are not proficient readers, by third grade—forget about college. They're going to have a really hard time passing high school," he says.

It's suddenly hard to hear over the delighted squeals of kindergarteners playing in the classroom behind me, unaware of the high-stakes conversation we are having about them. But the grim urgency Carnaghi is trying to communicate is not misplaced. Failure starts early in communities like Mott Haven. Nearly 90 percent of US first graders who struggle in reading are still struggling in fourth grade; three out of four third-grade readers who are below grade level are still below grade level in ninth grade; and one in six children who are not reading proficiently in third grade do not graduate from high school on time—a failure rate four times greater than among proficient readers. If the ninety-odd kindergarteners of Bronx 1 steer clear of this grim vortex of failure that has been all but inevitable for children in this community for generations, it will be in no small part due to what Syskowski, Carnaghi, and the rest of the kindergarten teachers are doing this year—aided and abetted by fully engaged parents.

"I assume right now that every single parent in this room knows exactly how to teach their kid because nobody comes up to me and asks me, 'What can I do? How can I help my child? Is there anything else I can do?'" Carnaghi is making demands, almost hectoring, but his tone is plaintive, nearly pleading. "We're here for your kids. But you're not showing us that you're here for your kids right now, because these routines are not getting set up. If you need to know what to do, raise your hand now."

Syskowski takes up the call. "Any question at all!"

Now there are lots of hands. Parents ask about how to handle behavior problems at home. One says she has a hard time getting her child to focus. Another mother expresses frustration at how poorly her child is performing on sight-word quizzes. "When he's in the house, he does the work perfectly fine. But when he comes here, I guess he gets a little bit scared. Whenever we do words in the house—'they,' 'were,' 'was'—he does it perfect. When he gets here, he usually gets one right or two right. Sometimes he gets all three right. So, I'm a little bit . . ." She trails off.

"Think about environment, right?" Carnaghi replies. "At home, your child is in such a relaxed environment. Do you time him?" Mom says no. "Start timing him. Get him used to timing in both environments. When he's at home, he gets all the time in the world, he's relaxed. That's not a problem. But if you really want to see something different, put on a timer." In other school settings, the suggestion that parents time their children, conduct weekly tests of sight words at home, or be forced to sit and listen to their child's teacher lecturing them that they're not living up to their parental responsibilities would cause an insurrection. But none of the parents raise an eyebrow, whether out of deference, intimidation, a shared sense of urgency, a reluctance to make waves, or some combination of these factors. Carnaghi adds, "Being timed makes anybody anxious, right?" He turns to the crowd. "Silent thumbs-up if that's what makes it anxious for you?" and many turn their thumbs up while several chuckle audibly. "It's not easy!"

"We have an open-door policy here," Syskowski reminds them, returning to her main theme. "Tell us the time you're scheduled to be off from work. Tell us the time you want to come in. Schedule some time. Please!"

Syskowski calls on a mother who is having trouble keeping her child's frustrations in check. "Nyelle has that same problem. If she doesn't know a word like 'what,' she actually gets angry. She cries and then we have to end it," she explains. "I feel like she's a little behind. I know she's got a C, but I feel like she should already be at D. But the last, maybe, two weeks, we had to shut down early because she gets so emotional." Syskowski senses a teachable moment. "You said something really awesome I wanted to get out in the open. Nyelle is very much a high flier in my class. It's very hard for me to challenge her, because she gets it in a snap," she explains, pointing at the mother, but directing her comments to the whole group. "Right now, Nyelle's mom is saying she's really not doing her best. Yes, a C is past where we need to be right now, but knowing your child and saying, 'That's not good enough,' keeps that bar high. Yes, it *is* going to be frustrating, and we will give you strategies to handle that frustration. They *totally* get frustrated here."

"We had a visitor in our class today, and he was like, 'That's the first time I saw tears today,'" Syskowski adds, and I realize she's talking about me. She tells the parents what happened with the little boy who won't be going to blocks tomorrow. "That was really tough for him to hear. At the same time, did I say, 'It's OK if you don't finish your book review?'" Now it's Syskowski who starts to tear up. "No. It's *not* OK. Because why would I let him fail when other kids are surpassing it and they'll go to first grade? You would not want me as your child's classroom teacher. You would not want Mr. Carnaghi or Ms. Skinner to be your child's teacher if we were like, 'You know what? You're right. It *is* really hard. Let's just let them be a B.'" How about if they get two out of the four sight words correct? 'That's good enough.' Where are they going to be in thirteen years? Then we won't talk about college. And that's something that . . ." Syskowski lowers her gaze to the floor. "I get chills. That's something that's really hard for me to . . ."

Syskowski doesn't finish the thought. She can't. She's crying. "I *do* get emotional. Because your children are *amazing*. They are absolutely amazing. I try to . . ." She quickly gathers herself. "We will never lower that bar because it's too hard. We will figure out other paths to get to the destination." She hammers every word—"Other. Paths. To *get* to the destination." She adds, "We will *not* lower it."

Syskowski is spent. The meeting breaks up with a smattering of applause from the parents, who pull on their coats, collect their kids, and begin to melt away down the hallway. Vandlik emerges from her office and shoots me a smile as she heads down the hall toward the main office. It's the biggest tell of the afternoon. In most schools, this kind of whole-grade, all-hands-on-deck meeting would be a major event. At Bronx 1, the principal didn't even participate.

As I join the crowd heading down the stairs and out into the lengthening late-afternoon shadows on Morris Avenue, it occurs to me that what I have just witnessed was not a parent-teacher meeting, but a Rorschach test, one that reinforces whatever preconceived notions people have about Success Academy, charter schools, and even the entire testing-and-data-driven education reform movement. If you're so inclined, you can see a pair of privileged white teachers spending thirty minutes dressing down parents, many their own age, and all of them low-income people of color whose lives they can understand only in the abstract. If you take a dim view of all this, you see children reduced to data points and the pitiless transparency of it all—the data walls, the immutable trajectories of five-year-old lives based on their kindergarten reading level. You see warning and rebuke, delivered like the Ghost of Christmas Future, with a wagging finger—the shadow of things to come if parents don't wake the hell up, step up, and get with the program.

Or you can see Carolyn Syskowski, with her giant heart and Pez-dispenser grin, who calls every student "love bug" and spends hours each day on the floor with other people's children, wipes their noses, pulls on their coats, sends them home, and then worries into the night about their reading and math scores. You can see, if you are so inclined, an unusually gifted and competent teacher, with emotional gears you cannot fathom, who can issue a consequence to a five-year-old like a bank examiner rejecting a loan, then an hour later bring herself to tears in front of a hundred strangers when for a single moment she catches herself weighing the cost of not doing so.

CHAPTER 16

Plan of Attack

A SIGN HAS APPEARED ON THE DOUBLE DOORS LEADING INTO THE fourth-grade wing. In bold type, it warns that there are seventy-five days left until the NYS Science Performance Exam and eighty-two days left until the NYS written science exam. It is in the network's trademark orange color and font, and spiral-bound so that the number of days can be flipped from now until the day of the test at the end of May. A nearly identical sign hangs in Albert Barabas's classroom: forty-two days until the state ELA exam and sixty-two days until the math exam. Two more posters, also network-issued, hang on either side of the smartboard. One is labeled "Math Plan of Attack"; the other, "ELA Mastery Plan of Attack."

MATH PLAN OF ATTACK

While working through a problem, a true mathematician always thinks carefully to ensure they are solving accurately.

* *I read the problem to make sure I understand it.*
* *I make a plan to solve it.*
* *I use my plan to solve the problem.*
* *I check to see if my answer makes sense.*

ELA MASTERY PLAN OF ATTACK

Tackling the text
* *Preview the passage.*
* *Closely read the passage with the thinking job in mind.*
* *Jot a main idea that answers the thinking job.*

Tackling the Questions
* *Read and interpret the question.*
* *Answer the question by coming up with a CLAIM supported by EVIDENCE from the text.*
* *If it's an open response: plan, write, and re-read. If it's multiple choice: read and evaluate each answer choice.*

A graphic shows the letters A, B, C, and D stacked atop each other, with all but B crossed out.

After math, it's time for close reading mastery, or CRM. Barabas and Lindsay Alexander hand out white athletic sweatbands for the kids to wear during the lesson, part of the latest contest among the fourth-grade classes to keep them motivated; they are competing for the highest scores in practice tests. Lynch's kids have purple ones; Richter's wear red. Alexander, who divides her time between Barabas's class and Richter's, will have to switch her color when she changes rooms, "but we know where her true heart lies," Barabas tells the class. "We need to let them know we're not playing around anymore," he says while cueing up a clean version of "Ante Up" by the Brooklyn hip-hop duo M.O.P. He orders his kids to "come to the rug like a boss" with pencils and whiteboards. The song starts. It's loud enough to be heard not just in the other fourth-grade classrooms but also down the block. Competitive flourishes come naturally to Barabas, the sports nut from Cleveland whose infectious energy fills the room. "Wooooo! It's *goin' down, baby!*" he cheers. The kids take up the chant their teacher has written as they march to the front of the room.

> *Fordham fourth*
> *slams the exam!*
> *Fordham fourth*
> *attacks with a plan!*
> *Achievin' 3s and 4s*
> *together through hard work!*
> *We never finish last*
> *forever we stay first!*

By the time the rap ends, the kids are in place on the rug, ready for CRM. "Woooo! I love what I see," he says. "Lookin' ready to go, hands locked, eyes right on me." The students in Fordham are "already masters of main idea." Today's "teaching point," which he has written on a large piece of chart paper, is that "close readers determine the meaning of unknown words or phrases using evidence from the text." The word "evidence" is in red. There are four "tips for understanding" unknown vocabulary: rereading, using context, reading around, and looking for parts of the words you know. "We've practiced those strategies *many* times," he reminds his class. "We're just gonna drill down today on that specific skill and share our strategies on how you did that."

The children each have a test booklet almost exactly like the one they will work from two months from now, but with the Success Academy logo instead of the State Education Department's. Barabas tells his students to turn to the first practice test passage, a nonfiction selection about an octopus titled "Escape Artist." He gives them seven minutes to "come up with a high-level main idea," and he sets the timer. "Before we start, though, I want someone to give me a quick preview of what this text is gonna be about." A boy named Reyli observes that it's nonfiction.

"What's the thinking job for nonfiction?" Barabas presses.

"Teach and the author's point of view," Reyli answers in Success Academy shorthand. "What is the author teaching me and what's the author's point of view," Barabas elaborates. "So, as you're reading, you're gonna be snowballing, thinking and making connections about how what you read connects to your idea."

The lesson is structured identically—down to the genre and thinking job—to the one Barabas and Lynch modeled for the second-grade team in the fall. The teaching point on the chart paper and the four tips for understanding come from a network-written lesson plan. This same lesson is being taught in dozens of Success Academy classrooms all over the city this morning. The first portion is "guided practice" and is scheduled to last fourteen minutes: one minute to discuss the teaching point and preview the reading passage; seven minutes for students to read, write down what they believe to be the main idea, and circle unknown words; two minutes to share a checklist of "main idea nonnegotiables" and "transferable takeaways" that can help them figure out the meanings of unfamiliar words; and four minutes of answering multiple-choice questions as a group. The kids will spend the rest of the class period, about forty minutes, working independently on the remaining passages and questions. While they busy themselves with the text, I open my laptop and search for the source of their reading passage. Google instantly reveals that the passage and questions are from a reading test given to *sixth graders* in four states on the 2012 New England Common Assessment. The practice lesson prepared by Success Academy for its fourth graders uses a passage pitched two years above their grade level.[1]

The kids finish their scanning. "We know it's nonfiction, but what's your initial idea?" Barabas asks. "What do you think this is gonna be about, Amina?" The girl runs her finger over the passage, which is about an aquarium octopus that learned how to get out of its tank to feed on fish in nearby tanks, and says, "I think this text is gonna be about how this octopus keeps on stealing other animals." What is she basing that on? "'Cause I looked at the first paragraph, and it said that he's sneaky and that the fish kept on disappearing." Barabas starts the timer. With two minutes left, he prompts them to finish reading and jot down their main ideas. "Answer what the text taught you and what you believe the author's point of view on the topic is."

"Pencils down and breathe," Barabas says as time expires. "Give me some things that *have* to be in your main idea. Key words. Non-negotiables. Ikram, read 'em off for me." The boy lists "octopus," "smart," "sneaky," and "disguised." Barabas asks Ikram to put them together. "Give me your whole main idea now. Nice and loud," he challenges.

"I wrote, 'Octopuses are masters of disguise. Octopuses can shape-shift,'" Ikram reads from his paper. His main idea is "Octopuses are amazing because of their natural abilities." He looks up to see his teacher smiling at him and nodding. "I like the way he identified each of the features," Barabas affirms. "He didn't just say 'amazing' without saying what they were." He gives the kids thirty seconds to "revise your main ideas," adding the traits that their classmate has just highlighted. The "teaching point" is figuring out the meaning of unfamiliar words, so Barabas steers the conversation back to it. "Anybody circle one and have a skill they used [to figure it out]. Josiah, what about you?"

"I circled 'radula,'" he replies.

"Yeah, I've never seen that word before. What paragraph is that in, bud?"

"It was in paragraph one."

"Paragraph one. OK, what does it mean? How'd you figure it out?"

Josiah decides it means "tongue," because in the reading passage, just before the unknown word, it says an octopus has a beak like a bird and a tongue—called a radula. "Ahhh!" Barabas smiles. "So which strategy did you use? Rereading? Using context? Reading around?" Josiah says he "read around," looking for help elsewhere to tease out the meaning. The explanation was right there. "Reading around!" Barabas elaborates. "This is *so essential*. This is a close reading exam, right? And you're developing these thinking skills that—it doesn't matter about the exam—your whole life you're gonna be reading millions and millions of texts, of books, of magazine articles, and there's gonna be words that you don't know. You've gotta be able to use the words around it to be able to come up with the meaning on your own."

Barabas has gone well past the fourteen minutes allotted to "guided practice." It's time for the kids to return to their desks to practice the skill they've just learned. He cues up the music again for the class chant. "When the song comes on, pop up," he directs. "By the time you get back to your seat, I want everyone ready to go. Pencils up so we can all start at the same time." The tables in his classroom are named for NBA teams, and the table that gets the highest score on each day's practice test earns the right to wear the basketball jerseys that he keeps hanging in the back of the classroom. "Let's make this whole school rattle!" he calls as the music swells. Barabas picks up the beat—WUHP, WUHP, WUHP, WOOOOO!— and the class rises, returns to their seats, and yells along.

> *Fordham fourth*
> *slams the exam!*
> *Fordham fourth*
> *attacks with a plan!*

"Let's go, baby! I'm lookin' for fours!" Barabas pumps up the volume to arena levels as the kids bop and bounce their heads. "Who's getting their jerseys today? Who's wearing their jerseys around the school today? Pencils up! Can't wait to see those initial ideas! Thinking while you're reading! On your mark. Ready! GOOOO!"

The music ends and the kids throw open the booklets with something approaching fury. While they're hunched over their work, Barabas shows me his lessons plan and data tracker for the next thirty minutes of "targeted teaching time." He will check in with Amina, Josiah, Jayden, Ibrahima, and Isabel to ensure they have a "complete main idea" and "keep track of the characters." He'll look to ensure Dwight, Brian, Brihannah, and Violetta "used their prior knowledge" to aid their understanding of each passage. The lesson is prescriptive and directive, but not scripted; teachers do not read lines written for them by someone else. Free time is built into the end to reward students who demonstrate particular focus and effort.

A half hour later, Barabas reviews their answers out loud. He and the kids are exuberant, genuinely excited by their right answers. "Did you just become, like, 2017 Queen of the Universe?" he praises one student who answered every question correctly. On the schools' color-coded data-tracking system, a child who is meeting grade-level expectations is said to be "on green." Blue is for those exceeding it. "I'm just gonna start calling you 'the Ocean' 'cuz you're blue all day long!" he gushes to another. One child gets a perfect score, and Barabas's enthusiasm is heartfelt as they high-five. Students at the Cavaliers' table are today's CRM winners, earning the right to wear NBA jerseys over their school uniforms for the rest of the day. One of the Cavs, a girl named Isatu, pulls a gold LeBron James jersey over her head, grinning proudly. It fits her more like a ball gown than a basketball jersey. She disappears inside it, and it nearly touches the floor.

It would be disingenuous not to call Success Academy's CRM "test prep." It certainly is. But, for good or for ill, it doesn't deviate much from the day-to-day features of its literacy program. A common criticism of Success is that it brings its curriculum to a halt during test-prep season. It doesn't. A savvier appraisal would be that the ELA curriculum feels like test prep year-round, not just during Think Mastery season.

The lines get blurry. But is it cheating?

Standardized testing—and its uses and misuses—is among the most contentious issues in American education and enormously difficult to unwind. Start with the obvious: any institution that runs on tax dollars will in some way be held accountable to justify its expense, its continued existence, and the public's goodwill. It won't do to say, "Just trust us—and send more money." Parents, the most deeply invested stakeholders in a school, want and deserve some objective validation that their children are learning and on track to meet their goals, whether it's college readiness, career preparation, qualification for military service, or simply to emerge as a competent and literate citizen. At the same time, few parents want their children's experience of schooling to be dominated by the demands of testing. If we are fair-minded, it is difficult not to be troubled by the degree to which, in too many schools, preparation for annual state tests has come to feel like the primary reason we send our children to school. The testing tail has been wagging the schooling dog for at least two decades.

The logic of test-driven "accountability" as public policy is clean and simple, even elegant. Test every kid in every school every year. Use the data that emerges to determine what's working and scale up success where it exists; ferret out chronic failure, whether it's individual teachers or entire schools, and give them the resources they need to improve. If failure persists, shut a school down, or in the case of teachers, counsel them out of the profession. What has too often occurred instead are any number of unintended but foreseeable consequences: curriculum-narrowing, aggressive test prep and cheating scandals, each a manifestation of Campbell's law, an adage coined by social science researcher Donald T. Campbell, which has become the cri de coeur of anti-testing activists: "The more any quantitative social indicator is used for social decision-making, the more subject it will be to corruption pressures and the more apt it will be to distort and corrupt the social processes it is intended to monitor."[2] Campbell extended his observation to testing, noting that "achievement tests may well be valuable indicators of general school achievement under conditions of normal teaching aimed at general competence. But when test scores become the goal of the teaching process, they both lose their value as indicators of educational status and distort the educational process in undesirable ways." Campbell's law is the heart of the brief against standardized testing: it has distorted education, giving tests a role they were not designed for and a power they were not meant to have. Testing was intended to identify and encourage best practices in American classrooms, but it's had close to the opposite effect: encouraging poor practice aimed at solely boosting test scores, not necessarily enhancing learning.

But it is equally important to recall the impetus for all this: a genuine and well-warranted concern about the quality of American education generally and the low quality of education afforded to low-income kids of color in particular. In *No Excuses*, Samuel Casey Carter placed a premium on student assessment as one of the traits common to the better schools he profiled. "Rigorous and regular testing leads to continuous improvement," he wrote. "High expectations without a means of measurement are hollow."[3] The education reform movement draws its moral authority and financial and political support from the data gleaned from testing. Without it, there would be no charter schools, no voucher programs, no Teach For America or small-schools movement, nor any of the other efforts, large and small, aimed at closing the achievement gap. There would *be* no achievement gap. Disparate outcomes would obviously still exist, but we would lose little sleep over them: The achievement gap *is* a test score gap. It pricks our conscience only because awareness of test scores make it impossible, even immoral, to ignore it.

Cheating scandals have led many of us to assume that the undesirable responses to testing and accountability mostly involve deliberate fraud. In 2009, the American Association of School Administrators named Atlanta superintendent Beverly Hall the National Superintendent of the Year and hailed the city as "a model of urban school reform."[4] A year later the state of Georgia was investigating potential cheating in nearly two hundred of its schools, including fifty-eight in Atlanta, and uncovering a pattern of "organized and systemic misconduct." Nearly three dozen educators were indicted; eleven stood trial, and all but one was convicted.[5] Hall passed away before she could stand trial. As in Atlanta, a case in Philadelphia mostly involved teachers erasing wrong answers on student tests and penciling in correct answers.

Such egregiously unethical behavior is easy to condemn. The picture gets considerably murkier, however, when you consider the myriad ways in which schools have changed their practices over the last few decades. "Test-based accountability has become an end in itself in American education, unmoored from clear thinking about what should be measured, how it should be measured, or how testing can fit into a rational plan for evaluating and improving our schools," notes Daniel Koretz in *The Testing Charade*. "It is hard to overstate how much this matters—for children, for educators, and for the American public."[6]

Koretz is neither an anti-testing zealot nor an ideologue, but a Harvard University psychometrician and a former public school teacher. He first came to my attention in 2009, when he and several colleagues demonstrated convincingly that encouraging gains on New York State math and reading tests over the preceding decade had been largely a mirage: over the same period, students' scores on the gold standard National Assessment of Educational Progress hadn't budged. It made no sense that the same kids' results should be up smartly on one test but flat on another. There was no charge of cheating per se; the state tests were simply getting easier. This confirmed what I had seen in my own fifth-grade classroom: Children I saw struggling in math, in some cases still performing basic calculations by counting on their fingers, were somehow deemed proficient in the subject, scoring a Level 3 on state tests. As comforting as it might have been to congratulate myself for their performance, it was obvious that something else was at work. By demonstrating that New York was creating a proficiency illusion with easier tests and by lowering the scores needed to be deemed on grade level, Koretz and his colleagues were holding accountability itself accountable: the entire point is to improve student outcomes, not define proficiency downward. In the years since, Koretz has become a serious critic of the downstream effects of testing on classroom practice. Overt cheating may be the most visible problem, but it's not the most common one.

There have been no credible allegations of outright fraud at Success Academy, nor are there likely to be. Given the intense scrutiny the network operates under and the significant numbers of disaffected former parents and teachers eager to knock Moskowitz down a peg, it is nearly inconceivable that its results could be achieved by the kind of systematic cheating that occurred in Atlanta and Philadelphia; it wouldn't go undetected or unreported for long. The network is more vulnerable to charges that its aggressive test-prep regimen itself constitutes a form of cheating, exerting such an extraordinary level of influence over classroom practice that it blurs the distinction. If this charge were to stick, however, Success Academy would have plenty of company.

Is test prep cheating? The answer is not as clear or obvious as one might think. While test prep has a generally negative connotation, it is not inherently bad. Schools have assessed student learning for as long as there have been students and schools. When critics complain about "teaching to the test," the standard rejoinder among accountability hawks is that test prep isn't an issue if high-stakes tests are "tests worth teaching to." The assessments associated with Common Core State Standards, adopted by all but a handful of states starting in 2010, were pitched at higher levels of rigor and sophistication; they were intended to be precisely this kind of test worth teaching to, while at the same time incentivizing various instructional shifts in math and literacy. Together this would make up a virtuous circle, where good teaching is good test prep, good test prep is good teaching—all of it validated by tests that reward rigorous curriculum and thoughtful teaching.

It hasn't worked out that way. "High-stakes testing has generated a vast amount of test prep that bears no resemblance whatever to these positive examples," Koretz notes. "At its best, bad test prep wastes precious time. Often it does much more harm, corrupting instruction and producing . . . fraudulent gains. And some of this test prep, even when carried out openly, shades into cheating." In

Koretz's view, there are three types of bad test prep. The most common is reallocation between subjects. Nearly every public school student in grades three through eight sits for an annual test in reading and math, which has been enshrined in federal law since No Child Left Behind went into effect in 2001. While states may require additional tests in subjects like science and social studies, reading and math have been emphasized nearly to the exclusion of everything else as a measure of school and teacher quality. It should thus surprise no one that schools "reallocate," spending more time on reading and math and less on other subjects. Success Academy has largely avoided the sin of reallocation or "curriculum narrowing." While history and social studies are not studied as discrete subjects until middle school, students get science every day starting in kindergarten and more hours of music, dance, art, chess, and sports, by far, than most urban elementary schools and charter schools, which have often responded to testing pressures by eliminating any "frills," up to and including recess. American children, on average, get a mere sixteen minutes of social studies per day in grades K–3, and nineteen minutes of science. The average increases slightly in grades 4–6, when forty-five minutes a day are devoted to both social studies and science.[7] ELA consumes roughly ninety minutes a day, math one hour.

A more slippery problem is "reallocation within tested subjects." A test, like a public opinion poll, represents a tiny sample of a much larger domain, or body of knowledge. A pollster surveys a representative slice of the population to draw sensible conclusions about, say, who's likely to win or lose an election. Test makers cannot test everything there is to know about a subject, so they sample key elements. Educators frequently refer to so-called power standards, a subset of math or ELA standards that is most likely to appear on state tests; those become the highest priority to teach and emphasize. That might sound benign, even savvy, but it can interfere with student mastery, or give a false sense of proficiency. Koretz draws an analogy with car manufacturers, which until recently built vehicles to ensure the safety of the driver's side but not the passenger side; until mid-2016, the Insurance Institute for Highway Safety conducted critical crash tests on the driver's side only. Customers had no reason to assume the passenger side was any less safe; the crash-test ratings created a sense of security and safety that may not have been deserved. Similarly, if teachers overprepare students on the standards most likely to appear and de-emphasize content that tends not to be tested, they risk engaging in the same kind of deception. Students could get a misimpression that they are more proficient in a subject than they really are; the score potentially offers a false positive.

The third type of bad test prep Koretz cites is explicit coaching. "Coaching focuses on unimportant details of the particular test," he says. "These details also include small, incidental aspects of content, things that aren't of any substantive importance but that can affect how students respond. Coaching entails focusing test prep on these details, rather than on the underlying content that matters." Most readers, particularly those who have hired expensive tutors for their children before they sit for college entrance exams like the SAT or other high-stakes tests, might not consider coaching "cheating" per se, but Koretz is emphatically against test-prep techniques that "at their worst teach students nothing of value whatsoever. These are really just a sleight of hand."

Is it really cheating if everybody does it? Not everybody does, but if affluent families continue to ferret out every conceivable advantage—and there's no way to keep them from doing so—it can only further cement inequity. Why should low-income students be denied the same opportunities? Kerrie Riley put forth this precise rationale in her training for third- and fourth-grade assistant teachers. "It's only fair that we give our kids the opportunity that other kids in the state are able to have that our kids otherwise may not have access if we didn't provide it for them," she told her colleagues. It's easier to close the test-prep gap than the achievement gap.

Koretz laments that test prep has corrupted the idea of good teaching altogether, and we may not be able to un-ring that bell: "High-stakes testing and undesirable test prep have been in place for so long that many young teachers have spent their entire careers immersed in them." At urban charter schools, this extends to the time many teachers, probably most of them, were students. Testing deeply informed their own experience of school. As Dan Koretz observes, teachers' understanding of the difference between teaching and test prep has been eroded. "To an alarming degree," he writes, they have "been taught that test prep and good instruction are the same thing."[8]

None of the examples Koretz cites is generally regarded as cheating by parents, teachers, or the media. But all three "really are cheating, because they can only produce fraudulent gain," Koretz insists. "I think most schools and most people in the media define 'cheating' much too narrowly . . . You're doing something that will deliberately mislead parents and taxpayers."[9] For good or ill, urban charter schools in general, and Success Academy notably so, in degrees ranging from very intense to extremely intense, do all in their power to push, prod, and cajole their students to perform capably on high-stakes tests. But if our definition of a "good school" is one with impressive test scores, then it should surprise no one if schools extend all efforts short of deliberate fraud to improve them. We have functionally demanded through decades of public policy that they do so.

———

It's raining and the second graders are taking recess indoors as I wander into Kowalski and Whitaker's classroom. Kowalski stands by the window with her arm draped around a child's shoulder admiring the girl's drawing. "Boys and girls, if you continue working so nicely," she announces, "Mr. Whitaker and I will put on some music." The kids are enjoying their free time when one boy leaps from his seat and yells to another, "Leave me alone!" Kowalski beckons him with a crooked finger. They speak out of my earshot, and then the boy goes off to join a group of his classmates drawing on the rug while Kowalski engages in shuttle diplomacy between the two boys. The drama, whatever it was, is resolved. Science teacher Amanda Sommi comes in to pick up a few of the children who have earned a pizza lunch with her. She whispers to the boy who set the other one off, squeezes his chin with one hand, and brings her face down to his level, touching her forehead to his.

Suddenly, something sets off Adama, who starts jumping up on Whitaker, attempting to grab a paper he is holding. His para pulls him off, but the boy continues to struggle. "Adama, you need to stop!" Whitaker repeats in a firm but calm voice. Order is briefly restored, but soon Adama is in a full-on meltdown, verbalizing angrily and incoherently, standing on a chair and screaming, "NOOOOO!" while Sommi and the para try to calm him down. When Ms. CeeCee arrives, drawn by either the ruckus or a teacher's distress call, Kowalski takes the rest of the class down to lunch. From well down the hall, Adama's angry screams can be heard as the class heads downstairs to the cafeteria.

CHAPTER 17

"Teach Me!"

A COMMON AND PERSISTENT CRITICISM OF URBAN NO-EXCUSES charter schools is that they impose middle-class values on children. What such criticisms elide is that those schools do not impose a set of values on families as much as they appeal to families already in possession of them; parents are attracted to schools that reflect and reinforce their ideals and beliefs, or at least do not actively undermine them. But the complaints persist and cut deeply. "'Paternalism,'" as David Whitman noted, "remains a dirty word in American culture."[1]

There is an equally unhelpful blind spot among many education reformers and charter school operators, who, consciously or unconsciously, often view urban communities and the families who live in them through a lens of dysfunction. It is commonplace to describe parents as partners; however, even the best charters tend to ask very little of them. The "partnership" is mostly limited to entering your child in a charter school lottery, delivering them to school on time, and showing up for parent-teacher conferences. Moreover, the self-regarding narratives that have grown around efforts to close the achievement gap have tended to create a kind of ed reform machismo in which results are discounted, even dismissed, if schools do not serve the very hardest-to-teach children growing up in the most dire poverty and with the most severe disadvantages.

These various story lines tend to overlook or ignore families like Vanessa and Andre Farrer, who are hiding in plain sight: working class, married, deeply religious, and heavily invested in their children's education. They are Success Academy's core constituency: focused, committed, and with expectations of their children that match or exceed those of their sons' teachers. It is not possible to say with certainty what percentage of the network's students live in stable homes with both parents, or to make a comparison to students at public schools in the same districts, but dual-income households appear to be overrepresented among the Success parent body.

I first met Vanessa Farrer in September at Bronx 1's Family Recess event for students who had completed all their summer homework. She and Andre live with their three sons on the tenth floor of a new apartment building on St. Ann's Avenue. When I visit, their two youngest boys, Antwan and Avery, are at the kitchen table hunched over their math homework, practicing for the upcoming state test. Vanessa has worked for the New York City Police Department for twenty-four years; she supervises the civilian workforce at one of the local Bronx precincts. Andre also works for the city, as a Section 8 housing inspector for the New York City Housing Authority. They met at church, Great Redeemer, an evangelical congregation that convenes in a storefront in the Soundview section of the Bronx. Their faith is central to their lives and how they raise their sons. Vanessa's email signature features a verse from Colossians: "Having disarmed principalities and powers, He made a public spectacle of them, triumphing over them in it."

If Antwan and Avery were students in the New York City public school system, they would be at PS 277, which is where I taught fifth grade and just down the street from their apartment and past Intermediate School 162. When I taught in the neighborhood, it was not unusual to see brawling students spilling out of IS 162, on at least one occasion drawing a crowd that swelled to more than one hundred kids egging them on. A plurality of my students went on to IS 162, a school so persistently low-performing that the city finally announced in 2016 that it would be closed. Antwan and Avery will never set foot in either. Vanessa loads the boys into a minivan each morning and drives about a mile and half down 149th Street to get to Bronx 1 before the doors open at 7:30. The couple's oldest son, Myshonne, a tall, rail-thin youth with a warm, shy smile, has attended a series of schools, public, private, and charter, in an attempt to find the right fit, including New Covenant Christian Academy and Bronx Prep, one of the borough's first charter schools. In middle school, he went to Mott Hall, a public school not far from their home. Vanessa says the school pegged her son as a "scholar-athlete," using his love of basketball to motivate him. "That was the phrase they used constantly: 'He's going to be a good scholar-athlete,'" she recalls. "I was like, 'Please, I need him to focus on academics.'" They pulled him out.

Vanessa first heard about Success Academy watching TV one night when she happened upon *The Lottery*, a 2010 documentary that follows four children from the Bronx and Harlem as they try to win a seat at a Success Academy school. *The Lottery* debuted at the Tribeca Film Festival at a time when the halo over no-excuses charter schools was shining the brightest. In the *New York Daily News*, columnist Errol Louis compared the movie to the Al Gore environmental documentary *An Inconvenient Truth* and predicted it would create and energize charter supporters by the thousands. "It conveys the desperation and urgency of urban public education better than the anti-charter forces can defend a status quo that is shockingly unfair and wholly unacceptable," he wrote.[2]

"I saw that movie, and I was like, 'Wow. I want my son to go to that school,'" she said. Antwan was not yet even in pre-K, but Vanessa resolved that when it came time, he would go Success, which, having crossed her radar, now seemed ubiquitous. She started noticing students on the subway in their orange uniforms and blue logoed backpacks; there were recruitment advertisements on bus shelters and phone kiosks. "I started seeing the billboards, and I started ringing my husband's ear about it. 'I'm going to try to put him in the lottery for Success Academy,'" she told Andre. "I would have tried for pre-K if they had pre-K." Hedging her bets, she applied to multiple charter schools in the neighborhood, winning seats at Bronx Charter School of the Arts, a local Montessori charter school, and Success Academy. Vanessa visited the others, but there was never any doubt in her mind that Antwan would go to Bronx 1. "I wanted him in there so bad from what I saw in the movie," she says, "and from other reports of other people," including a member of the Farrers' church. Local churches like theirs are another quiet driver of enrollment to high-performing charters. Almost without exception, all the families that I got to know at Bronx 1 and other Success Academy schools were either regular churchgoers or deeply spiritual. Many had attended religious schools as kids and expressed a wish to send their own children to Catholic schools or something similar.

With Antwan enrolled at Bronx 1, Success Academy's sibling preference made the path straight for his younger brother, Avery. "He kicked the door in, so now his brother's going to be right in there," Vanessa remembers thinking. Her resolution was driven by her frustration with Myshonne's various schools. While we are speaking, Myshonne says goodbye and heads off to a local basketball tournament. There have been times, his mother says, when he was not allowed to play ball because his grades were poor. "His grades are on point now—thank God for that," she says after he leaves the apartment. "He's gotten the understanding that your grades are first. That was hard for him to understand at first."

Andre Farrer spent his childhood shuttling between New York City and Charlotte, North Carolina, where he was an unmotivated student, but with grades good enough to earn acceptance to St. Augustine College and Appalachian State, neither of which he attended. "I was fairly smart in school, played sports, but I didn't do anything with it. I chose the fast life," he says, with a hint of sadness over lost opportunities. The phrase "I should have" comes up often as Andre reflects on his youth. He lived two blocks from West Charlotte High School, where his first-period class in the twelfth grade was Latin. He made straight As and was in the school's Latin Club, even though he was never on time, typically rolling into school when the class was half over. There were more interesting things to do, like the time some buddies took a road trip to Chapel Hill to see the national championship–winning University of North Carolina men's basketball team. "We snuck in, we were under the bleachers watching them practice. Got to meet James Worthy and Sam Perkins and Michael Jordan," he recalls.

He "wasted so much time on foolishness," eventually drifting into selling weed on the streets of Charlotte. "I'm horrified with my past," he says, which included a four-year prison sentence. But it could have been even worse. One night in Charlotte, "I saw some white dudes driving through the neighborhood, so that represents they're looking for some," Andre recalls. He had a quarter pound of marijuana that he had divided for sale into five-dollar bags with another full pound stashed in the trunk of his car. "I had one bag left, so me and my greed," he says. "I see the white guys, I turn my car around and chased them down, blew the horn, held the bag up." The guys in the other car weren't looking to get high; they were undercover police officers. "I gave the guy the bag, he pulls out the gun," Andre says. Had they searched his car and found the bulk of his stash in the trunk, Andre would likely have been facing a felony charge, but he talked his way out of it. "It came out so smooth. It's like, 'Listen, I just bought this, it's no good. I saw you guys and I'm trying to warn you.'" The cops fell for it—or cut him a break. "They never searched my car. They left it right there. They took me and locked me up. I got right out on my own recognizance." Close brushes with the law didn't scare him straight. "When you get away with stuff like that, you develop this mindset that you're invincible."

"I had the most profound thing said to me once by my probation officer," Andre recalls while his two sons work math problems at the kitchen table a few feet away. "He said, 'You are so smart you're stupid.' His meaning was, you think that you can outsmart everybody, and ninety percent of the time you can." Andre insists that he is blessed by God. "I am a chosen son, through prayers from my mother and family," he said. But his regret over lost opportunities drives his determination to see his three sons take a different path. "Now I raise my children to appreciate things. I teach them discipline. Just stay on the path," Andre says. "I'm fifty-three. By the time they get to fifty-three, I want them to already have a house. I want them to have already gotten their education and work in a good job."

This focus on education, discipline, and personal responsibility, lessons learned the hard way, makes Success Academy an obvious fit for families like the Farrers. Andre has little patience for those who criticize the school's rules and discipline. "I don't get it, because I'm all for structure," he says. "In our communities, black neighborhoods, they have to have that. It all starts at home." Nor does he have patience for complaints about the school's demands that parents be actively involved: "Unfortunately in black neighborhoods, most parents think you just go and drop the kids off and be done with them for six hours." Vanessa and her husband want to be involved, but some parents have told her that the demands are too much. "There's a lady in the building right now that took her daughter out, and now she's looking at mine and she sees them thriving," says Vanessa, who lobbied Bronx 1 to take the girl back but "they said, 'I'm sorry, she's got to go through the whole [admissions] process all over again.'"

The two younger boys are thriving at Bronx 1, particularly Avery, who showed inner determination from an early age, often being hard on himself when he struggled to understand something or even write his name neatly in pre-K. "If he couldn't do it, he was devastated. We would be like, 'It's OK, calm down!'" his mother says. Avery's teachers saw his drive and gifts too, and the boy quickly advanced as a reader. Carolyn Syskowski was his kindergarten teacher and wanted him to go directly into first grade, a move Vanessa resisted. "I was like, 'No, no. I want him to experience kindergarten.'" She and Andre were not eager to have their son become the youngest first grader at Bronx 1, or to be classmates with more socially advanced children.

Instead, Syskowski and Gisela Skinner, who was an assistant teacher at the time, would send him home with extra work, which he always blew through. He continued to outperform his classmates on assessments and march his way up through reading levels. Ms. CeeCee, who had been Antwan's kindergarten teacher and now supervises all kindergarten classrooms, soon took up Avery's cause, pushing the Farrers to let their son skip a grade. "Miss CeeCee is the one that called us in for the meeting. She said, 'Listen, mom and dad, we got to challenge him. We got to skip him. Please.'" The Farrers relented. Avery finished the year in Syskowski's class, but skipped first grade entirely, returning in the fall as a second grader in Charita Stewart's classroom.

Vanessa Farrer is rhapsodic about Syskowski. "She is beautiful. She is God-sent." When their son developed a digestive ailment, his teachers "would text us and send work home, and it was beautiful. I loved the way they pushed him. That spoke volumes to me and Andre. They really supported us." Andre appreciates Bronx 1's advocacy for Avery, "but I appreciate them more for Antwan, because he struggled." The boy's troubles have been mostly in reading comprehension, struggles that play out in frustrating tests of will over homework. "I would get frustrated with him," Andre confesses. "You could tell him something, and then ask him a few things and then go back to it, and he couldn't tell you. I'm like, 'I just told you!' I'd get mad at him. Now I've learned to calm down." The Farrers credit Antwan's third-grade teachers, Kaitlyn Walsh and Christopher Mikulka, for the change. When they asked the pair to send home extra work for their son, the teachers declined. "They said, 'No, no, no. We work him hard in school. We will send him something home on the weekend,'" Vanessa said. "They would send two math, two readings, and that was it. They said, 'No, we don't want to burn him out.'"

Antwan is taking state tests for the first time this spring; Avery has until next year. As testing season got underway, the volume of calls to the home increased noticeably. Ms. Walsh calls constantly with feedback gleaned from Antwan's practice tests. "She'll say to me, 'Listen, he didn't do too well today. He worked too slow or he went too fast; he didn't check his answers,'" Vanessa said. "Every night, *every night*, Mr. Mikulka or Miss Walsh will call Antwan and ask him, 'What's your strategy? What's your plan?'" The nightly calls have taken some getting used to. "If they call my house, then the house phone would ring," Andre says. He would check caller ID. "Then no sooner than that hangs up, your cell phone is going off, and you get an email, you get a text, and another phone call. I thought it was overwhelming," he said. "But then I'm like, 'This is really good. This shows that they care.'" Chaperoning field trips has given Andre additional respect for his children's teachers. "I was like, 'Oh God, I couldn't do this!'" he says, laughing. He and Vanessa are sitting on the couch, and as we speak, Antwan wanders over to ask his dad to check his homework. "I have to walk ten flights of stairs every building I go to. This is twice as hard as my job."

Working as an inspector for the city's Housing Authority brings Farrer in daily contact with slices of life that are invisible to most New Yorkers and that reinforce his commitment to his children, their education, and his faith. Section 8 tenants are subject to annual inspections, which Andre conducts. "We go in just to make sure that the ceilings are not collapsing, the toilets are working." Inspectors are told to apply "reasonable living accommodations" as a standard, but Andre sees abuses every day. "We know how many people are supposed to be in the house, most often a mother and her children," he says. "There's always some John Doe in there with his boxers on saying, 'Oh, I don't live here. She had to go on an appointment; she told me to be here,'" Andre says, shaking his head. "I walk in the bedroom—'All your shoes and clothes are in there. I know you live here. Whatever, man. Listen, I don't really care,'" he replies. "'I'm not here investigating. I came here to do an inspection.'" Some days he finds the job rejuvenating; other days, depressing. "When you go in, they're so sad sometimes, because you go in apartments and it's horrible conditions. It's filthy, nasty, roaches and mice, mold around the tub. I don't care if you're grown and you choose to live that way, but when there are children, that bothers me," he explains.

He sees signs of disorder everywhere. "When I get on the train or a bus and I look at the youth and the lack of respect for others . . ." he says. During his own childhood, he says, "Your neighbors had the authority to spank you and then take you home. By the time you get home, they called, and you get another spanking. Now these children walk with their pants down, cursing. Just on the train, the bus, just cursing like it's nothing." If I closed my eyes, I could be sitting not on Vanessa and Andre Farrer's couch in the South Bronx but in my childhood home on Long Island, listening to my dad fifty years ago complaining about "kids today."

Andre dreams about getting his family out of New York altogether, perhaps down to North Carolina and into a house. When he drives through the neighborhood with his sons, he points out grown men hanging around the streets. "I just show them. Because if you walk out the door, you see the guys just standing on the sidewalk— that's what they do." Even though the Farrers live in a new building, he points out that 40 percent of the tenants are subsidized tenants who came here from shelters. Before he quit smoking, Andre would go outside for a cigarette and see tenants setting up grills to barbecue even though it was approaching midnight on a weeknight. "I'm like, 'Aw man, we've got to move.' Because that's just crazy." But as long as they're in the city, the plan is to stay in this building so Avery and Antwan can finish school at Success Academy. In 2016 Moskowitz announced Success had purchased the iconic and long-abandoned Bronx Borough Courthouse, three blocks from the Farrers' home, as the site of its second high school and first in the Bronx. It will be where Andre and Avery go if they stay in the Bronx. "As long we're here in New York City, that's where they going to be," Vanessa says flatly.

As I prepare to leave, I mention that I'm scheduled to see Moskowitz the next day. Vanessa grows animated. "I pray for her, because I know that she is not liked. It's not even a fair dislike," she says. "People say, 'Oh, but they treat the children like robots.' Teaching them respect is teaching the children to be like robots?" Andre seconds his wife. "The one thing that I know about life is that misery loves company. There should never be any derogatory statements against Success. There should always be support from the community that we live in." When I tell the Farrers about a conversation I had with Moskowitz many months ago when she commented offhandedly that she'll "never win," Vanessa brings up the Bible verse in her email signature. "Jesus has won the victory for you, so just walk in the victory," she says. Both of the Farrers were recently ordained as ministers in their church. "You're not fighting for victory; you're fighting *in* victory," Andre adds. "Tell her she's already won," Vanessa says as I say my goodnights. "Give her that message from me. Tell her she's got us praying for her."

In 1966, the sociologist James S. Coleman published the landmark report *Equality of Educational Opportunity*. It arrived one year after the passage of the Elementary and Secondary Education Act (ESEA), a far-reaching piece of legislation that dramatically increased the federal role in American education, primarily via Title I funding. No Child Left Behind and the Every Student Succeeds Act, the latter passed in 2015, are reauthorizations of the 1965 ESEA. Commissioned under the 1964 Civil Rights Act by the Office of Education of the US Department of Health, Education, and Welfare (the US Department of Education did not exist at the time), the "Coleman Report," as it's come to be known, was among the largest and most authoritative studies of educational inequality ever undertaken—and still one of the most controversial. The report was expected to reveal a need for federal action to equalize educational opportunity, a centerpiece of Lyndon Johnson's War on Poverty.[3] Drawing on a data set covering nearly 650,000 children, 60,000 teachers, and more than 3,000 schools, Coleman's work did not find significant disparities in per-pupil spending and resources between black and white schools within given communities. What he found was that the greatest drivers of inequality were parental education level, other family background characteristics, and peer-group effects. The Coleman Report was famously released on the Fourth of July weekend 1966 in the hope that it would be ignored, since what he found did not support Johnson's "Great Society" call for federal action to equalize educational opportunity. It became, instead, among the most important studies in the history of social science, and one whose echoes are still heard today.

It is not much of an overstatement to say the education reform movement is a decades-long attempt to rebut the Coleman Report and to show that determined schools alone can close the "achievement gap," a phrase that was not in use in the mid-1960s. That attempt has been far less successful "at scale" than most reformers are comfortable acknowledging. Schools founded and run by urban charter school networks have been one of the few bright spots of the past few decades, but they serve relatively few children. After several decades of reform, the "rising tide of mediocrity" grimly described in the landmark 1983 federal report *A Nation at Risk* cannot be said to have receded much at all. Neither is it unreasonable to think that academic gains, where they exist, are driven—or at least made more achievable and sustainable—by the effects of parents self-selecting into schools that focus on raising achievement on standardized tests.

A few blocks from the Farrers' apartment is the headquarters of Public Prep, a small network of single-sex charter schools that serve almost exclusively low-income children of color from pre-K to eighth grade. The CEO is Ian Rowe, a middle-age African American man whose close-cropped hair is shot through with gray. For the last several years, in articles, op-eds, and speeches at education conferences and think tanks, Rowe has pressed an argument that is far more volatile than any that Eva Moskowitz has made. Rowe has persistently called out education reform for its unwillingness to confront and address the role family structure and stability play in school, and more pointedly, the reluctance to tell low-income children what we have known since the Coleman Report: that personal choices related to education, employment, and "family for-mation" impact life outcomes and prospects for upward mobility.

Frequently seen in the South Bronx neighborhood where Rowe's schools educate two thousand children are a pair of baby-blue Win-nebagos, which have been converted into mobile DNA-testing facil-ities emblazoned in mock graffiti with the words WHO'S YOUR DADDY? Rowe sees the vehicles as a symptom and illustration of the destabilization of the American family, a trend that hits hardest the low-income black and brown children who have become the near-exclusive focus of reform efforts over the last two decades, and a trend that he insists that school leaders "must confront head-on." Rowe, a product of New York City public schools who held senior positions at MTV and the Bill and Melinda Gates Foundation before taking the helm at Public Prep, takes care to ensure his argument is not perceived as "blaming the victim" or exclusively an issue among people of color. In addition to the Coleman Report, Rowe invokes the equally controversial 1965 report by Daniel Patrick Moynihan, *The Negro Family: The Case for National Action*, which warned that "at the heart of the deterioration of the fabric of Negro society is the deterioration of the Negro family."

"Three centuries of injustice have brought about deep-seated structural distortions in the life of the Negro American," Moynihan wrote. "At this point, the present tangle of pathology is capable of perpetuating itself without assistance from the white world." At the time Moynihan sounded his alarm, the non-marital birth rate among African Americans was about 23 percent. "Moynihan said this is a crisis of unbelievable proportion, and he was vilified for it," says Rowe. But today among whites, nearly 30 percent of births are out of wedlock; and among African Americans, non-marital births have more than tripled to 71 percent; among Hispanics, it's 53 percent. This rate of family disruption, Rowe contends, exerts a force that no amount of ed reform energy or do-gooder earnestness can surmount. "All that stuff doesn't matter, because our schools should be able to overcome all that, right?" Rowe asks sardonically. "It's just not true." The question he asks is what role should schools play in bringing attention to the effects of family disruption and taking the lead in encouraging subsequent generations not to go down the same road.

Rowe's pitch leans heavily on the work of the Brookings Institution's Ron Haskins and Isabel Sawhill, who described a "success sequence" in their 2009 book, *Creating an Opportunity Society*. "First comes education," they wrote. "Then comes a stable job that pays a decent wage, made decent by the addition of wage supplements and work supports if necessary. Finally comes marriage, followed by children." Haskins and Sawhill even argued for "marketing campaigns and educational programs to change social norms: to bring back the success sequence as the expected path for young Americans."[4] Rowe, nearly alone among education reformers and charter school leaders, is committed to taking the recommendation seriously. When a low-income person graduates from high school, finds full-time employment, gets married, and has a child—in that order—the chance of remaining in poverty as an adult drop to a mere 2 percent. "There is no public policy that comes even close to those kinds of results. This isn't even public policy," says Rowe, who insists schools have a moral obligation to ensure that children growing up in poverty, or at risk of falling into it, are at least aware of the success-sequence data. Low-income children in communities with the highest rate of family instability are the least likely to hear about it, grow up with it as a social norm, or to have parents and other adults in their communities pressure them to abide by it, Rowe explains. Of course, there's no guarantee that if you're born into a two-parent household, a positive education or life outcome is foreordained. But the odds are overwhelmingly in your favor, compared with those of children growing up in less stable homes. "If we don't acknowledge that, then we're being delusional," Rowe insists.

If Rowe has found few disciples for his crusade, it is because the vast weight of education reform thought and ideology leans in an entirely different direction. Sobered by the lack of significant progress despite decades of efforts to close the achievement gap, it is rare to hear education reformers and charter school executives arguing anymore that schools alone can end poverty. But what has replaced that conviction is a belief that poor academic outcomes are largely an effect of racism, particularly an implicit bias that reveals itself in higher suspension rates among children of color and black boys most specifically, in less challenging assignments and course materials, and in other demonstrations of low expectations. Moreover, education reform is still dominated by white men and women, both at the executive and classroom level. This makes problematic any discussion of marriage and child-rearing norms, no matter how compelling the data—and regardless of how many have adhered to those norms in their own lives or who would be deeply disappointed in their own children if they failed to follow suit.

Neither is it consistent to dismiss Rowe's argument as "blaming the victim" or insist it is inappropriate for schools to "shame" children, stigmatize their parents, or moralize to them. Schools praise and condemn behaviors and attitudes as a matter of course. We preach the virtues of kindness and sharing to small children; inform middle schoolers of the dangers of smoking, drinking, and drug use; and preach college attendance to their older siblings. Schools are closer to culture-imposing *machines* than to being neutral and values-free. If the success sequence is the raw material that enables families to set their children on a path of upward mobility, it seems irresponsible not to share this with children potentially to shape their behavior and inform personal decision-making, much in the way schools do at present without a second thought when it comes to anti-bullying initiatives or celebrating diversity. It is odd, inconsistent, and defensive to overtly try to shape students' attitudes and choices about a range of attitudes, beliefs, and choices, *but not that.*

Family stability appears to be a significant contributor to student outcomes at Success Academy. While there is no empirical data to prove the point, the phenomenon is observable every morning on Morris Avenue at drop-off in front of Bronx 1, where fathers are present in observably high numbers. Success Academy does not overtly praise or promote it in the way Rowe's nearby schools do, but a compelling argument can be made that its policies and practices are either a proxy for family stability or a significant challenge to keep up with in its absence. Managing the logistics of transportation, reading to children nightly, staying on top of homework and reading logs—even participating in political rallies and lobbying elected officials more than a hundred miles from home, for example—are more easily achievable by families with the kind of resources and bandwidth that are less likely to be available in single-parent homes, or in the absence of trustworthy child care. Even its controversial no-backfill policy of refusing to accept new students after fourth grade is a potential impediment to low-income families who are more likely to change addresses; high mobility has been shown to lower student achievement—particularly when the students are from low-income, less-educated families. Whether by design or happenstance, success-sequence families appear to be much closer to the norm than the exception in Eva Moskowitz's schools, and certainly when compared with families in traditional public schools in the same neighborhood.

February 2 is Groundhog Day, and the hundredth day of the school year. To mark the milestone, the entire staff and most of the students come to school dressed as if they're one hundred years old. A handful of kids are in their school uniforms, but most get in on the fun. One boy dons a checkered newsboy cap, red suspenders, and thick glasses. Another little girl has come to school in a pink fuzzy bathrobe and lavender nightcap, complete with a nasal cannula (the clear plastic tubing that delivers oxygen into the nose of elderly patients with respiratory trouble) secured behind her head with a rubber band. It's a convincing costume; she looks like a tiny escapee from a geriatric ward. A few other kids betray unusual ideas about what one hundred years old looks like, perhaps making do with whatever they could get their hands on at home. One fourth-grade girl is in a 1960s-style blouse and a black beehive wig, looking like she fell off a Shirelles album cover. Ugly dresses, old flannel shirts, and bow ties dominate. Most of Bronx 1's twentysomething staff and many of the kids have powdered their hair or sprayed it gray. In Mr. B's class, I notice a few fourth-grade scholars shooting me glances, chattering to one another in urgent whispers, and trying to squash giggles. The joke is on me. My hair has been gray all year. Vandlik swoops through the fourth-grade classes, unrecognizable in her hundred-day costume, a blonde fright wig, purple nightdress, and compression stockings. If there needs to be a serious conversation with a staff member or parent today, it will be hard to pull it off.

The building is crawling with adult outsiders—prospective parents who are considering entering the April charter school lottery. A cheerful network staffer named Jessie Diaz greets about a dozen of them for a tour of Bronx 1 and a chat about academics, school culture, and values. Several weeks ago, at a similar meeting for prospective parents at the Upper West Side campus, the visitors from one of Manhattan's most upscale neighborhoods peppered staffers with questions about foreign-language classes, sports and art programs, homework policies, and school uniforms—the kinds of questions parents tend to ask when the range of options available to them is good, better, and best—not bad, worse, or "holy crap." When Diaz opens the floor, the first hand up is a mom who lives in a school district many miles from the nearest Success Academy. Her question is direct and blunt:

"What are the chances of getting in?"

The candid answer would be "not very good," but Diaz explains that kindergarten is their best chance. Depending on which of the four Bronx Success Academies the woman applies to, there are anywhere from sixty to ninety kindergarten seats available in the lottery. If she can get to any of them, her chances of winning a seat improve. "Apply to any school you're willing and able to get to," Diaz advises. Like most oversubscribed charter schools, Success offers sibling preference. If one child gets in, the other moves to the top of the list for the next available seat. Priority is also given to families in the district's catchment area. Diaz is trying to be encouraging, but none of this is likely to help the mother who asked the question. She has come all the way from Co-op City, a thirty-minute drive when there's no traffic, and as far as one can travel from where we are sitting and still be in the Bronx. Worse, her son is not entering kindergarten; he's in second grade, and this will be the third year in a row his mother enters him into the lottery. Her chances are effectively zero. I spend a few minutes speaking with her afterward. It's hard not to be moved by the persistence and frustration that her willingness to commute is insufficient to overcome. But the math just doesn't work for her. Neither does the geography or the politics.

A few weeks later on a mild winter day, there is an even more vivid display of parent intensity and the raw emotions attached to their children's education at the annual Festival of the Arts, featuring theater, dance, and musical performances from about a dozen Success Academy schools. Performers from each campus must audition to be chosen for the showcase, held at Washington Irving High School, which used to be one of the New York City's most notoriously low-performing and persistently unsafe schools, with a graduation rate that had slipped below 50 percent. In 2003, a stool thrown from the upper floors struck a pregnant woman walking by. A few years later, a melee between kids from Washington Irving and another school sent shoppers at the crowded nearby Union Square Greenmarket scurrying for cover; a sixteen-year-old boy was stabbed to death. The city finally closed the school in 2015. Success Academy Union Square opened in the building that same year.

Many of the dozen student performances take up Black History Month themes; some of the pieces are pointed and political. Harlem 1's dance troupe performs to Dinah Washington's "This Bitter Earth," holding up signs that read RACISM, SEXISM, POVERTY, TRUMP, and PENCE. Middle schoolers from Harlem North West present a theatrical piece titled "Being Black in America" in T-shirts reading WE WILL NOT BE SILENCED. The backs are emblazoned with the names of Tamir Rice, Sandra Bland, Eric Garner, and others who have been killed by police.

Midway through the evening, the lights come up on the stage in the cavernous auditorium revealing six hard-backed wooden chairs in a row. Two girls stand on the chairs and dance to hip-hop music, while four other children chase one another around. A school bell rings, and the middle schoolers from Success Academy Bronx 2 take their seats, raising their hands and pleading for the attention of an unseen teacher, calling out, "Pick me!" "I've got it!" and "I know the answer!" Each is wearing an identical black hoodie. An unseen teacher hisses, "Shhhhh!" and the kids fall silent and sullen. After a moment, one boy rises and starts to speak, reciting "Teach Me" by the poet and spoken-word artist Nytesia Ross.

Just so you know, I am not in that percentage of kids that you automatically think drop out of school and head directly to the streets. No! You will not catch me doing that classic nod, drive by, handshake, money in narcotics trade. That is not me. Contrary to your belief, I actually have a desire to go to school and get an education!

The auditorium breaks into murmurs. A few people spontaneously applaud, catching the next student off guard. She pauses before adding her voice to the piece.

But you see, the problem is when the condition of the school that I attend is determined by the neighborhood in which it is in, when I am expected to learn in an environment that isn't even suitable enough to be taught in. When my teachers are conducting class in janitors' closets or in the hallways or in the gym!

Somewhere in the darkened auditorium, a woman lets out a shout. The crowd is riveted as the third girl starts to speak. Feeding

off the rising energy in the room, she spits out her monologue angrily, her head bobbing in daggerlike thrusts.

> *The problem is when my teachers already have preconceived
> notions on the rate in which I will learn because they don't
> think kids of my social class can retain information as
> quickly as other kids that attend school in the wealthier part
> of the city. Therefore, I am not challenged.*

Shouts of encouragement from the audience grow louder as the
kids recite their lines, one after another.

> *Because they know that I am already dealing with problems
> at home, they don't want to give me a heavier load, and in
> their eyes they're helping me. But what they don't realize is
> that they are crippling me, making me dependent on them.
> They may or may not be purposely producing lower-class
> citizens, but this is not OK with me!*

Several voices shout, "Yes!" and "That's right!"

> *Regardless of what you think of me, my destiny is not tied
> to being in prison or on the streets. I was told the key to a
> better life is education, so give me the opportunity to
> obtain it!*

"*Teach me!*" all six kids shout in unison.
Now the audience's cheers and applause are so loud and sustained that someone backstage mistakenly assumes the piece is over;
the stage lights go out. After a few seconds they come back on.

> *Do not rob me of my education! Teach me! Tell me about
> my history. Do not assign it to just one week in February!
> And in that time do not intertwine fabricated lies to make
> my country seem prettier.*

A father two seats from me leaps to his feet and yells, "No fabrication!" The boy who speaks next literally shouts to be heard, his voice breaking.

Do not filter the truth, because history is living proof how mistakes can be made. But as a country, we can overcome difficult times and reach better days!

The performance ends with all six children shouting in unison:

Teach me! Because I have a desire to learn. Because the only way we can successfully lead is if you teach. So teach! Teach me![5]

At the final "Teach me!" the kids peel off their hoodies and throw them defiantly at their feet, leaving them standing in their Success Academy school uniforms. A dam bursts. The parents in the auditorium lose their collective minds. Several dozen take up a chant of "Teach! Teach! Teach!"

The ovation goes on and on.

CHAPTER 18

Joy and Vomit

Carolyn Syskowski comes to Charita Stewart's classroom one afternoon to collect Luis, a round-faced kid with a bit of mischief about him. They are scheduled for a reading evaluation. Reading is a struggle for Luis, who has a December birthday and is younger than most of his classmates. Success students sit for these one-on-one assessments multiple times each year to determine their reading level and progress. In the Fountas and Pinnell Level A–Z reading system Success Academy follows, second graders generally read between Levels I and M.[1]

Reading out loud from a nonfiction book about whales, Luis comes to an unfamiliar word, "calf," and gets stuck. He repeatedly tries to sound it out, initially settling on "calph" as the correct pronunciation before realizing that doesn't make sense. He changes to the correct pronunciation and continues reading out loud as Syskowski listens and takes notes. After a few more minutes, it's time to see how well he understands what he's just read.

"So what did you learn in this book?" she asks. Luis begins to rattle off random facts from memory. Whales send messages to other whales. They communicate with "whistles and burps and . . ." He struggles to recall a word. "They click," he says finally. Syskowski presses for more. "What other information did you learn about whales?" Luis describes their ability to "bounce sounds off of fish" to find food. "A blue whale is as big as twenty-five elephants. They're the giants of the sea," he adds, a phrase that comes directly from the book. To ensure he's demonstrating reading comprehension, not just prior knowledge, Syskowski asks Luis to show her evidence for the facts he's just cited. The boy turns to the table of contents to find the source.

Syskowski's class begins clattering back in from the blocks room with Ms. Hanania, so she and Luis move to the hallway. "OK, Lu, let's get back to the book. How are whales like people?" she asks. "They find food. They send messages to each other," the boy answers. "They have babies." And how are they different? Luis twists his face and looks to the book to jog his memory. "When people need help with something, they don't cry or whistle or click. They just call for help. Like on the phone," he answers. "And whales can't speak. They speak, like, *whale*." Syskowski continues jotting notes as Luis empties his head of all that he's just read. "Is that all the questions?" he asks. Syskowski, poker-faced, asks, "How do you think you did?" Luis looks up at her with a hopeful expression but says nothing as Syskowski holds her expressionless gaze for another moment.

"*You did really good!*" she says, laughing and breaking into a grin. Luis gasps. "You're definitely an L!" The boy throws his head back and jams both fists under his chin as a "Wheeeeeeeee!" escapes from between his teeth. The look on his face is unbridled eight-year-old joy. "I'm gonna cry!" Syskowski blurts out. "Gimme a hug! Remember yesterday when I asked you what your goal was and you said K? What did I say?" she reminds him.

"'Make it an L!'" answers Luis, who is laughing and bouncing in his seat. "Am I L?" he asks, in disbelief or just wanting to hear it again. Syskowski nods and smiles down at him. "C'mon! We gotta go cheer in your classroom," she says, and Luis jumps up and starts to run down the hall. "Hold on! I wanna be there too!" she calls, taking off after him, as I join the pursuit. When we arrive at Stewart's classroom, Syskowski throws open the door and in her most booming teacher voice shouts, "We've got some *BIG NEWS!*" All eyes turn to her and Luis in the doorway.

"I'm Level L!" Luis blurts out.

At six feet tall, Charita Stewart projects a stoic, even solemn air. Now her reaction is almost shocking. She throws her head back and shouts, "YESSSSSS!" a guttural bellow that comes from deep in her chest. I remember the day her girlfriend proposed. Her response today dwarfs it. She lifts Luis off the ground and twirls him around in the air. "I'm so proud of you!" His classmates break into spontaneous cheers. "Way to go, Luis!" several call out.

Syskowski watches from the doorway, still beaming. "Should we go tell Ms. Belkin too?" she asks. Belkin is Luis's teacher for guided reading. Stewart and Syskowski quickly hatch a plan for Luis to prank Belkin. "Do serious face!" they urge the boy and head next door to tell Belkin he just got tested. "Oh? What level did you get?" she asks cautiously, taking the bait. "I'm a L!" Luis bursts out. Belkin hugs him. Assistant teacher Alex Gottlieb covers her mouth with both hands and her eyes well up.

For all the drama, real or imagined, that surrounds Success Academy's policies and practices, one that has not been seriously questioned is its slavish devotion to "leveled reading." Public classroom displays of reading levels start in kindergarten; the network uses them to drive grade promotion and retention decisions. The likely reason leveled-reading instruction has not faced much scrutiny at Success and other charter schools is its dominance in American education, particularly at the elementary school level.

In leveled reading, a teacher listens as her student reads a piece of text at a given level, just as Syskowski did today. If the child makes two to five mistakes per one hundred words at Level L, for example, that is considered the student's "independent" reading level. One mistake or none means the book is too easy; six or more mistakes is said to be at the child's "frustration" level. Levels are not determined by "decoding" alone; fluency and comprehension are also considered. Armed with these insights, teachers steer students to books in their classroom libraries at their "just right" level, the sweet spot at which a child can read independently with understanding and pleasure and an appropriate level of challenge. A child's "instructional" level for guided reading with a teacher in small groups would be the next letter up. In Luis's case, he will be encouraged to "book shop" in his classroom for Level L titles to read independently, but he'll read Level M books with teacher support to encourage further growth. In theory, if a child is motivated to read extensively and independently, language growth and reading proficiency will follow organically, setting the child on a steady climb through higher levels. Many students (although I did not see this method employed at Success) are taught to use the "five-finger rule" when choosing books: open to a random page, start reading, and hold up one finger every time you get to a word you don't know. If you run out of fingers before you get the end of the page, the book is too hard.

As intuitive as leveled reading may sound, it is one of education's false orthodoxies. Despite its prevalence in US elementary and middle schools, the research base is surprisingly thin. Many different leveling schemes exist. "Lexile scores" determine text complexity based on a computer algorithm that measures various attributes, such as sentence length and the number of challenging vocabulary words. The ubiquitous Fountas and Pinnell leveling system considers not just the physical features of a text but also genre, content, themes and ideas, and illustrations. This all lends reading comprehension a sense of precision and certainty that doesn't hold up to scrutiny. In *Reading Reconsidered*, Doug Lemov, Colleen Driggs, and Erica Woolway use the examples of George Orwell's *Animal Farm* and the middle school warhorse *The Outsiders*, by S.E. Hinton. Both are a Level Z in the Fountas and Pinnell system even though "one was among the most challenging books our seventh graders read, while the other was among the easiest," they wrote.

Not only are books different; children are too. A reader's motivation and prior knowledge of a topic can dramatically affect her comprehension. When you know a lot about a subject, that knowledge can fill in gaps in your comprehension. In his 2009 book *Why Don't Students Like School?*, University of Virginia cognitive scientist Daniel Willingham illustrated this point with these two examples.[2]

EXAMPLE 1

Motor learning is the change in capacity to perform skilled movements that achieve behavioral goals in the environment. A fundamental and unresolved question is whether there is a separate neural system for representing learned sequential motor responses. Defining that system with brain imaging and other methods requires a careful description of what specifically is being learned for a given sequence task.

EXAMPLE 2

A chiffon cake replaces butter—the traditional fat in cakes— with oil. A fundamental and unresolved question in baking is when to make a butter cake and when to make chiffon cake. Answering this question with expert tasting panels and other methods requires a careful description of what characteristics are desired for a cake.

Willingham lifted the first paragraph from a technical research article and wrote the second one about baking to mirror precisely its structure: the first sentence provides a definition; the second poses a problem; and the third states what it will take to solve it. "Which do you think you will remember better tomorrow?" he wrote. The second paragraph "is easier to understand (and therefore will be better remembered) because you can tie it to things you already know." You can, with effort, make sense of the first paragraph, "but some richness, some feeling of depth to the comprehension is missing. That's because when you have background knowledge your mind connects the material you're reading with what you already know about the topic, even if you're not aware that it's happening."

Seen through this lens, it becomes obvious that one child's Level L book might be another's M or H. Interest and motivation also matter. Call it the *Harry Potter* effect: millions of kids have made it through every word of J.K. Rowling's series with comprehension and enjoyment, even though in many cases the books, which range from Levels V (*Harry Potter and the Sorcerer's Stone*) to Z (*Harry Potter and the Deathly Hallows*) were far into their supposed frustration zone.

Given its air of precision—and its ubiquity in classrooms—you might expect that leveled reading has a rich research base demonstrating its efficacy. But Timothy Shanahan, a distinguished professor emeritus of urban education at the University of Illinois at Chicago, has traced the origins of "independent, instructional, and frustration" reading levels to a 1946 textbook by Emmett Betts, *Foundations of Reading Instruction*—and a single study conducted by one of Betts's doctoral students. "I tracked down that dissertation and to my dismay it was evident that they had just made up those designations without any empirical evidence," Shanahan wrote. When the study was replicated, it yielded wildly different results. "Basically we have put way too much confidence in an unproven theory," he concluded.[3]

The Fountas and Pinnell system is the most common leveled reading system in elementary and middle schools. Professors Fountas and Pinnell, however, would likely be aghast at how it's implemented at Success Academy. "It is our belief that levels have no place in classroom libraries . . . or on report cards," the two insisted in an interview with *School Library Journal*. "We created the levels for books, and not as labels for children, and our goal was that these levels be in the hands of people who understand their complexity and use them to make good decisions in instruction."[4] Success Academy disregards nearly all this guidance. Classroom libraries have book bins sorted by levels; children's nightly reading logs have a column to record each book's level. Data walls in every classroom indicate each child's current reading level. When Bronx 1's kindergarten teachers warned parents in January that their children would not go to first grade unless they were at Level D, they were not making it up. It is, by several teachers' and administrators' accounts, a common Success Academy practice, even though chief academic officer Michelle Caracappa insists that "holdover decisions are not based on a single metric" and "are strongly discouraged in kindergarten in general." But without exception, every single child at Success knows her reading level, and parents routinely cite them and credit children's teachers with moving them up the scale over the course of a year.

By mid-March, the flip chart in every fourth-grade classroom now reads:

NYS ELA Exam: 11 Days Left
NYS Math Exam: 31 Days Left

"I would like twelve of us to get 4s, sixteen of us to get 3s, and absolutely zero 1s and 2s." Kerri Lynch is setting expectations in Fordham-NYU, where her students are about to spend two hours on a Book 1, a twenty-four-question multiple-choice reading test modeled on the first section of the state exam they will sit for at the end of the month. "We can completely achieve that if we're doing our best thinking," she encourages.

Lynch wants her students to focus on four things. "Main idea is king," she says, repeating the mantra every scholar will hear thousands of times by the end of the fourth grade. "But keep your understanding of the whole text in your head," she reminds them. "It would be very unusual to have an answer choice that has nothing to do with what the whole text is about.

"Plan of attack, always," she continues. "If you don't find evidence that answers the question, don't just mark it in a random place that's kind of related. Keep looking. It's in the text. It's your job to find it." Lynch, who studies her students' work obsessively, has recently noticed several of them getting sloppy, making more mistakes on practice tests as test day draws nearer and the practice sessions get more intense. "Stamina, stamina, stamina," she now tells the class. Her final reminder for today is "be your own coach." Lynch and the other fourth-grade teachers usually circulate and confer with students during practice tests, guiding them as they eliminate incorrect answers and narrow down answers to "magic maybes" and reminding them to "counterattack" by circling back to passages and questions they found difficult after completing the test. But with the ELA exam less than two weeks away, she concludes, "I'm not going to be coaching you today."

A large cache of prizes has appeared in Lynch's room and the other classes in testing grades: dinosaur stamps, a spin-art kit, chess sets, darts, Nerf footballs, headphones, woven bracelets, a flower-pressing kit. To motivate kids to follow their "plan of attack" and meet their personal goals, Lynch and the other third- and fourth-grade teachers can hand out rewards. "Does anyone want to share what they're working for today?" she asks. Casildo has his eye on a football. Carlos and Christine covet the darts. Lynch puts on music and encourages the kids to walk around for a few minutes, relax, stretch, high-five, and encourage one another. When the music goes off, the kids settle back into their seats. "Look at me," Lynch says. "We're down to the wire. I want nothing but your best today."

Through the windows, clouds are thickening. A nor'easter is bearing down on the city, forecast to dump as many as two feet of snow on the South Bronx. Blizzard warnings are in effect from Boston to Washington, DC. Barring a last-minute turn out to sea, the storm will wreak havoc on Success Academy's carefully orchestrated "dress rehearsal." Immediately before every state test, each school in the network runs a full simulation under test-day conditions and following the precise administration plans, down to the time slots when each teacher takes their class to the bathroom. New York City schools rarely close, and Success could conceivably remain open tomorrow. But Moskowitz has been criticized in the past for keeping her schools open when DOE schools are closed for weather.

About twenty minutes in, Lynch pauses to conduct a raffle, the first opportunity for kids who have shown particular focus and effort. Normally she dispenses incentives and prizes freely during practice tests. But soon the clouds darkening her face start to match the sky outside. She told the kids she would not be coaching them, but as she circulates up and down the rows of desks, she can't help herself. "Stop. *Stop!* Listen to me. That's just not possible," she says, looking over Christine's shoulder and stabbing at her bubble sheet. "You've got to answer questions without looking at answer choices." Stopping at James's desk, she sputters, "Are you *kidding* me?" then squats alongside his desk, whispering urgently. Rising to her feet, she encourages him—"You've got this"—and moves on. A few minutes later, she calls a halt to express her frustration with the entire class. "My friends, the second passage is not looking good. I'm looking at your work and you're not thinking. Your evidence is not in the right place; you're not interpreting the questions. That whole second passage is just plan of attack. And yet I'm seeing answers that make no sense. *Get yourself going!*"

Hosinatou gets up and turns off the air conditioner in the back of the room above where she sits. Lynch barely looks up. "Nope. Put it back on." You could hang sides of beef in the classroom; the chilly temperature keeps the class awake and alert. Vandlik wanders in and tells Casildo to fix his body, which is spreading over his chair and desk. So little of his bottom is in contact with the edge of his chair that he appears to be levitating. Jaden is growing agitated, verbalizing the passages. Vandlik intervenes. Then Lynch. The boy slumps over onto his desk.

At the ninety-minute mark, the fourth graders are still at it. Casildo searches for an answer in the fluorescent ceiling lights. Hosinatou sits with her chin in her hand, her test booklet in her lap. Christine is as still as a statue, focusing intently. Even Jaden, who was so unsettled a short time ago, is slugging away. Carlos raises his hand to use the bathroom and literally sprints from the room when Lynch signals permission. Two hours in, nearly all the kids are done attacking and counterattacking, turning "magic maybes" into best guesses. They start to fidget and bounce, reading and drawing while Lynch scores the tests, her irritation visible and rising. "If you're not finished, put your pencil down and lock your hands," she says, bringing the class to attention. "I have to say I'm very disappointed today. You guys did not come in and bring it today. I'm seeing really sloppy work, really sloppy answers. This is just sad. We've put in work all year. This is the time when you've got to start showing what you know."

In the hallway, noise and chatter from the third-and-fourth-grade "effort party" starts to swell. Students who, in their teachers' judgment, tried their best are invited to spend the next half hour at a limbo contest or playing balloon volleyball. There's a Disney movie playing in Steven Madan's classroom; iPads and laptops are available next door in Richter's class. Science teacher Amanda Sommi has set up a kinetic sand play area where kids can be kids until lunch. "If I call your name, you can go to the effort party. The rest of you can wait until I come check in with you or you can continue working," Lynch announces sternly. About half the students in the class hear their names called and bolt.

If there are rules to balloon volleyball, they are known only to the fourth-grade boys and unenforced by anyone, adult or kid. The object seems to be to jump and swat at balloons to blow off steam and scream as loudly as possible when one pops. When Adrian, freed from Lynch's post-practice purgatory, emerges from the room, Casildo runs over and grabs him. "Adrian, come!" he says, and takes his friend's arm, leading him into the middle of the scrum. Within seconds, both boys are leaping, swatting, and laughing madly.

─

After the party, while the kids are at lunch and recess, the teachers huddle with Vandlik to review the results. "Overall, their results are good today," the principal reports. "*Are they?*" Lynch is incredulous. Across the grade, 80 percent of the kids scored at Level 3 or 4. Vandlik heads off to a conference call about the snowstorm and contingency plans; the teachers continue to pore over the tests. Seven of Lynch's students scored Level 2, but they were each one or two right answers away from a Level 3. By New York State's standards, most of them would likely be graded "proficient." Success Academy requires seventeen of twenty-four correct answers for a passing score. "For the state it might be more like sixteen or even fifteen," says Lynch, who is particularly disappointed in kids who passed but should have done better. "I'm looking at the answers they're choosing, and it's like, 'You couldn't have thought about that,'" she explains. "It's not even about passing. Are you doing the thinking we've been doing all year? You're a smart kid, and you chose an answer that makes no sense. Like . . . *what is that!?*"

She would never say it to her students, but Lynch concedes one or two will be hard-pressed to reach Level 3 two weeks from now. Hers is an integrated co-teaching classroom; several of her students are in special education and have individualized education programs outlining services to be provided, personal learning goals, and unique testing accommodations, although even after eight months in her room, I have no idea who the special ed students are. One is an English-language learner who came to Success just last year and is still well behind his classmates. "He's someone I don't expect to pass. It's not like he's not trying. There are some real gaps. He just might not be able to do it by test day," she explains. "By the end of the year, he'll be ready."

Ready or not, the real state test Book 1 is eleven days away. The DOE announces schools will be closed tomorrow. If the storm is as bad as forecast, the day after could also be snowed out, and maybe the day after that. Lynch is annoyed but not panicked. "The biggest thing is that they believe they can do it, and that they want to do it," she says. "Today I was hard on them. In the next two weeks, it will be more positive, like, 'You can do this, you can do this, you can do this. Whether you believe you can or not, I'm telling you, you can do this.'"

———

Early the following week, on the eve of the state tests, a line of chartered coaches idles seven deep on Morris Avenue, waiting to take Bronx 1's third and fourth graders and their teachers to Radio City

Music Hall, which Success Academy has rented out for its annual "Slam the Exam" pep rally. Nearly four thousand children from every network elementary school with children in testing grades are invited. Each prepares a pump-up chant to perform. In the auditorium, the kids are practicing a choreographed call-and-response march.

> *Everywhere we go,*
> *people want to know*
> *who we are.*
> *So we tell them . . .*
> *We are Bronx 1,*
> *the mighty, mighty Bronx 1.*

Each child is wearing a matching Success Academy T-shirt and a camouflage baseball cap reading BX1. At the end of their routine, they bow their heads and touch the brims of their hats with military precision.

A few minutes later, I join the kids and teachers and climb aboard one of the coaches. A fourth-grade boy named Joshua, whom I have not spoken with all year, politely asks me to sit next to him. He wants to be an athlete when he grows up, but he has questions about being a writer. He has three much older siblings, all adults. His mother, who works as a security guard, lived in Nigeria and Benin and came to the United States before he was born.

When we arrive in midtown Manhattan, several boys point and giggle at an art deco relief of a bare-breasted woman on the side of Rockefeller Center. Renting out Radio City for a rally to hype up kids for a high-stakes test is the kind of extravagant display that drives Moskowitz's critics into paroxysms of rage. While the event is underway, she is savaged on Twitter: "How much did you spend to rent out Radio City Music hall? While so many public schools can't afford supplies & computers. Shameless!" "4,000 kids dragged to propaganda event to lend support to school privatization." The education news website *The 74*, founded by Campbell Brown, one of Success Academy's board members, invites its readers to watch a live video feed from the event. "Why the hell would I watch a shit-ton of money being spent to rally for a BS test? Seriously?" someone responds, while other users promote the hashtags #SocialJustice and #PublicSchoolProud to register their criticisms and contempt. The account for New York City's teachers' union, the United Federation of Teachers, links to a *New York Daily News* piece and tweets, "ICYMI: Eva has chartered Radio City Music Hall for Success Academy pep rally."

None of it kills the buzz inside as kids sing along to pop songs, and their teachers dance in the aisles and take selfies with their students. The hall slowly fills to the rafters. Awards are given out, with the nominees projected onto a pair of screens high above the stage. Evelyn Ortega's son, Eleazar, is nominated for an ELA achievement prize, which gets his classmates excited, but he loses out to a kid from Bensonhurst. When Moskowitz takes the stage, the kids from Cobble Hill start chanting, "Eva! Eva!"

When Moskowitz tells the kids, "You are making history," she draws delighted shrieks and cheers. But it's a pep rally—nearly every utterance from the stage draws a response. Moskowitz seems to aim her brief remarks at politicians and critics far beyond Radio City. "You're going to show the nation, the entire country, the USA of America, what kids are capable of doing," she says. The loudest and most sustained cheers her remarks get are when Moskowitz asks the kids' teachers and principals to stand up for a round of applause.

Back at Bronx 1 that afternoon, after a celebratory pizza party, Albert Barabas settles his fourth graders for one last practice test. Richter's classroom down the hall is starting with a class cheer. It's so loud that it seems to be coming not from across the hallway but right outside the door.

Who rocks the house?
Marist College rocks the house!

Barabas rolls his eyes and shuts the door. "Everyone knows that whoever talks the loudest is the weakest inside." His delivery is deadpan, but a smirk tips off his kids that he's up to something. He lets it slip that he's made a bet with Ms. Lynch and Mr. Richter. "I'll tell you what it was in a minute," he says as he hands out the tests. The kids' interest is piqued; a few shoot each other quizzical looks. Barabas narrates the room, but it's his own thoughts he's verbalizing. "My faith is in these four walls," he says as the last practice test hits a desk. "Your hands are locked and your eyes are on me," he says as Vandlik wanders into the classroom. "Let me tell you what we're going for," Barabas says and clears his throat.

"The first day of school, I told you we had a special group. I said I really believed from the bottom of my heart that this could be the first class in the history of New York to get one hundred percent fours on the state test. And I truly believe that we're in a position right now to actually do it. Especially because of Dwight's domination yesterday," he says, singling out a scholar who got twenty-one out of twenty-four correct on yesterday's practice test. "I told the other two classrooms that I *guaranteed* that we would have every single person pass today." Savannah Jae, one of his scholars, gasps and slams both hands down on her desk in a melodramatic expression of shock.

Vandlik plays along with Mr. B's trash talk. "I feel like I shouldn't even be in here to hear this. This is like . . . *whoa*," she says, looking incredulous.

If every student passes the practice test and Barabas wins the bet, he says, "Yeah, I get to brag to my friends, and I feel good, like I'm a great teacher, blah, blah, blah. But if you win, you guys . . ." He pauses, drawing out the moment. "Throw out your homework for the weekend."

"*Yeah, boy!*" Savannah Jae yells and leaps to her feet, pointing one by one to her classmates to encourage them to *bring it*. The kids are whooping and hollering, and Barabas motions for calm. "We didn't win anything yet," he reminds them.

"Save the energy for the book!" Vandlik says as she turns to leave. "The stakes are high!"

"Most important is this mission we've been on since August,

and we're only a couple of days away," Barabas says, refocusing. "This will be one of the last practices we have, and I'm telling you, I've done this for years. We're ready. Every single person in this room can do it. So let Ms. Lynch and Mr. Richter hear it. We're gonna let them feel it." He asks his kids for their "strongest, loudest, most hype" cheer, cuing up a pump-up rap and putting it on blast. "Pencils up! One hundred percent! I believe in you, baby, and I'm so proud of you!" Barabas is shouting over the music.

"*GO!*"

The last practice test of the year is underway.

Most of the students are scribbling away, but Josiah is having difficulty settling down. Barabas hands him raffle tickets to incentivize him to stay on task. Vandlik returns and tries to redirect his focus. He sighs loudly. He kicks his feet. Barabas, unfailingly patient and encouraging, floats by every few minutes and asks him several times in a soft voice, "How are you feeling?"

Halfway through the practice and without any warning, a boy seated against the wall vomits prodigiously all over his desk and booklet. The smell is instantly overpowering. Incredibly, the other children barely react. Barabas can't leave, and assistant teacher Lindsay Alexander is in Richter's room, so I go off in search of the school nurse or a member of the ops team to deal with the spreading miasma in the classroom. As I round the corner, Carnaghi yells out my name, stopping me from my mission. He is zooming down the hall, flying a little boy, Superman style, in his arms. The kid is grinning from ear to ear, giving everyone high fives to celebrate . . . *something.* I high-five him and say, "That's awesome!" without even asking what he did, and hurry toward the main office. It's locked. The ops team is in the cafeteria setting out cookies and hot chocolate for parents to thank them for their support and ensure that they're just as prepared for tomorrow's test day as their children. Finally, I flag down a janitor, who heads off to get rubber gloves, disinfectant, and a mop. Ms. CeeCee scurries off to find Mahelia Mighty, and I jog back to tell Barabas that the cavalry is coming. The kids are still focused and diligently slugging away.

An hour or so later, at dismissal, kids and parents munch on cookies and hot chocolate. Many have stickers on their shirts and jackets that say, I GOT A 4! It's cloudy and chilly as they head out for the weekend, Barabas's students thinking about how to spend the weekend unburdened by homework. In front of the building, a Mister Softee ice-cream truck plays the familiar jingle that is to the Bronx what crocuses are to the rest of the country—the first sign of spring.

The day has been Success Academy in microcosm: a gaudily expensive pep rally, angry tweets, a teacher's faith in his students, test prep, joy, and vomit.

CHAPTER 19

Testing Day

THE SIGN ON THE DOUBLE DOORS SEPARATING SUCCESS ACADEMY from Bronx Letters commands, QUIET! TESTING IN PROGRESS! But neither quiet nor testing is in evidence on the other side at 6:30 a.m. on this gray and dismal March morning. Ty Redmond, a former kindergarten science teacher and dean at Bronx 1, now the founding principal of a new Success Academy in Far Rockaway, Queens, has set up amplifiers in the hall between kindergarten and first grade, and Justin Timberlake's "Can't Stop the Feeling!" plays at near-nightclub decibels. For the last three months, the staff has worked to get the children pumped up for the state tests. Now it's the teachers' turn. Coffee, bagels, fruit juice, energy shots, and Red Bulls wait on the semicircular table where the littlest scholars normally sit for small group instruction.

Students won't arrive for another hour. Third-grade teachers Anna Luker and Joey Patterson are the first to hit the spread before retreating to their classrooms. Matthew Carnaghi helps himself to coffee; it's his first testing day, but just another day at school for his kids, who are not in testing grades. The K–2 teacher's only job is to "keep the climate," which is code for ensuring cathedral-like silence in the halls. Science teacher Amanda Sommi's face lights up when she comes in and sees the array; nothing delights an overworked teacher more than free food. She sways to Jay-Z's "Run This Town" while helping herself to breakfast. Lynch, already wearing her game face, snatches up a 5-hour Energy shot and heads for her classroom.

By 6:50 a.m., every staff member has come through the door. The hallway bulletin boards are draped with blue plastic sheeting. State rules require that every chart, poster, number line, or board with student work—anything that could conceivably serve as a cheat sheet—be taken down or covered up. Bronx 1 looks ready for painters. Or a mob rubout. When I introduced myself to Redmond, he assumed I was a state inspector on hand to monitor test administration.

By 7:00 a.m., most of the kindergarten and first-grade teachers have shut their doors to block out the music blaring a few feet away. Ms. Kowalski comes down the hall for breakfast. When she taught at a DOE school, a dance party was not part of the test-day routine. Neither does she remember testing being so intense when she was a girl growing up in Greenwich Village, but her mom insists she's remembering incorrectly. Before No Child Left Behind made annual testing in grades three through eight the law of the land, New York, like many states, tested children in both math and reading in fourth and eighth grades. Schools put their best teachers in those "testing grades." For ten-year-old Alanna Kowalski, scoring a 4 in fourth grade meant getting into an honors middle school. She has a cousin who is a third grader at Success Academy Hell's Kitchen. "I called him on Friday to ask him if he had fun at the pep rally at Radio City. He said, 'Before the pep rally I was nervous, but now I'm not.'" Her students won't take their first high-stakes tests for another year, but their schedule for science and other specials will be disrupted, since those teachers have roles in the day's testing routine. Her second graders are "excited for their older siblings, but that's it," she says.

The music blares on as Vandlik cruises by in head-to-toe Success Academy orange, down to a pair of orange Chuck Taylor high-tops scrawled with student signatures. The network's level of detail for the physical setup on testing day far exceeds the state's mandate to cover posters and bulletin boards: all proctors are expected to wear quiet, rubber-soled shoes. Vandlik has had them since her last year as a classroom teacher, when she taught fourth grade. At the time, middle school students wore orange sneakers as part of their uniforms, so Vandlik bought her own pair. "We were talking all year about getting ready for middle school," she recalls. As testing season approached, if a student put in a notable effort or met an individual goal, they earned the right to add their names to her shoes. Her whole class ended up signing them. She's worn them ever since on testing days.

The party winds down, but DJ Redmond has one last number on his playlist. A recording of the Bronx 1 kids' Radio City pep-rally cheer—"We are Bronx 1, the mighty, mighty Bronx 1!" fills the hallways. The effect is ghostly in a school empty of children. The faculty congregate to hear from Vandlik.

"I feel great about today. This is our last Book 1 of the year," she says, referring to the practice tests the students have taken since January. "I really hope you guys are as excited as I am. I hope you feel as calm as I do." Turning to Redmond, she says, "Ty, we've been quoting you a lot the last couple of days. What do you always say? 'Today we just need to do . . .'"

". . . what we do better than it's usually done."

"Our kids are literally the best-prepared children in the state to face up to the challenge of today. They are so well prepared because of all of you," Vandlik continues. The staff bring it in for a cheer, then melt away to their classrooms and arrival posts. Vandlik confers with Jen Fuoco as they head downstairs. There have been subway problems, but everyone on staff is present and no parents have called warning that any students might be late. "I just checked again and there are no calls," Fuoco tells her. Today's game plan requires assistant principals to call the "top twenty culture offenders"—parents of students most likely to fail to arrive on time— to ensure they are aware it's testing day and to encourage them to leave early for the commute. If parents prove unwilling or unreliable, plans are in place to pick kids up in cabs. Charita Stewart already made one such run this morning.

"So the adults are all here, and the kids are in good shape," Vandlik responds. "Fahim's mom is here," Fuoco reports. By prearranged plan, one parent dropped her son off on arrival and then circled back into the building—apparently being held in abeyance in case the child needs emotional support during the day. One family is not sending their child today. It's Bronx 1's first "opt out." New York, and particularly the affluent suburbs on Long Island and in Westchester County, have become hotbeds of parents' refusing to let children sit for state tests. In 2016, as many as 20 percent of the state's eligible students didn't take the tests.[1]

"That's never happened before," Vandlik remarks, as she and Fuoco arrive in the cafeteria. Inevitably, there are raffle tickets for any child who arrives before 7:35 a.m. "Ready for all those little crazy people?" she asks before throwing open the door, where students and parents are lined up for the big day.

"You are ready, Jones brothers."

"You got this."

"I'm so excited for you!"

Camille McKinnon wishes her daughter, Blessing, good luck as she shakes the principal's hand and disappears into the stairwell. "Ready to slam it!" Vandlik encourages the girl.

As I watch the usual parade heading upstairs, the girl who is almost always first in line for middle school arrival every morning sidles up, curious about why I'm always here, scribbling in a notebook. "You're one of those people who sits in the back of the room and watches?" she asks, presumably referring to the constant flow of network staffers lurking at Success. I tell her I'm writing a book about her school, which she considers. "You look like that person who ran for president," she says. "Not Donald Trump. The other one." She rifles her memory before summoning up, "Mitt Romney." I laugh. We talk for a few moments about school and teachers. Michelle used to be in Barabas's class. He was her favorite teacher. I ask

her where she wants to go to college, maybe Fordham like Mr. B?
"No," Michelle says in a tone that suggests that she's given it a great
deal of thought. "I want to go to Princeton or Yale."

Hector, a student in Barabas's class, steps to the front of the line.
He has been sent to school this morning with his mop of unruly hair
brought to heel in a fourth-grade version of a man bun. Vandlik
smiles and pats him on the head. "Sometimes his hair gives him
power," she quips, "and sometimes it's just in the way." A second-
grade boy squirts under her arm, evading her attempt to give him a
hug, and runs up the stairs. "If he was closer, I'd force him into it,"
she says and laughs. It's almost 7:45, and she looks down the block.
"Run all the way to me, Matthew! You're right at the buzzer!"

Upstairs, the now well-rehearsed pretest routine is underway,
with a frisson of extra electricity among the teachers. Perhaps the
coffee, Red Bulls, and energy shots have kicked in. Vandlik puts her
arm around a girl in a purple hijab and asks her how she's feeling.
"We were so worried about your asthma!" The girl heads off to join
her class, which is lined up to use the bathroom during their assigned
seven-minute slot. Lynch is narrating over the sound of flushing
toilets, praising her students for their focus and calm as they wait
their turn in the hallway. "Adrian's standing up so straight and tall.
Samiyah's showing she's absolutely ready to go," she says. "Elyse, as
always, being an example, bringing it when we need it the most."

The vibe is quiet and serious, but the children do not look
stressed. The fourth graders use the bathroom from 7:50 to 7:57 and
then make way for the third graders from 7:57 to 8:04. As they
return to their classroom, Lynch reminds them to "stay in the zone."
Across the hall, Kerrie Riley monitors the traffic in the girls' room;
Ms. DiGirolamo supervises the boys. No one speaks. Middle
schoolers stream by on their way upstairs, carrying their breakfasts;
a few smirk at the younger kids while teachers remind them to pass
"in zero noise."

By 8:10 the hallway is empty. The only sound is the steady ca-
dence of toilet flushes from the third-grade wing. Steven Madan's
class gets a six-minute bathroom slot from 8:04 to 8:10. His voice

reaches my ears. "Take this time to go over your goals to make sure you get every point," he says and high-fives every student as they pass back into the classroom. "I know you're rockin' it today."

Kellie Grant, special education teacher Alexandra Margolis, and Carson Rockefeller prepare the test packets in the leadership office. Kanye West's "Stronger" is playing in Lynch's room as she kneels in front of one student's desk. Not bothering to get up, she shuffles on her knees from one desk to the next, offering last-second reminders and encouragement. Some of the students busy themselves reading or coloring; others wait silently. Across the hall in Barabas's room comes the now familiar opening riff of the Who's "Eminence Front," which he plays before every practice test. When the song ends, the hallways are deathly quiet.

The silence is short-lived.

Kerri Lynch is shouting at the top of her lungs, "Let's go, let's go, let's go! This is it. This is the day! This is the *real* day! The *first* day!" It's 8:20 and "pump-up speeches" start spilling from every classroom; these locker room–style motivational pep talks are scheduled to end by 8:25 precisely. Jen Fuoco sidles up and taps a finger in my notebook. "If it's not already in there," she says, "today's the day you write, 'They're *crazy*!'"

She smiles and steps away, to where Hector has stepped out of Barabas's classroom, his face a rictus of irritation. He's tugged his bun loose, and Fuoco starts pulling his Niagara Falls of hair into a ponytail. "He prefers a ponytail over a man bun," she says. "But only for testing." The ops team keeps a supply of hair ties on hand. Just for testing days.

In my notebook I jot, "They're <u>crazy</u>."

And it *is* all just a bit crazy. The fourth-grade teachers have turned off the lights in their rooms to add extra drama to their speeches. "Keep that in your head!" Richter implores. I can see him pacing the room through the window in his classroom door. "When you're feeling frustrated, when you're feeling tired, when you're like, 'I can't possibly do this,' that's when it all comes together. That's when you need to dig deep and keep pushing! Because that's when champions are made!" He cues a video of a song I don't recognize, with a driving guitar riff and a soaring children's choir. "Sit up straight and tall and track me. I need to see you in the zone. I see Luis in the zone. I see Zaid in the zone!" Richter is either a gifted actor or deeply into this moment. "We've been working toward four goals. All. Year. Long. I've got 'em up here," he says, pointing to his temple, "but you've got 'em in your heart. I'm going to ask you a question, and I want *everyone* in this school to hear you." He pauses for effect and to scan the faces of the kids sitting upright and staring back at him.

"*Are you going to work smart?*" he shouts.

"YES!" the answer comes back even louder.

"Are you going to work hard!?"

"YES!"

"Are you going to work consistently?!?"

"YES!!"

"And are you going to work *confidently?*"

I'm grinning despite myself. It seems impossibly goofy—and just plain impossible—to get kids this wound up to take a reading test, but by the time they get to the fourth "YES!" the class is on as much of an adrenaline rush as the English army at Agincourt. Students still in their beds will count themselves accursed that they were not here with them on State Testing Day.

He's not finished. "You know that a strong main idea is what's going to be able to help you answer those questions. Main idea is king. You're going to get to that main idea by snowballing. You've got your initial idea? Add on to it and jot while you read. Plan of attack on every question. Plan of attack is your best friend. It helps you out when questions are challenging. Make sure you're counter-attacking."

"Start strong, finish strong," he shouts. "Say it with me!"

"Start strong, finish strong!"

"*Not good enough!*"

"*START STRONG, FINISH STRONG!*"

"That's what I'm talking about. *THAT's* what I'm talking about!"

It's 8:25.

"You know Ms. Margolis is going to walk through that door any second," Richter says and lowers his voice. "You can do this. You can do this, and we all believe in you. I believe in you. Ms. Vandlik believes in you. Ms. Margolis believes in you. Your parents believe in you." From Lynch's room, a chant of "We are, we are Fordham! NYU!" to the rhythm of Queen's "We Will Rock You" comes through the shared wall. "They're getting loud," says Richter. "I want to hear *our* chant."

Who rocks the house? Marist College rocks the house . . .

Richter circles the room fist-pumping as the kids chant and stomp. After a minute, he's panting. "Take some deep breaths," he concludes. "This is your moment."

At 8:30 precisely, the pump-up portion of the day is over. The morning now belongs to New York State and the dry bureaucratese of testing. The only sound now is Richter's voice reciting the instructions that every teacher from one end of the state to the other is required by law to read verbatim.

You cannot have any communications device, including a cell phone, with you during this test or during any breaks, such as a restroom visit. Such devices include, but are not limited to cell phones, iPods and MP3 players, laptops, notebooks, or any other personal computing devices . . .

Richter reads from the testing manual, even though Success Academy forbids its students to bring most electronic devices to school anyway.

If you keep a cell phone or any of these items with you, your examination will be invalidated and you will get no score. Is there anyone who needs to give me any of these items now?

Unhidden by the blue plastic sheeting in the hall are dozens of eight-by-ten color pictures of fourth graders still visible, and I find myself examining each closely like they're paintings in a museum—Hosinatou, Ikram, Savannah Jae—as the sound of test instructions fades into background noise.

You will be taking the 2017 Grade 4 Common Core English Language Arts Test. There are three books for this test. Today, you will answer the questions in Book 1. You will answer the questions in Book 2 tomorrow and the questions in Book 3 the following day . . .

This is the only experience of elementary school Christine, Adrian, and Eleazar will know. Children, especially elementary school children, have no basis to compare a traditional public school, a charter school, or a Catholic school. They know only their teacher, their friends, their favorite subjects. Which teacher was nice, or funny, or introduced them to a book they loved; who put the fear of God into them or got them excited to take a test and made them feel like they could crush it. Who *expected* them to crush it.

All of your answers must be marked on your answer sheet. You may, however, make notes, underline, or highlight in your test book as you read. Are there any questions?

The test begins. Vandlik and Fuoco circulate from room to room, peering through the windows in each classroom door, observing the kids like they are fish in an aquarium.

Later that day, I head for the subway down 149th Street, the broad thoroughfare that leads to the Hub, the retail heart of the South Bronx, past the check-cashing place, a funeral home, nail salons, a Goodwill, and the storefront *abogados*. I find myself thinking about Michelle and her ambition to go to Yale or Princeton. I wonder if there's a soul within a mile radius of where I stand who graduated from either. At the other end of my subway ride, Ivy

League grads outnumber the delivery people who bring Seamless orders to multimillion-dollar apartments and the taxi drivers who take moms and dads to their offices in the financial district or midtown after dropping their kids off at fifty-thousand-dollar-a-year private schools. When those kids hit high school, they will apply to elite colleges. Their applications will be backed by well-connected parents, letters of recommendation from alumni, SAT scores inflated by tutors charging a thousand dollars an hour, professionally coached and edited personal essays describing service missions in the third world, and earnest tales of passions for the arts and achievements in athletics. Michelle will have Liz Vandlik, Albert Barabas, a few other teachers, and her test scores.

It's not a fair fight. But it will have to do.

Day two of the ELA test goes much like the first, absent the pump-up speeches. Ms. CeeCee flies from the building to pick up a scholar whose family was in a minor fender bender. In the moments before the test begins, Vandlik sits with Casildo, who is prone to bouts of anxiety. "Look at me," she tells him, placing a finger under his chin and lifting his face toward hers. "Are you nervous? That's good! It's good to be a little nervous!"

There's a small but discernable drop in crispness and energy from the previous day; the task turns to keeping focus and stamina up. Assistant teacher Varshini Srinivasan is doing jumping jacks and stretches in the hallway with a third-grade boy, after which she envelops him in a hug. "You got this," she says softly and steers him back to his classroom. Alyssa DiGirolamo comes out of her classroom leading a girl with an enormous bow in her hair. They pace cartoonishly in a circle, arms pumping madly, then reverse course, making a few more circles in the opposite direction. The girl skips to the water fountain; DiGirolamo puts her hands on her knees and catches her breath. Madan emerges with a little girl; they also walk in quick circles. "Remember your goals," he reminds her.

While the third and fourth graders are ensconced behind closed doors, children in the lower grades are working, their teachers charged with "keeping the climate" while testing is underway. Kowalski is monitoring a few students as they use the bathroom. Students usually start going to the lavatory on their own from kindergarten, but today, teachers supervise to ensure nothing interrupts the testing. Back in the classroom, Kowalski's students are reading independently. She punctuates the quiet by giving "dojo points" to children who are reading silently on ClassDojo, a technology platform used to reinforce positive behavior. As the children transition for reading groups, she takes out her phone to call a parent. "Can you talk to Emir?" she says, without pausing for pleasantries. "He's rolling around the floor and not doing any work." Chloe is eager to talk with me about the book she's reading, one in the Geronimo Stilton series about the adventures of a talking mouse. For two minutes she maintains a nonstop monologue. When I compliment her excellent summary, she proudly tells me she's a Level P.

There's a new sign next to the door of the second-grade classroom that used to say HUNTER COLLEGE. It now reads, CONCORDIA–CITY COLLEGE, the alma maters of Brandon Whitaker and Alanna Kowalski. After lunch, Whitaker is working to get kids to transition to the rug, narrating, issuing corrections, and trying to get "one hundred percent." We're closer to the end of the school year than the beginning, and it's still a little ragged around the edges, with kids cross-talking and chattering. There are still small conflicts and the occasional hissed "shut up." Whitaker issues at least a half-dozen corrections before everyone gets settled. But the class is as focused and orderly as I've seen it. As the new name beside the door suggests, it is every inch their class now.

And Adama isn't in it anymore.

CHAPTER 20

The Lottery

ENVISION THREE MOTHERS, IDENTICAL IN AGE, RACE, INCOME, employment, and marital status. Each has a four-year-old due to start school next year. The first registers her child at the zoned public school down the block. The second worries the school is unsafe; she doesn't like the way its kids act on the street, and she's heard there are lots of fights. She fills out the application for a few local charter schools thinking she'd rather send her child to nearly *any* of them rather than the neighborhood school. The third mother has visited, researched, and talked to friends and neighbors about Success Academy, and that's where she wants her child to go. She enters the lottery and prays. These three parents might be identical on paper, but they're not comparable at all. Even if the third parent started out like the second, seeking *any* alternative, it is highly unlikely that her child could end up at Success Academy by accident or happenstance. The network's admissions and enrollment process requires an unusual level of parental bandwidth and persistence to complete, even compared with that at other charter schools. A common narrative among ed reformers and charter school advocates is that student outcomes are determined by which school door a child walks through each morning. But this elides the differences in parental motivation and engagement that determine which child walks through each door. These three mothers might be "matched" demographically but not *psychographically*. Their values, opinions, attitudes, and aspirations make them more different than alike. There is nothing to be gained in pretending otherwise.

The process of separating out these parents starts every April.

"Welcome to the seventy-fifth annual Hunger Games," announces Holly Saso, managing director of enrollment at Success Academy. The few dozen staffers gathered in a sixth-floor conference room chuckle at her wry joke. Today is the lottery for admission for the coming school year. By state law, charter schools that have more applicants than available seats must hold a lottery to randomly select students for admission. New York City has well over two hundred charter schools. All but a handful have waiting lists or are oversubscribed and hold admissions lotteries; Success Academy is among the city's most oversubscribed, averaging about six applications for every seat, although demand fluctuates both among individual schools and across the network from year to year, running as high as ten applications per seat and more than twelve-to-one for particular schools. Demand is particularly high for charter school seats, Success included, in the Bronx, Harlem, and central Brooklyn.

A decade ago, Success and other charter schools used their admissions lotteries to draw media attention and score political points. They were held in rented gymnasiums and auditoriums, with nervous parents and children in the audience hoping for a low number that meant a lifeboat out of dismal neighborhood schools— catnip for local television and newspapers doing stories about a public school system that had failed generations of kids. Gleeful winners went home sporting I WON THE LOTTERY! stickers. Losers were devastated, in tears and on camera. The high- (or low-) water mark for the pageantry and pathos is the 2010 documentary *The Lottery*, which Vanessa Farrer stumbled on by accident one night on TV. But by the time the film came out, the lotteries were already losing some of their luster. The backlash became fierce, even among supporters. "Charter schools, please, stop," wrote the *New York Times* columnist Gail Collins. "I had no idea you selected your kids with a piece of performance art that makes the losers go home feeling like they're on a Train to Failure at age 6. You can do better. Use the postal system."

Now the admissions lottery is a low-key affair involving a few staffers seated behind a computer. While it's still technically an open public meeting, it would make for terrible TV. Accordingly, no news crews are present. When Saso starts the proceedings, it's just two to three dozen Success Academy employees and me, at the network's office in the financial district of lower Manhattan. She runs aloud through the process anyway. This year there are thirty-one Success Academy elementary schools to which new students, mostly kinder-garteners, will be enrolled. There are 17,058 "on time" applicants for 3,017 seats. "We say 'on time' because we continue to take applications, but they will be late applications, and they don't run through the lottery," she says. By the end of the summer, an additional 500 or 600 applications will come in this way—roughly six applicants for every available seat. For their first lottery in 2006, there were 440 applications for 155 seats, a ratio of 2.8 applicants for each slot. Since then, the numbers have increased geometrically, peaking at 22,000 applicants in 2015. This year's drop to 17,000 applicants has been attributed to a variety of factors, from an increasingly crowded charter school market to a series of armor-piercing articles by Kate Taylor of the *New York Times* that have frightened prospective parents away.

"So we can start the lottery," Saso says. With a keystroke, the software randomly separates the applications into winners and losers in less time than it takes Saso to explain the weighting and preference system, which gives first shot to the brothers and sisters of current students. The network obtained permission from its authorizer, the State University of New York, to give a preference to the children of Success Academy employees as well; more than two dozen are currently enrolled, including Eva Moskowitz's two youngest children. The next level of preference is families within the school district in which a school is located. Even though Bronx 1 has no operational connection to New York City's Community School District 7, it is located within its geographical boundaries. A child with a sibling or employee preference might get in first, but with those exceptions, no child may be admitted from outside a district as long as there are still families within it who want a seat.

One last factor that can improve a family's chances is if a child merits a "weighted preference," like being an English-language learner. Echoing the advice given to prospective parents touring Bronx 1 on the hundredth day of school, Saso says every applicant is encouraged to apply to as many of its schools as they can conceivably get to by 7:30 every morning. The more schools applied to, the better the chance of acceptance; there is not one lottery but one lottery for each campus. "So we ask them to rank in order of which schools they would most prefer to go to. And the reason we do this is so that we can have one applicant and one seat," not one applicant taking up six seats, for example. Ranking by preference assigns the highest-ranked school a child gets into as their accepted seat. "And if they got into any schools below that, we take that acceptance away," Saso explains. Remaining applicants are placed on a waitlist according to their lottery number.

A few minutes later, it's over. Within days, roughly three thousand applicants will be offered seats for the school year starting in August. More than twice that number have no chance and will receive a letter saying as much. The remainder will be notified that they are now on what Success Academy calls the "likely" list for admission and are required to continue the enrollment process. "It's the luck of the draw," Saso tells her colleagues as the low-key lottery wraps up. "It's a shame that education has to come down to that. But it really is the luck of the draw."

Winning a seat in Success Academy's lottery does not guarantee that a child will be enrolled. Instead, it sets in motion a series of meetings and steps that parents must complete. Parents whose children have won a seat outright, as well as those with a low waitlist number, are invited to a welcome meeting in early May. Moskowitz herself hosts several of these meetings, which are scattered among various Success Academy schools. Attendance is mandatory, even for likely-list families.

Bronx 1 has roughly ninety kindergarten seats to fill and anticipates a few dozen openings in grades one through four come August. In its land-that-time-forgot auditorium, dozens of parents sit on the hard wooden seats, many with their children. At six o'clock precisely, Shea Reeder, the principal of Bronx 4, Success Academy's newest school in the borough, rises from her seat in the front row. Eschewing a microphone and speaking from the pit in front of the stage, she introduces herself as a seven-year veteran of Success Academy. She's been a teacher, an assistant principal, a dean, "and then they finally were crazy enough to give me my own school," she quips. She introduces Liz Vandlik, who waves from the doorway.

A tall African American woman, Reeder, when I last saw her, was serving as the MC of the "Slam the Exam" test-prep rally at Radio City Music Hall. She also hosted the network's Liberty House kickoff event last summer. There's a world-weariness to her face and voice; she smiles infrequently, and when she does, it projects as much sadness as joy. This makes her an unconventional choice for high-profile hosting duties, but her air of authenticity connects with parents and teachers alike. With two children at Success— one in middle school, one in elementary—it wasn't so long ago that she was sitting in this meeting not as a principal but as a parent. "When I came to visit, I said, 'Listen, I need to work for this organization. I believe in what you stand for. I believe in what you're doing for kids,'" she says. "That's how much I believe in Success Academy."

What comes next is more of a warning than a welcome. Echoing the language students hear daily in their classroom, Reeder tells the parents that she has a "thinking job" for them this evening. "Keep this question in mind during this entire presentation," she says. "*Is Success Academy the right fit for me and my child?*"

Most schools would ask parents to consider only if the school is right for their child, not the parent. But Reeder's question is neither accidental nor ill considered. At the start of the assembly, parents might be wondering whether their kids can handle the school. By the end, many are surely left wondering if *they* can handle the demands Success Academy places on parents, its logistical challenges, and how well they will mesh with the culture and environment of its schools. "Although you're going to hear a lot of great and amazing things about us, there are some things you may say, 'Mmm, doesn't work for me,'" she warns. "And that's fine too. Success Academy is *not* for everyone." She hits the word "not" emphatically. Nor is she free-lancing or going off-message: As she speaks, a network-designed PowerPoint is projected on a screen above the stage behind her. The words "Is SA right for you?" loom over her. "We want to make sure you are making an informed decision about coming to our schools. Because we expect that you accept us one hundred percent," she continues. Parents cannot say that they like the curriculum but not the way Success Academy manages its classrooms. "It's not Burger King. You can't have it your way." Some parents chuckle, but Reeder's not joking. The first bullet point says, "We love and support your kids like they are our own!" The next says, "Our school design is everything—it's all or nothing. Nothing is optional!"

Reeder recites a brief history. Eva wanted more for her kids and the community. She started Harlem 1 ten years ago and has been expanding ever since. Demand is high. "Some of your zoned schools are not really great options, as you know. You want something more and better for your child," she says, eliciting a teeth-sucking sound and an "Mmm-hmm" from a mother seated behind me. "We believe in teaching kids to critically think, to analyze and question each other, question the teacher, and truly, truly think," she continues.

"We do not allow scholars to fall to the wayside or get lost in the classroom. We're on top of every single child that comes into our school because we believe that all children can learn. We try to support them in every way possible," Reeder goes on. "When they come to us, four years old in kindergarten, we are telling them, 'You are going to college! That is not optional. *You are going.*'"

Again, the PowerPoint states it bluntly: "You need to be on-board," it reads, followed by a list of nonnegotiables, including early start times; a spring break schedule that does not line up with public schools'; safe and orderly schools with "the possibility of suspension." Nothing is soft-pedaled. "In terms of behavior, we suspend, all right? Let me be clear with that. We suspend," Reeder says. "We do not tolerate hitting, biting, kicking, fighting, *anything.* And we suspend kindergarteners if they do that. If you have a problem with that, this might not be the school for you." Every incident or behavior that might result in a suspension is thoroughly investigated, she promises, but "any type of behavior that does not fit into our model and our expectation, we *will* suspend your child." Yet again, she reminds parents that Success might not be for them. "Eva likes to say this is a marriage. We are partnering up and raising this child together. We expect that you guys are on board with everything we're doing." I have come to recognize this mix of straight talk and tough love, equal parts harassment and encouragement, aspiration and unsparing demands for compliance, as the signature feature of Success Academy's culture. Like Carolyn Syskowski's "Come to Jesus" meeting in January, the welcome meeting is another Rorschach test.

Few schools would be comfortable telling parents how to conduct themselves in their own homes. It is stamped on Success Academy's genetic code. "It starts with you. If you're with your child and most of the time you're on your cell phone, that's the habit they're picking up," Reeder lectures. "You have to set an example. If you want your child to be a reader, you have to be a reader first." I glance around to see how this is landing with parents, but it's hard to tell. It's hard to imagine a gathering of Upper East Side private school parents sitting quietly while being lectured about the need to establish a reading culture at home, to put down their phones, or the blunt "my way or the highway" talk about school culture. It is one thing to say that "it takes a village" to raise a child. It is quite another to be lectured by the village school leader on exactly what that must look like. Reeder betrays no sense of discomfort. "We are raising this child together," she says again.

When she stops her monologue to play a promotional video about Success Academy's curriculum and teaching methods, I watch the parents instead of the screen. My eye settles on a mother who is beaming and nodding her head animatedly. The video ends, and Reeder ticks off the features of Success Academy's elementary school routines. Reading logs. Six books a week. Hands-on science daily. Art, chess, dance, and music—not as extracurriculars but as part of the curriculum—outdoor recess every day that it's not raining. High expectations, even for special education students. "We don't lower the bar for *anyone*," she insists. "We have the same expectations for them as we do for all of our students." If parents are unsure of their ability to work with their children, Success will help. "We have math nights. We have literacy nights. We have lots of family events so you can come learn how to support your child," she explains.

Success Academy issues cell phones to every teacher and requires them to respond to any phone call or text from a parent within twenty-four hours, but it's a two-way street. "If we call you, we expect you to return that call within twenty-four hours," she says. "That's really important." Since there are no parent-teacher conferences, "we meet whenever we wanna meet," Reeder explains. "If you say as a parent, 'I'm noticing something at home'"—Reeder pantomimes speaking into a phone—"'Teacher, hello. Can we meet tomorrow? Great.' We have meetings starting at seven o'clock in the morning. Whatever it takes for your child to succeed." Parents should expect to hear from teachers and administrators at the first sign of trouble. "We communicate *a ton. A whole* lot," Reeder says. "We're constantly calling you, texting you, like, 'Hey! Your child didn't do homework. What's goin' on?' Sometimes things happen.

That's fine. But we expect you as the parent and the adult to reach out to say, 'Hey. Got a little caught up last night. Something's going on. We'll make it up over the weekend,'" Reeder says. "No problem." Conflicts between parents and Success start when communication fails. "We keep things clear and open," she says. "Communication is *everything*."

She turns back to the PowerPoint. "Uniforms are big," not optional. "It can't be, 'Oh, I didn't get to the laundry, so I sent my child to school in jeans.' Your child will be sent back home. Uniforms every day. Clean every day. Make sure you have a system so that the uniform is on your child's back every day." Uniforms are monitored for compliance. "And that incluuuuuudes socks," Reeder says, drawing out the word in a way that implies, as a school principal, she has seen enough wrong-color socks to last a lifetime. "We pull up pants, and we check socks. No white socks allowed." Ties for boys. Navy stockings for girl. She counsels kindergarten parents to send an extra uniform to school, "because sometimes they do have accidents. So be prepared for that."

Inevitably, the other half of Success Academy's dual mission comes up. "Before I came to SA, I never even thought about advocacy," Reeder says, but now "it makes total sense." Bronx 4, Reeder's campus in the Soundview neighborhood of the Bronx, "would not be in existence unless there were parents who came before us who marched," she says. "And that's a part of your role too. Some of you are probably sitting there saying, 'Listen, I don't have time for that. I gotta work.' You gotta have time for it. Right? Because if you want your child to succeed and go through Success, we need that support."

She cues up another video, this one describing Success Academy's advocacy work. It's an evocative piece of filmmaking, with Success Academy parents talking earnestly about their commitment to fight for more space and more schools. Again, I watch the crowd. The new Success parent who caught my attention a few seats away from me wipes a tear from her face. If the theme and purpose of the welcome meeting is to ensure parents are walking in with eyes wide open—Is Success Academy right for you?—this young mother is the newest acolyte.

Reeder starts to wrap up. She has put a lot on these parents' plates, not trying to sell them, but to steer them. "So"—she pauses—"going back to that question I started off with." A longer pause.

"Is Success Academy right for you?"

Reeder paces, her footsteps echoing in the quiet auditorium. Finally, she stops moving and faces the parents. Her voice drops a register. "We ask for a lot," she says, breaking the silence. "We ask for a *whole* lot. It's for a reason. We believe that your scholars can be the absolute best version of you. We believe that your scholars can be something great. We start them out really young. But you have to be on board to make sure that we are in this partnership together, supporting one another. So when we call you with a problem, you're like, 'No problem. I got it. I'll work with 'em on it tonight.' Same language. Same expectations. Your kid will grow so much in a year, it will blow your mind," Reeder concludes. "Blow. Your. Mind."

Then, almost as an afterthought, Reeder mentions transportation. Success Academy does not offer buses. For some parents, the logistics of getting a child to and from school present an even bigger challenge than complying with culture demands, reading logs, and homework. Every Wednesday, children are dismissed at 12:30 so that staff can attend their professional development sessions. "That's something else you gotta keep in mind," Reeder adds. "'Will I be able to pick up my child on time? Will I be able to have somebody to support me with that?' School lets out at 3:45 but every Wednesday is "12:30 no matter what." She hits "12" and "30" hard, hammering the point home. "And we do *not* have after-school, so you guys have to figure that out."

The meeting lasts just under an hour, but it opens a portal into the model and culture that explains in no small part the network's consistent results across its schools. Suddenly it all makes sense: The common criticism leveled at Moskowitz and her schools is that they cherry-pick students, attracting bright children and shedding the poorly behaved and hardest to teach. This misses the mark entirely. Success Academy is cherry-picking *parents*. Parents who are not put off by uniforms, homework, reading logs, and constant demands on their time, but who view those things as evidence that here, *at last*, is a school that has its act together. Parents who are not upset by tight discipline and suspensions but who are grateful for them, viewing Success Academy as a safe haven from disorderly streets and schools. Charter schools cannot screen parents to ensure culture fit, but the last hour in the auditorium is a close proxy for such an effort, galvanizing disciples and warning off the indifferent and uncommitted. At the same time, there is something undeniably exclusionary about it. If you don't have the resources to get your child to school by 7:30 and pick her up at 3:45—at 12:30 on Wednesdays—Success Academy is not for you. Literally.

After the meeting ends, I introduce myself to the mother who caught my attention for her apparent enthusiasm. Her name is Ayan Wilson and her son, Darren, has won a seat at Bronx 1 for kindergarten. We exchange email addresses and agree to meet for an interview. But when I reach out to her the following day, her reply is heartbroken, nearly despondent. She misunderstood her status. Darren has *not* been accepted. He's merely on the "likely" list.

"It's a devastating blow," she writes. "However, I am not giving up hope. My kids are my world and I will not stop trying to give them every opportunity to have the best education." She is still willing, now eager, to be interviewed about what she says is the "gruesome process" of trying to get her son into a good school. "I hope this interview allows people to see the desperate need for good schools in our neighborhoods," she writes. "The betterment of our children depends on it."

CHAPTER 21

The GAS Factor

THE LAST MAJOR STATE TEST OF THE YEAR IS FOURTH-GRADE science. The first day comprises "performance tasks" with children rotating among three workstations where they are expected to use beakers and rulers to take measurements; collect data and classify objects; or use a ball-and-ramp apparatus to gather data and make inferences. It's far more predictable than ELA and math, making the test relatively easy to train and practice for. In 2016 just over half of all fourth graders statewide scored a Level 4, with nearly nine out of ten scoring "proficient" (Level 3 or 4). One former Success Academy science teacher dismisses the test as "a joke." Even so, an unblemished record of 100 percent of fourth graders earning the very highest score is a significant accomplishment and a point of pride.

Bronx 1 falls into the familiar pattern of dress rehearsal for the exam, which is held over two days in late May. All testing conditions and protocols are observed. The fourth graders are shepherded into one of the two science classrooms on the third floor, nine at a time, divided among the three stations. Matthew Casildo, the bright and studious boy from Lynch's class, is once again having a bout of anxiety. He's in the hallway with his third-grade teacher, Kaitlyn Walsh. Her arm is wrapped around the boy's head, and she is gently rubbing his left ear with her thumb, the boy's head nestled in the crook of her elbow. Science teacher Amanda Sommi gives the kids a pep talk, just as she will on the day of the test.

The practice test begins, and I watch the fourth graders through the window of the classroom door. When a student drops a weight, Sommi pounces to grab it. A second science teacher, Ella Schwarzbaum, is standing by with tissues in case there's a spill. After a few minutes Casildo starts to melt down; Kellie Grant darts in to pull him out as the other children continue their work. She and Kerrie Riley try to console the boy, who has wedged himself in a corner of the hallway and refuses to make eye contact. A few seconds later, Vandlik emerges from the stairwell. "We're going to have to face it eventually, but you can choose," Riley is telling the boy. "You can choose to face it today or you can choose to face it tomorrow. It's really up to you."

"Casildo, can I make a recommendation?" Vandlik asks. He is still sandwiched between the water fountain and the wall, looking as if he wants to press himself into the cinder blocks and disappear entirely from view. "Turn around. Let me see your handsome face." He resists and she cajoles. "Oh, c'mon. *Come on!* C'mere, you." She is smiling beatifically at him. "Look at me. Do you want to hear a story from my life?" she asks. It's a rhetorical question. Vandlik launches into a monologue about learning to drive back home in Illinois. One day, her dad let her drive on the highway for the first time on the way to her grandmother's house. "I was driving the family minivan, and my dad sat up front with me. My mom, my sister, and brother were all in the back. So I was responsible for my *whole* family." She interrupts herself, sits down at a desk in the hallway, and starts to draw a crude map. Casildo, hooked and curious, has peeled himself out of his hiding space and steps toward her. "Do you know what a 'median' is?" He shakes his head. She has sketched a four-lane divided highway on a piece of paper.

"Picture me, Casildo. I'm coming down the off-ramp, and I had to make a left. But I'm not used to making left turns onto very big roads." She draws a thick line dividing the map into two lanes in each direction. "Whether I didn't look carefully, or I just didn't know"—she adds a looping arrow—"I made a left *here*, instead of going across. See what happened?" Sixteen-year-old Lizzie Vandlik had steered the minivan, with her entire family inside, straight into oncoming traffic. Her dad grabbed the wheel, directing the vehicle onto the median. "I was freaking out, right?" Vandlik says. "I almost killed my family. I almost got in an accident. It was terrible. My first time on the highway. I was like, 'I'm never going to do this again.' Guess what my dad did?" She looks up at Casildo.

The boy guesses that her father took over. Vandlik shakes her head. "Nope. He told me to get my life together"—one imagines the word her father used was not "life"—"then he made me turn the car around and drive the rest of the way. Do you know why he did it?" She waits several seconds to allow Casildo to consider why any rational adult might let a frightened teenage girl continue to drive home with the rest of his rattled family in the backseat.

"Because he knew you could still do it," Casildo replies. A statement. Not a question.

"He knew I could still do it," Vandlik repeats. "But he told me that if I freaked out then, and decided that I was too upset to do it, or if he took over and had me try again another day, he knew I would never have gotten in the car again. He made me fix the problem right then." She laughs at the memory. "If I gave up or put it off until later, I was gonna have a lifelong fear of driving. Does this make sense?" Casildo is nodding with a tight-lipped smile. "Do you think you should fix your problem today? Do you think I'm going to let you put it off until tomorrow?" They both know the answer.

"I have lots of Mr. Vandlik stories," she tells him, rising from the desk. "C'mon," she says, putting her arm around Casildo and shepherding him back inside the science room. A few minutes later, he is hunched over his paper, completing the final station of the practice test. Sommi and Schwarzbaum hover just out of his field of vision, ready to pounce should he falter again.

———

As testing season wore on, I was surprised by my reaction to the efforts at Bronx 1 to push, prod, and cajole students to "slam the exam." As a classroom teacher, I had been deeply uncomfortable with test-prep rallies; frankly, I resented attempts to get kids jazzed to sit for standardized tests; such efforts seemed to benefit teachers and schools more than kids. In the years since, I've often described my "complicated relationship" with testing.[1] The resulting data is critically important to evaluate the effectiveness of policies and programs; however, it's impossible to ignore the outsize effects of test-driven accountability policies on K–12 education.[2] The temptation to turn a child's entire experience of schooling into a dry regimen of test prep is too much for many schools to resist. When parents complain, it is generally the effects of testing culture, not the tests themselves, to which they object. Those complaints are valid and serious. That testing culture was what I was seeing at Success Academy—*on steroids.*

So why didn't it irk me?

As the aggressive test prep of Think Mastery season came and went, as prizes accumulated at the front of classrooms—bribes students could collect by showing good effort and following their "plan of attack"—and as I sat in Radio City Music Hall for what must have been the most expensive test-prep rally in history, I wondered if I was falling victim to a kind of Stockholm syndrome. Watching Liz Vandlik tell Matthew Casildo about driving the family minivan into oncoming traffic, a parable to encourage him to go back to finish his practice science test, was the moment I began to unravel my own conflicted response.

To put it mildly, the historic relationship between low-income children of color and schools in the United States has not been a good one. If you are black or brown and poor, particularly in a large city, school is the place where, as often as not, you learn the low regard in which you are held. The message you often receive is that you are not very capable and not much is expected of you. The relationship between communities of color and schools has been characterized by some combination of low expectations, failure, and coercion, often tinged with racism, either tacit or overt. We have warehoused generations of children of color, given them little, and expected less in return. Evelyn Ortega's experience, tearfully recalled in that hospital coffee shop, is depressingly common: "Why were they just passing me?"

What I was seeing at Success Academy—what felt different and potentially powerful—was a consistent pattern of high expectations, warmth, and encouragement. Tough love, to be sure, but also a focus on specific and measurable outcomes. The engagement of Liz Vandlik, Albert Barabas, Kerri Lynch, and Carolyn Syskowski is personal, authentic, and intense. Whether they could articulate it or not, the children under their care surely sense the investment their teachers have in them and in their success. Frustrated by my inability to name this quality, let alone quantify it, I started referring to it as the "GAS factor"; GAS stands for—forgive the indelicacy—"give a shit." It describes the signals communicated to children by their school that there are adults in their life outside their immediate family who are invested in them.

Much of my work, both as a teacher and in education policy, has focused on civic education and ways to enhance and improve the civic mission of schools. Educators and scholars often fret about whether schools pay sufficient attention to developing students' civic engagement. It is seldom observed that schools are not where children go to learn civic engagement but to experience it, to feel the effects of the civic engagement in their community. This is the "hidden curriculum," the unwritten, unofficial, and often-unintended lessons, values, and perspectives that students absorb. If you are a child, you see it in the interest teachers take in you and the signals that your education is going to lead to some meaningful end. You are not just here marking time and filling a seat. School matters. *You* matter. Your teachers aren't punching a clock and cashing their paychecks.

They give a shit. By extension—since teachers act on behalf of the state and society, which authorizes and administers the vast majority of our schools—so does your country.

Empathy is part of the GAS factor, but only a part. Highly effective teachers care deeply about their students, but so do a lot of highly *ineffective* teachers. "They won't care what you know until they know that you care" goes an expression repeated endlessly to new teachers. The advice, like so much about education, is offered in earnest. But it is easy for this kindly bromide to mutate into low expectations, even condescension. How can we expect a child to pass algebra when he's hungry? How can I ask this teenager to do her homework when her mother works nights and she's responsible for her younger siblings? Why should we expect children to read and understand Shakespeare when it's so far removed from their lives, interests, and personal experience? The brand of tough love practiced at Success may not be for everyone, but it is authentic and effective. The first and most important relationship a child has with a civic institution in our society is with her school. As that relationship goes, so go all the others. When you are surrounded by adults who are demonstrably invested in your success, who do not assume your inevitable failure or condescend because they perceive you as *less than* or other, who do not dwell on your deficits or perceive you as oppressed or a victim, you are pointed in a specific direction in life.

But why standardized tests? Why not art, music, writing, or a student's personal passions? Why must a reading or math exam be the referendum for a child's relationship with their school? It needn't be, of course. But in this context, there is something powerful about an objective measure of achievement. It is one thing when your mother or teacher expresses pride in your accomplishments. It is quite another when the state of New York tells you that your performance equals or exceeds anyone's in the state—particularly when kids who look like you have historically rarely reached those levels. While test scores might be Success Academy's calling card—the thing that has made the network an object of fascination, envy, and scorn—the possibility exists that Success Academy and Eva Moskowitz's greatest achievement may have less to do with test scores than with the signaling value of those scores and the methodical creation of a school culture, reinforced at home, in which every adult in the child's life is focused on a set of behavioral and academic expectations that reaches its fullest expression at testing time. When it works, it changes urban education from a forlorn hope—one that runs on gauzy promises and sentimentalizing poverty, and whose signature feature is failure—to one that offers a measurable, externally validated return on a family's investment, a return that is both expected and widely distributed in a school community.

The clearest insight into the Success Academy's culture and performance predates the network's founding. In 2002, Nobel Prize–winning economist George A. Akerlof and his colleague Rachel E. Kranton published a paper titled "Identity and Schooling: Some Lessons for the Economics of Education" in the *Journal of Economic Literature*.[3] They observed that schools not only impart skills; they also impart an image of ideal students, their characteristics, and behaviors. "School rituals—pep rallies, home-room announcements, assemblies—and day-to-day interactions in classrooms, hallways, and gymnasiums reveal the nature of this ideal. Teachers, administrators, and coaches praise and reward some students, while they disapprove of and punish others. These features and occasions define what we call a *school's social category* and its *ideal* student. Students with backgrounds similar to this category readily *identify* with the school. Others, however, do not fit in so easily."

Akerlof and Kranton were building on the insights of renowned sociologist and researcher James Coleman, who described how students divide themselves into familiar social categories—nerds, jocks, burnouts, and such—which influence academic performance. Students choose a social category and with it their level of effort. "When choosing categories, students try to fit in: They consider the match between their own characteristics and the ideal characteristics of jocks, burnouts, and nerds. When choosing effort, students also try to fit in. They consider the match between their own actions and the ideal behavior of their chosen categories," wrote Akerlof and Kranton, whose goal was to "bridge a critical gap in the social sciences" bringing identity and norms to economics. "People's notions of what is proper, and what is forbidden, and for whom, are fundamental to how hard they work, and how they learn, spend, and save. Thus people's identity—their conception of who they are, and of who they choose to be—may be the most important factor affecting their economic lives. *And the limits placed by society on people's identity can also be crucial determinants of their economic well-being.*"[4] (Emphasis mine.)

—

Schools validate and valorize certain ideas and behaviors, which affects how students perceive themselves, their level of effort, and who they want to be. Akerlof and Kranton's takeaway, which reaches full flower at Success Academy, is that you have to establish and promote a culture of achievement and inspire a critical mass of students to embrace it. "If you're able to get a majority of the students to buy into it, it becomes self-perpetuating, because young people like to fit in," explains Patrick Wolf, an education policy professor at the University of Arkansas. "Even if a student is not oriented toward valuing achievement, if they enter a school in which that's the dominant culture, they will accommodate themselves to it."[5] By aggressively messaging its expectations to parents, followed with constant demands for compliance, even monitoring and evaluating parental effort, Success Academy puts into practice the most muscular conceivable version of Akerlof and Kranton's theories.

The effort to create and sustain a coherent culture is unmistakable. It's in the first-day-of-school demands for uniform compliance and Liz Vandlik's concern for lensing her staff and teachers who "aren't seeing the world the way we do." In Shea Reeder's "this isn't Burger King" speech at the welcome meeting. In Carolyn

Syskowski's "Come to Jesus" intervention with kindergarten parents. In Eva Moskowitz's "education crimes and misdemeanors." Success Academy's culture is unusually clear and consistent. It presents an unmistakable vision of who students are expected to be and why it matters. Driving that culture into the home magnifies the effect. And all of it stands in sharp relief to the neighborhood schools that these kids would otherwise attend.

If you accept the idea that school culture can be a significant driver of student outcomes, even the primary one, it leads to an uncomfortable conundrum for education policymakers. The ability to "control for culture" is baked into the opportunities afforded the children of affluent Americans. If you are reasonably well-off and you want your child to go to school surrounded by peers who take school seriously, behave well in class, care about their grades, and put forth significant effort, and whose parents are as engaged and invested as you are, you have your choice of private or public schools in higher-income zip codes that offer honors programs and Advanced Placement classes. It is challenging but not insurmountably difficult to steer your child into a productive learning environment alongside equally motivated peers who embrace an academic identity. You have de facto school choice. More importantly, your right to self-select and pursue an excellent education for your child is unquestioned and unremarkable.

If you are a similarly minded parent but without the means to pay your way out of a chaotic or low-performing neighborhood school—if you are Ayan Wilson, Evelyn Ortega, or the Farrers—your options are limited. Moskowitz seems nearly alone among major charter operators in understanding or intuiting the connection between school culture, parental buy-in, and student outcomes. She spends an extraordinary amount of time and energy ensuring "culture match" and on efforts to ensure families remain committed to Success Academy's approach and vision. Perhaps aware of the unwelcome scrutiny acknowledging this would attract, Moskowitz insists that even if she were allowed to, she would not screen and handpick applicants instead of admitting families by lottery. "I wouldn't do it," she told me, "because I don't think I could tell who they are."

The oft-stated belief among the reform-minded is that a good school or an effective teacher should be able to inspire children and maintain a high-performing classroom culture. Two generations of Teach For America recruits have been drilled to believe in the "self-fulfilling prophecy of high expectations," for example. "When a teacher combines the urgency and focus of measurable outputs with the motivation of high expectations with the direct relevance of students' interests and needs, the teacher creates a big goal that drives extraordinary accomplishments," wrote Teach For America's chief knowledge officer Steven Farr in *Teaching as Leadership*, his 2010 manual for the organization's recruits.[6] This overstates the amount of control even the best and most energetic teacher has over outcomes, particularly when students receive conflicting signals from peers or other adults right outside the classroom door. For some small number of schools led by a charismatic principal or for unusually gifted teachers, the ability to inspire high expectations and student investment may indeed work. But it is clearly neither the default nor dominant feature in public education, particularly at schools serving disadvantaged and disaffected communities, where students and parents have come by their disaffection honestly. Starting with a substantial number of engaged parents, even if that means merely a willingness to have their engagement directed and focused, is a significant advantage for any school or school community. It is also enormously difficult—perhaps impossible—to replicate "at scale."

If "culture-aligned" students, families, and teachers are sprinkled about a given community in numbers too small to create the critical mass needed to drive or dominate a school culture, we arrive at a nearly insurmountable public policy dilemma: if we prevent such students and families from self-selecting, it is tantamount to a kind of enforced mediocrity. If this is a critical component of successful outcomes for affluent families, what justification can there be in denying to low-income and minority families—*and only to those families*—an essential prerequisite of educational success, economic opportunity, and upward mobility? While such policies might not be intentionally racist, good intentions do not guarantee good outcomes.

The most common objection to charter schools and publicly financed private school choice initiatives is that schools of choice "siphon resources away" from traditional public schools.[7] One such "resource" is engaged and invested families. This is more true than most choice and charter school advocates like to acknowledge, but it will resonate with anyone who has ever stood in front of a classroom, grateful for her most motivated children. Classroom dynamics change substantially based on who is in the room and their level of effort—Akerlof and Kranton's insight writ small. It should go without saying that most parents are uncomfortable thinking of their child as a public resource. No affluent parent is asked to view her child that way. But the price of our egalitarian impulse is to enshrine an aristocracy: Those with resources who value safe and orderly schools and a culture of academic achievement have largely unfettered access to it. Those with the same priorities and values but without resources struggle to gain admittance. Given Akerlof and Kranton's observation that children seek to assimilate into social groups and their concomitant achievement level, this suggests not merely acceptance of a vicious circle but *insistence upon it*, deepening poverty and despair, limiting access to good schools and school cultures—all in the name of equity and fairness. Well-intended efforts to leverage schools as a means of ending generational poverty are perversely doomed to perpetuate it—unless we allow like-minded parents to self-select into schools in the greatest numbers possible.

If the counterargument is that encouraging this kind of self-selection concentrates poverty and dysfunction in other schools, the candid answer is to acknowledge the risk, not dismiss it, and to account and plan for it. It is both poor public policy and immoral to demand that low-income families accept their fate as school-culture outliers, limiting their children's potential in poor-performing schools in the name of "equity." It is a burden that affluent families are never asked or expected to bear.

One former Success Academy school leader was philosophical about all this. "Is it really such a bad thing that this is basically an elite private school that admits by lottery?" he asked. "It's the first time folks in the inner city have had that chance."

CHAPTER 22

Proof Point

KELLIE GRANT HAS LINED UP THREE COLUMNS OF INDEX CARDS IN double rows on the rug in Ms. Syskowski's classroom. Each card lists the name of a kindergarten student; each column is made up of one row of boys and one row of girls: Class A, Class B, and Class C. It's her initial attempt to sort this year's kindergarteners into next year's first graders. Four of the cards have the names of current first graders who are going to be held back. "Gather around," Grant calls to the kindergarten teachers. "I've separated some scholars who have behavioral challenges." There are ten such students. "That's literally all I've done so far," she says. The kindergarten team, who knows them intimately, is being asked to troubleshoot each prospective class roster, separate students who don't get along, and ensure an even mix of personalities—the attention seekers, nice kids and needy ones, quiet children and boisterous ones—the archetypes in an elementary school classroom. "We want to make sure we didn't create new problems," Vandlik says as the teachers start milling about, examining the ad hoc rosters.

"We have a 'girl clique' here," Syskowski says, pointing out three girls in her class who need to be broken up next year. "OK, we'll put one of them in each class," Grant says, and starts moving cards around the rug. Each child's card designates them as "OGL," "BGL," or "AGL," for on grade level, below, or above; the teachers try to ensure each class has a similar mix of each. Syskowski spots one of her students that she wants to move up to second grade, just as she did with the Farrers' youngest son, Avery, last year. "Is Cindy being skipped?" she asks.

"We're keeping a list of 'trial skips,'" Vandlik replies. One or two of the kindergarten students are sufficiently advanced, but "we want to make sure there's no regression over the summer. We've been burned a few times," she adds. The teachers continue shuffling students between classes. "Girls good?" Ms. CeeCee asks. The teachers nod and murmur their assent. "Lemme do the boys," Grant says and reads each name off the cards, class by class. Vandlik wants to ensure the first-grade boys who are holdovers are in different rooms next year. The teachers identify several others who need to be separated. Two children are leaving—one to Bronx 3, the other to Harlem Village Academy, another charter school—leaving an imbalance in the numbers. After the horse-trading comes the final test. "On your own, without talking to anyone else, rank the classes you would want to teach," Grant instructs, asking everyone to list Class A, B, and C in their order of preference. "If everyone has the same answers, then we didn't do a good job making even and balanced classes." There's a minute of silence as the teachers look at each class and envision leading it. "This is hard this year!" says Ms. CeeCee.

"It's good if it's hard," replies Vandlik.

They hand their answers to Grant. "Three for C, three for B," she counts. "But A is not first on anyone's list."

Grant and Vandlik try to draw the teachers out about why no one put Class A as their first choice. Syskowski points out three low-level boys. "Instruction's going to be rough" with those kids in the same room. She also identifies three girls "with a lot of needs," she adds. "Very low, very quiet, and often off task." The reshuffling resumes. This child is stubborn. That one has a difficult parent. One class ends up with eight low-level students, as many as the other two combined. In one iteration, there is only one "high flier" in a class, but it's Cindy, the girl Syskowski wants to skip a grade. "I just don't see her in first grade. She's a very well behaved child, but she's not challenged." Finally, balance is achieved.

"You guys feel OK about it?" Vandlik asks. As the teachers start to drift back to their classrooms, Grant gathers up the index cards. "It's a good first draft," Vandlik says, as she and Grant prepare to repeat the process for the older grades.

The school year is racing toward its end. It's Field Day, a red-letter day on the calendar of every elementary school kid. The staff as much as the children can taste the end of the year, and there's a holiday atmosphere at Bronx 1. Kids come to school in play clothes, not uniforms; the staff, too, is decked out in athletic gear. Syskowski leads her kindergarteners onto the ballfield in a Carmelo Anthony Knicks jersey. Vandlik wears a Success Academy baseball shirt, with a lanyard and whistle around her neck. Ms. Kowalski, ever the outlier, is the only staffer not in sports gear.

Everything is giddy chaos. The most popular activity appears to be a game called Extreme Simon Says, in which players who are eliminated are doused by a Super Soaker water gun, gleefully wielded by Mr. Morales. Inside, three little girls are an exception to the casual dress and mood; they appear as if they're dressed for church. They have each been named "principal of the day," an honor earned by maintaining perfect attendance for the entire year. They've brought their play clothes to change into once they have discharged their official duties, which include shadowing Vandlik and accompanying a VIP on a tour of the school.

The VIP is Eva Moskowitz, who has in tow a VIP of her own, Tiffany Dufu, an author and activist, whom Moskowitz is courting for her board of directors. But something else is brewing. A few weeks ago, Jen Fuoco took me aside to make sure I would be there for Field Day, promising a "major surprise." Whatever Fuoco is cooking up is given ample cover by the visit from Moskowitz and her guest, whose tour starts in the third-grade room named Marist-Clemson. Ms. Walsh is in a Marist T-shirt; Mr. Mikulka, in a Nike shirt with a Clemson Tigers paw print. As always, their classroom shows well; the kids are on point as Vandlik explains to Dufu Success Academy's "conceptual math" curriculum. The entourage moves to Lynch's room, where the fourth graders are studying westward expansion, which Moskowitz, the former history professor, says is her favorite project-based learning unit. "Expansion is something you know all about," Dufu needles her with a smile. On the way to the art room, their final stop, I ask fourth grader Dorcas, in her role as principal of the day, can she please get the cafeteria to serve pizza for lunch today? The fourth grader explains patiently and politely that it's a half-day today so there's no lunch served. When Moskowitz asks the girls, "Are there any improvements we need to make?" the three suggest that Bronx 1 could use a retractable gym divider so that more than one class can play without interfering with one another. Moskowitz, omnipresent Starbucks cup in hand, gives the girls her full attention, nodding as they make their pitch.

The women retreat to the principal's office to debrief. Dufu peppers Moskowitz with questions about everything from school lunches and real estate to race and politics. The chief leadership officer for Levo, a professional networking website for millennials, Dufu is a friend of board chair Daniel Loeb; she notes that in the classes she visited, she saw "a lot of what I would call 'discipline,' for lack of a better term." Having thirty-two kids in a class requires a very well-managed classroom, answers Moskowitz, explaining her belief that "with tight classroom management you can release kids' intellectual potential." Freedom is expressed not in student behavior, but intellectually, in the progressive pedagogy the network ostensibly favors. "The world has changed," she says. Nothing at Success Academy would have been remarkable or even noticeable in 1940 when schools were more formal. "School was sort of like going to church." Teachers were respected and had "a certain amount of cultural capital," she continues. Today if you go to a typical school, you're likely to see teachers in flip-flops and midriffs. "We're kind of reacting against that." Nor does Moskowitz believe that asking students to speak at conversational levels implies a straitjacket or that kids aren't free to express themselves. "It's in the service of self-expression and thinking and ideas," she explains. More pertinent, the school tone, culture, and what registered for Dufu as discipline are, in large part, why parents choose Success Academy in the first place. The network often does focus groups asking parents why they have chosen to send their kids there. "I'd love the answer to be 'science five days a week' and 'blocks play in kindergarten.' It isn't. It's safety." When Dufu asks if safety over academics is really an appropriate choice, Moskowitz doesn't miss a beat. "It is for them."

I have not attended any of these focus groups, but nearly without exception, in my interviews with Success Academy parents and those hoping to get in, school safety is a primary concern, and almost always brought up unbidden. It seems to extend to charters as a whole. No authoritative study exists, and the New York City Charter School Center keeps no data on the question, but it is widely assumed among the city's charter school operators that much of the demand for seats is driven by the perception that charter schools are safer and more orderly than district schools. It's a mixed blessing. When I visited one well-regarded network of classical charter schools not far from Bronx 1, the founder said that one of his goals was to attract parents who explicitly chose his schools for their unique curriculum, but safety and proximity remain the primary drivers of his parents' choice.[1] While education policy wonks and advocates may want the word "charter" to be synonymous with "innovation" or "excellence," among many parents it mainly remains a synonym for "safe."

Dufu has done her homework. She presses Moskowitz about the network's backfill policy. "It is challenging. It takes [students who don't start at Success in kindergarten or first grade] a little while to get used to the way we do things here," Moskowitz concedes. Vandlik points out that among the three girls who accompanied them on their tour was a third grader who is new this year to Success Academy and is flourishing. Dufu notes that nearly all students she saw were brown while the vast majority of teachers and administrators are white. Is that the case in all the schools? Moskowitz has the data by heart. Across the network, 37 percent of faculty, just over one out of three, are people of color. Those numbers are "lower than we would like," Vandlik interjects. She points out that she has "a significantly higher percentage of people of color in [her] associate teacher pool" who are getting promoted to lead teacher roles. "It's not as fast as any of us would like," Moskowitz says, "but it gets significantly easier every year." Dufu asks if Success has hired "diversity consultants," but Moskowitz dismisses the idea. "I've had it with outside consultants. They don't understand," she says. Her greater challenge, she counters, is making sure every employee understands that there's a difference between race and class and "making sure that you're not making assumptions that families are poor because they're of a certain race or ethnicity." There is no adversarial tension in the exchange, but it surfaces the clearest statement I have heard all year from Moskowitz about her views on education and race. "We have a design," she explains, "and we didn't design schools for black people, or poor people, or Latinos. We designed what we thought were world-class schools for any race, socioeconomic class, or ethnicity. That's a radical notion."

It *is* a radical notion and a clear example of Moskowitz's willingness to swim against the tide of fashionable ideas in education. Another radical aspect of Moskowitz's model is seldom remarked on: Changes in education travel a one-way street. Innovative school models and pedagogies tend to be birthed in affluent neighborhoods and then migrate to less advantaged schools and districts once they are "proved" effective. What's rarely considered is that any number of those programs and practices don't work in affluent schools any better than in low-income settings. Their ineffectiveness is merely revealed when they are foisted on students who lack the cultural capital to compensate for their inherent weakness. A good example is the Teachers College Reading and Writing Project, a "balanced literacy" curriculum that has dominated New York City classrooms for more than a decade. In 2013, the New York State Education Department began wisely steering schools away from the program, in favor of curricula perceived to be more phonics- and knowledge-rich and more closely aligned to the Common Core standards. The Teachers College program was described by the *New York Times* as "unstructured and ineffective, particularly for low-income children." But it remained firmly in place in New York City, largely because it was favored by then-schools chancellor Carmen Fariña.[2] She was convinced of its effectiveness from her days running PS 6, one block from the Metropolitan Museum of Art in one of Manhattan's most exclusive zip codes, where many parents could just as easily have afforded elite private schools and whose children come to school with all the cognitive benefits accumulated by growing up in richly literate homes.

If the flow of educational experimentation, innovation, and fads is a one-way street, from privileged zip codes to poor ones, Moskowitz is driving aggressively into oncoming traffic. Success Academy opened dozens of schools in low-income neighborhoods, serving almost exclusively families of color, before locating in more economically mixed neighborhoods like the Upper West Side, Cobble Hill, and Union Square. The curriculum and school culture offered in these more mixed neighborhoods does not differ whatsoever from what is on offer in the Bronx, Harlem, or Bed-Stuy. In fact, affluent parents are knocking on Moskowitz's door wanting what she has created for low-income communities. Moskowitz tells Dufu that her biggest fear is that her leaders and teachers might apply a different set of standards to kids because they might be poor. "There are lot of sensibilities around the fragileness of children," Moskowitz says. "And I think to myself, 'You're a white girl from Long Island; *you're the fragile one.* The kids have actually been through a lot. Don't impose your issues on the kid.'"

But Dufu is not done pressing Moskowitz. How does she

reconcile that some elected representatives may support the school but don't want some of its families in this country because of their religion? The subtext is the offer made to Moskowitz to serve as Trump's education secretary, which she turned down. "We don't reconcile it, and I don't think it's possible," she replies, an answer she's given before. A few weeks earlier, when the Republican Speaker of the House, Paul Ryan, visited a Harlem Success Academy, protesters filled the streets outside. A few months earlier, a staffer at Harlem 2 emailed Moskowitz on behalf of a group of teachers, questioning her support for education secretary Betsy DeVos, her silence on the administration's attempt to ban travelers from certain majority-Muslim countries, and other policies that could directly impact their students and families.[3] "I really believe the enterprise has to be single issue. People wanted me to take a stand against Trump on immigration," Moskowitz responds, growing animated. "I can't start opining on global warming. Particularly with this president, I could spend every waking hour denouncing this, that, and the other thing." She did weigh on transgender bathrooms "because that's in my lane."[4] This stance, too, puts Moskowitz solidly out of the mainstream of education reform, which has drifted in recent years away from a focus on education policy and practice toward a pointed advocacy on immigration, housing, policing, and other issues.

The women talk about Moskowitz's ambition to reach one hundred schools and school funding issues before Dufu takes her leave and Moskowitz and Vandlik head downstairs to look in on the Field Day festivities. But the scene that greets them is not rambunctious children running relay races and playing kickball. There's a large and orderly crowd gathered outside, which includes dozens of parents and a television camera crew. A line of scholars is holding up a string of letters spelling out CONGRATS. Vandlik, disoriented and uncomprehending, mutters, "What's going on?" just before the entire staff, student body, and parents yell, "Surprise!" A chant of "Bronx 1! Bronx 1!" starts up, and someone hands a microphone to Moskowitz. She announces that Liz Vandlik is one of only two recipients nationwide for the Ryan Award, a prize given annually to a principal who has demonstrated "exceptional leadership in closing the achievement gap" over four years or more. The award, given by the Chicago-based Accelerate Institute, comes with a twenty-five-thousand-dollar honorarium and an invitation to be a guest lecturer at the Kellogg School of Management at Northwestern University. "Liz hates surprises, and she hates when anything's about her. So it's going to be a great day," said Fuoco, who was given a discreet heads-up about the award nearly a month ago; she alerted the teachers only last night; they rallied the parents, who have come out in force.

As Pat Ryan Jr., the head of the Accelerate Institute, announces the award and sings her praises, Vandlik stands awkwardly next to him. She shifts her weight and crosses her arms over her stomach, her body language telegraphing discomfort. When it is her turn to speak, she struggles to maintain her composure. Camille McKinnon is one of a dozen parents recording the scene on her cell phone camera. Afterward, Vandlik lingers on the playground, accepting the congratulations of families and colleagues, posing for pictures. I've witnessed her discomfort with praise before, but this seems different. Something isn't right.

It wasn't until weeks later that I learned what happened that afternoon. After receiving the award and the congratulations of her staff, students, and families, Vandlik retreated to the office of middle school principal Britney Weinberg-Lynn and sobbed. The school year that was days from ending had been, she was certain, the worst of her professional life: She was bad at her job. Failing. Now all the people she felt certain she had let down were standing on the ball field cheering and applauding, pretending that she is something she's not. There was nowhere to hide from a spotlight that could only reveal her incompetence. On my first visit to Bronx 1 more than a year earlier, Vandlik described her angst over the uneven quality of teachers and classrooms in her school. At the time, it sounded rehearsed and performative. Over time, I came to see it as her obsession. Most of us in this work would be delighted to get

90 percent of our students to proficiency in reading and math and would gladly bask in the accolades those results would bring. Vandlik seems incapable of seeing past the 10 percent who aren't making it, or the idea that a child under her care is spending even a day in a classroom with a weak teacher. It was, Vandlik was certain, *her* failure. And it was too much to bear.

The previous fall, when Bronx 1 was designated a National Blue Ribbon School by the Department of Education, Vandlik shrugged. Her parents back home in Chicago were dismissive. "Everyone gets a blue ribbon," her father had said. This time, her parents were not dismissive. They didn't even know. Overwhelmed by impostor syndrome, feeling like a fraud, and presented with an honor she was certain she didn't deserve and could not live up to, Vandlik didn't tell them. It wasn't until more than a week later that her boyfriend emailed her family the news. Vandlik's sister opened the email first and immediately called their parents. They both wept, proud of their daughter, who is very good at her job.

CHAPTER 23

Culture Clash

ON THE LAST FULL DAY OF SCHOOL FOR HER KINDERGARTENERS, Carolyn Syskowski comes to work in a white dress with a purple sash, the colors of Hunter College, her alma mater. The girls wear purple bows in their hair and faux grass skirts; boys pull purple and white Hawaiian leis over their necks to perform "We Know the Way," a song from the Disney movie *Moana*, at the end-of-the-year assembly. The school year will finish in the same place and under the same conditions it began ten months ago, in a hot and sticky auditorium.

The final assembly is "Success Stories," a celebration of the children's first year of school. The children read "résumés" that they wrote themselves to their parents, who are scattered throughout the auditorium. Several students line up on stage to speak, introducing themselves by name, classroom, and "Class of 2033," the impossibly distant year they are scheduled to graduate from college. The first girl says she loves number stories and wants to become an art teacher. "I am a Level I reader, and I like to play the cello," she concludes. Zian, from Ms. Syskowski's class, says he wants to be a firefighter. He also tells the crowd he'll "never give up my toys because I have to practice being an adult." Nyell says she "aspires" to be a nurse, and uses the word correctly.

Back in the classroom, together for the last time, with parents shoehorned into every square foot, Syskowski hands out awards for academic accomplishments, winning personality traits, or simply for being exemplary community members, singling out children with the best manners, best school spirit, and wildest imagination. Future authors, artists, teachers, engineers, scientists, and one "future mayor of the Bronx" are honored. Syskowski sings the praises of Allison, who goes out of her way to play with every one of her classmates, always noticing when someone has no one to play with and bringing them into the fold. Three kids who started the year in kindergarten were promoted to first grade before Christmas; that leaves Cindy to claim the prize for having advanced the greatest number of reading levels over the school year. She is reading at Level K, equivalent to second grade. A father goes slack-jawed. "I want her to read to me," he says. "I'm not a Level K."

There's one last bit of business Syskowski has to share, something she's known since March but has only just told her students, and now their parents: Speaking in her clear, firm teacher voice, she announces that she is leaving to become a Success Academy assistant principal next year, but not at Bronx 1. She will transfer to the network's school in Cobble Hill. "Oh, no!" one mother moans. The parents sigh loudly. "It's hard," Syskowski stammers, caught off guard by the response, absentmindedly rubbing her knee and trying to maintain her composure. "It's something I've wanted to do for years but . . . I don't want to leave Bronx 1," she sputters, abandoning her fight not to cry. Several parents also wipe away tears as Syskowski encourages them to continue to call for any reason at all. "Please contact me. I want to be a part of your children's lives," she says. "You have beautiful, *beautiful* children. And I really appreciate that you trusted us this first year. I know it's hard. I know there were maybe times when you didn't like me, but I told you that would happen!"

Syskowski is not the only teacher moving up the ranks. Albert Barabas, too, will become an AP next year. He lobbied hard to be assigned to the middle school upstairs, where he could walk in with established relationships with students and their parents, but Success Academy has other plans, assigning him to its original school, Harlem 1. "The flagship, baby!" he exulted when he told me the news. After seven years as a teacher, Carson Rockefeller, Bronx 1's lead science teacher, will also leave to become an instructional manager, overseeing several elementary schools.

The next day, a sudden downpour scatters students and parents at the last drop-off of the year, briefly threatening the fourth-grade graduation ceremony. For the first time, there is no pretense of classroom instruction. In Lynch's room, boys in khaki pants, white dress shirts, and orange bow ties gather in bunches, killing time before the ceremony talking boisterously and physically overreacting to one other, trying on the attention-seeking speech and mannerisms of the middle schoolers they're about to officially become. The girls are dressed even more formally in white dresses. Camille McKinnon's daughter, Blessing, looks like she's prepared to march down the aisle as a bride, not just to graduate from fourth grade.

Constance Smith is there, too. Several months ago, she was detailed to Harlem West to teach fifth-grade ELA. But she's back to see her students graduate. She joins the boys for an impromptu dance party and towers over them, making them instantly look again like little boys. The spirited vibe turns serious when it's time to go out to the ball field. "You look amazing. Present yourself the same way you've dressed yourself," Lynch instructs before issuing a few reminders on how to conduct themselves. "Your parents are right behind you watching you." During the song they will sing at graduation, "the first part is about love and gratitude toward your families," she reminds them. "Big smiles! Gesture toward them."

When the ceremony ends an hour later, the school year is officially over. Teachers hand out report cards, dispense hugs, and wish a happy summer to the children, who melt out of classrooms and down hallways. Two kids run past Matthew Morales, who calls after them, "Walk!" The boys come to a dead stop then proceed silently to the exit. Morales turns and smiles. "I just had to do that one last time." The father of a kindergartener comes to Laura Belkin's room to meet his son's new first-grade teacher. It takes Alex Gottlieb a moment before it sinks in that he's looking for her. She's been hired as a lead teacher for August, one of the few ATs to make the cut and be invited back to Bronx 1 for the fall.

Across the hall, Alanna Kowalski and Brandon Whitaker say their goodbyes in the classroom where they were the last to arrive, after Elena Ortiz's flameout and Nick Carton's midyear departure. It's been trial by fire in Bronx 1's most challenging class, but both will be "returners," Whitaker teaching in fourth grade with Ms. Lynch and Kowalski paired in kindergarten with Matt Carnaghi. For Kowalski, the midyear hire plucked from the DOE, it's been a challenge to master the culture, behavior management, pedagogy, and routines without the benefit of the network's exacting T School for new teachers. But she's made it through. As her last student prepares to leave the classroom, Kowalski wishes Ady a happy summer, makes him promise to read, and then notices something just as he's about to step into the hall.

"Tuck in your shirt," she orders.

The next day is the final one for staff. With no children in the building, teachers blast the uncensored versions of their playlists as they pack up their rooms. I've grown accustomed to seeing Bronx 1's teachers as authority figures—fake it till you make it—and their music reminds me how young most of them are. Piles of furniture and boxes grow in the center of each room to make things easier for the maintenance people who will clean and paint over the summer.

There's a bittersweet quality to the day, which I spend mostly helping Kerri Lynch pack up her room. She's a little cranky, a little blue. Her best friend, Barabas, has been ticketed for school leadership in Harlem, and now Brandon Richter is leaving, too. He's accepted a position at another charter school, Brooklyn Lab, for next year.

Smith will be back, but she's slated to teach third grade, leaving Lynch as the only returning member of this year's fourth-grade team. While they're boxing up their room, she and Smith find costume hats from their American Revolution unit. They take selfies wearing them to text to some of their students. Laura Belkin, who is getting married and transferring to Success Academy's newest school in Hudson Yards, west of Manhattan's Penn Station and closer to her New Jersey home, comes looking for Smith. She hands over the thick wad of play money that was the linchpin of Tyrone's behavior plan. One of the outlier scholars who was an object of the special friends' walk-through back in October, he passed second grade and will be in Smith's class next year. Tonight there will be a party at a nearby tavern. For many of Bronx 1's staff, it will be a final farewell. Lynch will leave directly from the party to board a flight to London; she plans to spend the next month bumming around Europe. She seems so down that I wonder if her return ticket might go unused, but I don't ask.

If you are in your twenties or thirties, there's a fair chance that at least some of your elementary school teachers are still at your old school, a little older and grayer, perhaps growing thick about the waist, but right where you left them. They serve for life, like Supreme Court justices. If Success Academy students visit just a few years from now, they might not see even a single familiar face. The de facto model that has evolved is more like the US Army or the Marines: a small and talented officer corps surrounded by enlisted men and women who do a tour, maybe two, then muster out, with new recruits reporting for duty. Teacher turnover, and lack of experience and continuity, is widely assumed to be a problem, particularly in urban schools. But it's never suggested that our military would be better if only soldiers stayed in uniform longer. So far, the relative inexperience of Success Academy teachers hasn't seemed to compromise their effectiveness.

None of this applies to Kerri Lynch, among the most competent and committed teachers I've observed in any setting. She's not a Teach For America corps member with a two-year obligation to honor and an eye on law school, public policy, or Wall Street. Someday she might think about school administration, she says, but not yet. For now, she is the rarest creature in a high-performing urban charter school: a seasoned veteran and the longest-serving upper-grade teacher at Success Academy Bronx 1.

She is twenty-seven years old.

———

A week after Vandlik collected her award from the Accelerate Institute, Eva Moskowitz traveled to DC to collect a major honor of her own. Every year since 2012, the Eli and Edythe Broad Foundation has awarded the Broad Prize to a large charter network that has "demonstrated the best overall academic performance while closing achievement gaps and serving low-income students and students of color."[1] YES Prep, Uncommon Schools, and KIPP are all past recipients of the award, which does not accept applications or nominations: a ten-member review board of education researchers and policymakers determines the winner based on student outcomes and "scalability." Success Academy was the consensus over the other two finalists, DSST Public Schools, which operates twelve schools in Denver, Colorado; and Harmony Public Schools, a Texas-based network with forty-eight schools serving thirty-two thousand students. The controversies that have dogged Moskowitz were very much on the minds of the judges, which included former US secretary of education John King. "The main sentiment was that [Success Academy's] results are just dramatically better. Not just better than the district, but also dramatically better than other high-performing charters," one member of the panel told me. "It was just hard to argue with that."

Not that they didn't try. According to several judges who spoke on condition of anonymity,[2] the committee pressed hard on attrition data, wary of honoring a CMO that might be deliberately ridding itself of low-performing students. But the data didn't support the charge. For example, analyses by the New York City Independent Budget Office and WNYC, New York City's NPR affiliate, calculated the student mobility rates of the school districts where Success Academy schools are located and compared them with the attrition rates of Success students in the same districts. Based on those comparisons, 1,061 students would have been expected to transfer out of Success Academy during the 2013–14 school year. The actual number was only 609.[3] If the network was deliberately shedding low-performing students, the attrition rate would have been expected to be higher. The data showed Success Academy held on to fewer of its students than all but one other charter network in New York City, but at a rate much higher than New York City public schools in the same neighborhoods.

That analysis doesn't answer, however, whether Success was more likely to shed *low-performing* students, a charge that has been persistently leveled at Moskowitz. A 2015 analysis by the Manhattan Institute and written by Marcus Winters, an associate professor at Boston University, while not specific to Success Academy, found that low-performing students are more likely to change schools than high-performing peers in *both* charter schools and traditional public schools. "No statistical analysis can confirm alleged isolated instances of charters inappropriately removing low-performing students," Winters concluded. However, the data "suggest that rampant claims that NYC charters systematically remove low-performing students—whether directly or indirectly, through 'counseling out'— are, at the very least, overstated."[4] Nevertheless, Diane Ravitch, the prominent critic of charter schools and Success Academy in particular, was withering about the Broad Foundation's decision, repeating the charge that Success sheds "those with disabilities, English language learners, nonconformists, and others who can't or won't produce high test scores."[5]

This dispute will never be resolved to universal satisfaction. Too much is in the eye of the beholder. If a charter school insists on holding over a poor-performing student to repeat the sixth grade while the neighborhood school across the street is happy to admit him to seventh, was that child encouraged to withdraw or "counseled out"? If a third-grade girl comes off the waitlist, but Success

Academy insists she must be placed in the second grade after assessing her, is the school maintaining high standards? Or is it dissuading those "who can't or won't produce high test scores" from enrolling?

The end of the school year brought an opportunity to explore some of these issues and also to resolve a lingering mystery: What happened to Adama? All I knew for certain was that the boy left Bronx 1 in March. His parents, who had been so determined to keep him at the school, withdrew him suddenly. During the year, I was dependent on Success Academy for permission to make observations; now, I was no longer at risk of losing access. A few weeks later, I was sitting on a couch in a small apartment overlooking the Harlem River and the Willis Avenue Bridge with Adama's mother, Maimouna Wouattara, who had emigrated from Burkina Faso ten years earlier with her husband and who had limited command of English; another Bronx 1 parent, a neighbor and friend, was present to translate.

The story that unfolded over the next two hours was deeply troubling. Wouattara had been encouraged to enroll her son by her friend, whose two children have thrived at Bronx 1. But the relationship soured quickly. Adama was suspended frequently, disrupting his parents' work schedule. Wouattara claims the school pressured them to withdraw their son and enroll him in a public school where he could be in the more restrictive classroom environment that they insisted he needed. Worse, there were about half a dozen incidents where the school called 911 and had the boy taken to the hospital in an ambulance because of his behavior. The conflict between the family and school grew so contentious, they claimed, that Success Academy called New York City's Administration for Children's Service, the agency that investigates claims of parental abuse and neglect.

Midway through Adama's first-grade year, the couple retained Nelson Mar, a senior staff attorney and parent advocate at Bronx Legal Services, who has represented a number of families in disputes with Success Academy. When problems first surfaced, Wouattara's husband, Saiba Sanga, recalled, the couple's response had been to take time off—he is a taxi driver; she is a hotel housekeeper—to spend time at Bronx 1 as a preventive measure. "It's like we have to go there and sit, like paramedics," explained Sanga. When Adama saw his parents at school, he didn't act out, so they visited frequently. But staff eventually dissuaded them from coming. "They said, 'You're not gonna go with him when he goes to college,'" Sanga recalled. "I said, 'No. It's because he's a kid now, so we do it now.'"

The couple insists there were no problems with Adama in kindergarten; however, one Bronx 1 teacher who worked with him that year and sympathizes with the parents, told me privately that he had behavior problems from the start. In first grade, he was suspended for disobedience, running around the school, and physical altercations with other students. On at least one occasion, he was alleged to have hit an adult staffer, a member of the ops team. At the same time, his parents claim that Success Academy began pushing the local Committee on Special Education (CSE), the Department of Education body that coordinates special ed services for students not enrolled in DOE schools, to approve an individual education program recommending that Adama be placed in a 12:1:1 classroom, with twelve students, one teacher, and a paraprofessional. Success Academy had seventeen such classes throughout its network, but none at Bronx 1. Charter schools are generally not required to provide them.

"We know that he has some problems," Sanga said, but the couple resisted placing Adama in such a restrictive setting or withdrawing him altogether. But Success persistently pushed them to accept an alternative placement for Adama. "They even ask me if I can take him to private school," Sanga said. "And they gonna ask the CSE to pay for it." Like many Success Academy parents, they valued the premium placed on discipline and wanted him to remain, but the pressure continued. "On multiple occasion, they ask me what I'm gonna do, when I'm gonna make the decision to take him out from the school," said Sanga, who told me that the school also suggested they have their son taken for a psychiatric evaluation and medicated.

In second grade, things escalated dramatically. On several occasions, including three times in a single week in December, the school called 911 and had Adama taken to nearby Lincoln Hospital. Finally, when Sanga was notified once again that his son was being removed, he told the school he would not meet the ambulance at the hospital. Attorney Nelson Mar had told them that during school hours, the child is the school's responsibility and Adama's parents were within their rights. But they claim the incident resulted in Success Academy calling ACS to investigate the parents for neglect. "Because of what?" asked Sanga. "Let me tell you, we are a poor family. But we love our kids." ACS made three separate visits to their apartment.

By March, they were finished. Adama, his parents said, was "suffering," and so were they. "Every time I see [Saiba] it looked like he's sleeping on the street because he's so stressed," said the friend who'd encouraged Wouattara to enroll her son at Success in the first place. "He ended up starting taking blood-pressure medication." Her son's frequent suspensions from school and the disruptions to her schedule contributed to Wouattara losing a job at a Manhattan hotel. "It was too much on her," said her friend. "It was too stressful. They're not giving Adama a chance to finish the school year. It's like they're pushing him out of the door. That's how she felt."

"We tired," added Wouattara, in English. "I don't want to do Success no more."

The couple's harrowing tale also included a shocking charge and an explanation for a second lingering mystery: teacher Elena Ortiz's sudden departure from Bronx 1 the previous fall. They claim she quit when she was asked to lie to the Committee on Special Education about Adama's behavior problems in order to justify transferring him from Bronx 1 and into a more restrictive classroom setting. Wouattara, Sanga, and Mar were at Bronx 1 the day Ortiz stormed out and never returned. They had requested a meeting to discuss their son's most recent suspension and brought their attorney. It was scheduled for 4:30. "We get there, we're waiting, and 4:45 comes, 4:50 comes, we see Ms. Vandlik walking back and forth. We're like, 'Well, this is strange.' Usually they're fairly prompt about starting a meeting," Mar recalled. Ortiz walked up and told them she'd just quit her job. "She said, 'They want me to say that Adama did this and did that, and I can't say that,'" Mar said. "The thing that I remember distinctly was that she said, 'They want me to lie, and I'm not going to do that.'" I reached out to Elena Ortiz to confirm this version of events, making plans to meet in person, which she canceled. I continued to reach out to her repeatedly over months, but she stopped responding to my messages. The last time I texted her, I received a terse reply: "Wrong number."

Four different staffers with whom I discussed the matter expressed skepticism, even incredulity, that Vandlik would ask Ortiz to lie. "It's possible she may have misunderstood something, but there's no way she would tell her to lie," insisted one who has worked with Vandlik for years. "Just no way." Others noted Ortiz herself had had a rocky tenure at the school and was erratic even before her flameout. One former colleague suggests she was looking for an excuse to quit.

But the story Adama's parents tell cannot be dismissed. It fits a troubling pattern of parents who have claimed that they were told that Success Academy does not offer special education services or the classroom settings that their children need; or that suspensions were meted out so frequently that work schedules and routines were disrupted, wearing families down and eventually forcing them to give up and pull their children out. In January 2016, more than a dozen Success Academy parents, New York City's public advocate, several children's aid organizations, and others filed a complaint against the network with the US Department of Education's Office for Civil Rights alleging systematic policies and practices that violate children's civil rights under the Individuals with Disabilities Education Act and other federal laws. The complaint alleged that Success Academy "discriminates against students with disabilities by failing to identify them or provide them with reasonable accommodations," and even retaliates against them by "taking measures to coerce them to leave . . . when they require services related to a disability."[6] Early in 2019, a fresh round of parent complaints resulted in New York State charging Success Academy and New York City's Department of Education with violating the civil rights of students with special needs following an investigation by state officials.[7]

There is a depressing sameness to the allegations in the lengthy OCR complaint: A Harlem 4 student required to repeat the second grade three times and suspended on multiple occasions. A Harlem 3 student recommended for 12:1:1 special education placement, which the school did not provide. A Bronx 1 student held over in the same grade three times. Staff urging parents to remove their children and enroll them in DOE schools. In nearly every case, the OCR complaint alleges that staffers pressured parents to remove children altogether rather than working with them to develop strategies to help them be successful. The allegations made by Adama's parents would fit in seamlessly. (In fact, Nelson Mar represents several families in the OCR complaint.)

The claims created no small amount of cognitive dissonance. What I'd observed over the year left me with an impression that was generally favorable. Far from a soul-crushing, militaristic, academic hothouse, the schools I visited were professionally run, safe, and supportive. This was particularly true at Bronx 1. Children, especially those of elementary school age, do not always control or express their emotions, but nothing that I observed was outside the range of what one would expect to see in any good elementary school: the children were held to high expectations academically and behaviorally. But just as clearly, they were treated with care and affection. Teachers differ in their personalities, motivation, classroom manner, and skill level, but in hundreds of hours of unmonitored observations, I never saw one behave toward a student in a manner that I would not want my own child treated. Moskowitz's characterization of the sweet spot of a Success Academy teacher—a "no-nonsense nurturer"—seemed consistently in evidence.

Equally clear and frequently noted across the network was the insistence that Success Academy is "not for everybody." That is easy to say in the abstract. It takes on a different dimension when it applies to a struggling child you know by name and face or a teacher whose classroom you have spent hours observing, or when you are sitting on the couch of an anguished mother, listening as she tells harrowing stories about a school whose staff you have come to respect.

My time with Adama's parents left me shaken and wondering if I'd been deceived, or if I'd deceived myself. I'd certainly witnessed several incidents where Adama was mischievous, inattentive, or badly behaved, including one major meltdown. I was not present or aware on any of the occasions when Bronx 1 staff called 911 and had him removed.* Moreover, Adama was not the only difficult child in a given classroom, nor on any given day even the most obvious behavior problem. I observed Success Academy staff working hard not to exclude Adama and other "outlier" children, but to ensure they were engaged, encouraged, and included—and that parents were informed of even minor behavioral issues as they arose. My impression was that his second-grade class pierced the veneer of perfection outsiders associated with Success Academy. With its rotating cast of teachers, a significant number of children with behavior problems, and, at least in the first months of the year, a

---

* Calling 911 in response to student behavior problems has a long and complicated history in New York City, in both traditional public schools and charters alike. In 2014, the city signed a settlement with eleven families who alleged their children were sent to hospital emergency rooms as a form of discipline, despite there being no medical emergency. Legal Services NYC, where Nelson Mar is an attorney, had documented approximately three thousand cases per year of children being removed from schools following 911 calls. Under the terms of the settlement, the city agreed to stop calling 911 as a form of discipline and to adopt guidelines for schools to use to de-escalate a crisis. At Success Academy, staff are instructed to call Emergency Medical Services "if there is a medical emergency, or if a student or adult is in danger." According to spokesperson Ann Powell, "Staff makes every reasonable attempt to de-escalate students in crisis," but if the situation rises to the level of risking the safety of the scholar or others, staff are instructed to call 911. "Throwing chairs and desks in a way that could injure another student or a student assailing another student or a staff member are examples when EMS would be called," Powell explained to me.

teacher who struggled to maintain basic order, it looked and felt the most like classrooms I'd seen while teaching in a public school in the same neighborhood. It was the primary reason I kept coming back: to see firsthand how Success Academy handled disruptive students, which, as nearly any teacher will attest, is perhaps the steepest challenge facing schools with large numbers of students growing up in poverty.

If Success Academy is a Rorschach test, revealing or challenging our preconceived notions about the education we offer to our least advantaged children, this is the final exam: A single disruptive child can bring a classroom to a halt. Put three or four such children in a single room and even minor misbehaviors can have a cascading effect, bleeding away a teacher's time and attention and student learning. When multiple children with serious behavior problems share a classroom, a level of disorder can ensue that tests the patience and skill of all but the most gifted teachers. When those behaviors become common across classes and grades, an entire school groans under its weight. Disruptive behavior becomes assumed, even normalized, exerting a gravitational pull that comes to define a dysfunctional school and undermines learning for everyone. One of the most significant moral accomplishments of the education reform era is that it has become unacceptable to hold low-income students and children of color to lower academic standards—the "soft bigotry of low expectations" famously condemned by President George W. Bush.[8] But the same soft bigotry applies no less to student behavior. When disruptive behavior comes to define a school's culture, it is impossible to overstate how damaging it can be to teaching and learning. The effect is cancerous.

In my second year of teaching, I had a student I'll call Natalie, one of the most magnetic and intelligent children I've ever known. She was also fragile and emotionally unstable, and on her worst days, a danger to herself and others. Natalie and her twin sister were larger-than-life figures at my school. Foster children prone to volcanic fits of temper, angry attention-seeking outbursts, and physical aggression, they intimidated adults in the building, including me.

Someone decided that what Natalie really needed was a male authority figure—a phrase I soon learned to view with alarm—which is how she ended up in my classroom. Except for days when she was absent, which were frequent, my de facto classroom model that year was 23:1:1. Twenty-three students, Natalie, and me. I planned lessons specifically to engage and interest her, or at least distract and occupy her. Small-group instruction and class projects became nearly impossible. If she was not the object of my attention at nearly all times, Natalie would *make* herself the object of my attention.

Writing was one activity that she enjoyed and did independently, and which occupied her for long stretches of time; I still have several of Natalie's journal entries and essays, including ones she wrote about her chaotic family life, which contributed to her poor behavior in school. When my principal's mentor, a kindly retired school administrator, saw her acting out in the cafeteria one afternoon, he was appalled and insisted that she belonged in an alternative setting. My response was fierce and paternal. If we can't save Natalie—I clearly remember using the word "save"—with her brains and talent, we should all just go home. She remained in my class. The day she found out she would not be going back to live with her father, we wept together in the hallway. Natalie had become my personal project and fed my sense that I was not just a competent teacher but also a caring and empathetic one. She remained a handful, but I learned how to reach and teach her.

Another girl in my class that year was Tiffany, the earnest and dutiful "not your problem" child I described at the outset of this book; the girl I was functionally ordered to ignore.

If one wants to argue that the problem in the classroom was me—that a competent teacher should be able to meet the needs of every child under his care—I will not argue strenuously in my own defense. But I will ask whether my experience is closer to the exception or the norm, and how many of the nation's 3.7 million teachers are able to adequately deal with the disparate skill levels and range of challenging behaviors present in a given classroom— particularly one where a disproportionate number children come bearing the weight of poverty, family instability, racism, and other ills and dysfunction that exist far beyond a school's walls and a teacher's control.

When a school or teacher fails to engage or manage disruptive behavior, children are cheated. But who, exactly? The disruptive child who is suspended and excluded from class? Or the diligent student whose education bleeds away hour after hour while her teacher responds to antisocial outbursts or focuses on her classmate to prevent them? The weight of education policy and practice, as enshrined in impulse, empathy, and the law, comes down on the side of the disruptive child. But not at Success Academy.

With its exacting school culture, Success Academy has set itself defiantly in opposition to current fashion in education; nowhere is that more visible than in the network's rejection of "restorative justice" in student disciplinary practice. A response to decades of zero-tolerance discipline and justifiable fears that learning time lost to suspensions creates a school-to-prison pipeline, as well as data demonstrating that African American boys in particular face disciplinary measures disproportionate in number and severity, restorative-justice practice aims to reduce forms of exclusionary discipline, instead favoring measures that "allow individuals who may have committed harm to take full responsibility for their behavior" by acknowledging harm done to others, making amends, and committing to avoiding the harmful behavior in the future.[9]

In a blistering 2015 op-ed in the *Wall Street Journal* titled "Turning Schools into Fight Clubs,"[10] Eva Moskowitz attacked a proposed disciplinary code promoted by New York City mayor Bill de Blasio. "The code is full of edu-babble," including "'restorative circles,' . . . a 'community process for supporting those in conflict [that] brings together the three parties to a conflict—those who have acted, those directly impacted and the wider community—within an intentional systemic context, to dialogue as equals.' This is nonsense," Moskowitz wrote. "If student A 'impacts' student B with a fist, they shouldn't 'dialogue as equals.' Student A should be disciplined."

Her refusal to make even polite noises at fashionable trends in education drives academics, advocates, and education policy wonks to fits, but it's bracing for parents for whom a good school is a safe school. Moskowitz is unyielding on suspensions as a tool for maintaining behavioral expectations and as a nonnegotiable condition of academic purpose and seriousness. "Suspensions convey the critical message to students and parents that certain behavior is inconsistent with being a member of the school community," she continued. "Proponents of lax discipline claim it would benefit minority students, who are suspended at higher rates than their white peers. But minority students are also the most likely to suffer the adverse consequences of lax discipline—that is, their education is disrupted by a chaotic school environment or by violence."

It is difficult to disagree without indulging in hypocrisy. There was never a day during my daughter's K–12 education that I did not take for granted that she was safe, or that her schools would be anything other than orderly and academically purposeful. In contrast, the parents in Mott Haven, where I taught, and in countless similar schools throughout New York City and the United States, have likely never known a day when they could take that as a given—a situation that would drive many well-off parents to madness. Or to their lawyers. School discipline remains a fraught and delicate issue, but the emphasis in US education at present is to weigh its impact almost exclusively through its effect on the disciplined student, not the far larger number of students who lose learning time to disruptive behavior. Refusing to follow suit is Moskowitz's line in the sand. It seems inconceivable that it will ever change as long as she runs Success Academy.

—

A few years ago, on a cold, early-winter morning, I was on my way to Democracy Prep Charter High School, where I was teaching a civics seminar to the seniors. A voice called out, "Mr. P. *Mr. P!*" It was Natalie. She was pushing a stroller and had another kid in tow—two of the four children she now had, at age twenty-two. She had dropped out of school in tenth grade.

A few days later I sat with her and her children at a nearby IHOP and urged her to enter the charter school lottery for her oldest boy. Her first choice, I told her, should be Success Academy. A few weeks later, over the holidays, Natalie sent me a text asking if I could help her buy a Christmas tree, holiday dinner, and presents for her kids. I asked her how much she needed. Five hundred dollars, she replied. The next day, I met her on the corner of Park Avenue and 125th Street, withdrew the money from my savings account, and handed it over. On Christmas morning, she texted to wish my family a Merry Christmas. "The kids are ecstatic," she said. "I can't thank u enough."

I don't know if she entered her son in the lottery for Success Academy or any of the other schools I recommended. My texts went unanswered; Natalie was gone again.

———

You want this to be simple. To be clear and morally uncomplicated. You want the stories we tell about public education—especially for the poor and the poorly served—to be bracing and edifying, tales of determined teachers, high expectations, tough love, and muscular accountability that elevate every child. Put those things under one roof and reap the benefit—equity, excellence, and upward mobility. It's not simple. It will never be simple. We cannot wash our hands of Natalie. Neither can we say Tiffany will be fine or blithely tell her teacher that "she's not your problem." The homilies of education and education reform do not apply. We must see things as they are, not as we wish them to be.

I am in no better position today than I was as an inexperienced fifth-grade teacher to say which child deserved more of my time or to weigh fully the cost of how my time was spent. Neither am I in a position to referee the painful dispute between Adama's family and Success Academy. I can, however, report what I observed and offer

my perspective as someone who has taught in classrooms with significant numbers of behavior challenges and special-needs children.
By the standards of the elementary school where I taught for several
years, much of the noncompliant behavior I witnessed from Adama
and other outlier scholars did not seem unusual; it was often well
within the range of what I saw almost daily in the neighborhood
public school where I taught. By the standards of Success Academy
and Bronx 1, however, those misbehaviors seemed outsize. Over
time, school culture shapes your responses to student misbehavior.
My old school was rife with Adamas. At Bronx 1, he was an outlier.
This seems a point worth dwelling on.

One of my clearest memories of my first months as a teacher was
an oppressive sense that my students' behavior was a referendum on
my competence, reinforced by unhelpful advice that kids are disruptive when they're bored and disengaged. Like every new teacher,
I struggled with classroom management. On bad days, I felt close to
a panic over it. I'd never experienced anything quite like the terror
of escalating misbehaviors, a classroom spiraling out of control, a
student calling out, "Do something, Mr. P!" and not knowing what
to do. In my first months as a teacher, I went to my administration
for help with one particularly difficult and defiant child who had
instigated several fights. An assistant principal chastised me, saying,
"This isn't your daughter's private school." My principal advised me
to consult with his previous year's teacher, since she didn't have any
problems with the child who was tearing apart my classroom and
turning my days into a waking nightmare.

It was an eye-opening conversation. The boy had behaved no
differently in her room than in mine. Why had she never sought help
from the administration? "Why would I?" she replied, acidly. "It's
not like they'd do anything about it." I got the message: the cavalry
isn't coming. It took a concerted effort, voluminous paperwork, and
dozens of written "anecdotal records," daily documentation of
every incident of misbehavior and the steps I took to address it,
before the boy was placed in a more restrictive special education
classroom in another school.

Walk into an elite private school or an affluent suburban school and poll the staff on who are the best teachers in the building. The list will likely consist mostly of those who have the best command of their subject matter and are passionate about sharing it with children and successful in firing their imaginations. In a high poverty school, the list might very well be the ones with exceptional "control" of their class. "Good classroom management" is too often synonymous with "good teaching." When there are high expectations and clear behavioral norms in place and disruption is the exception, teaching is a significantly different act. Success Academy operates at the nexus of these two impulses: high expectations for behavior *and* academics. Behavioral norms are clear, consistent, and aggressively messaged and monitored. There is a palpable pressure, both external and self-directed, to keep children focused and on task. I cannot discount the possibility that it causes inexperienced teachers and administrators to be overzealous in responding to misbehavior that by the standards of other schools might not merit much attention at all. It is easy to perceive this as a systematic effort to shed outlier children who are not up to the standards of conduct and performance. And maybe it is. The possibility cannot be dismissed. The administrative focus on outlier scholars, in evidence from the very first days of school, and instructions to teachers to identify them and "manage up," could be interpreted either as the first step to bring those kids into the fold or toward encouraging their parents to withdraw them and harassing them into doing so.

What also cannot be denied, however, is that the kind of focused and intentional culture that Success Academy works so hard to maintain is a standard feature, even a defining one, of private schools, gifted and talented programs, and public schools in affluent communities. Eva Moskowitz, nearly alone among major education reform figures, has the standing and backbone to come down emphatically on the side of students and parents who favor safe schools and strict discipline. "I've heard her say, 'What do you say to a conservative churchgoing woman whose granddaughter is in class with an emotionally disturbed child who has shouted at her, "Suck my dick!"'" recalled one New York City charter school leader who has crossed swords with Moskowitz but admires her willingness to take heat for her uncompromising views.[11] "You can't give that grandmother the pabulum about the need for equality and how suspensions don't work." That stance exposes the hypocrisy among elites and reformers who would never abide disruptive children in the schools their own children attend. "We had a kid like that in my daughter's school," he observed. "After two months of parents besieging the principal, that kid was gone."

Whether children leave charter schools by means fair or foul, by choice or coercion, the fact remains that they must go to school somewhere. Teachers and administrators in neighborhood public schools complain that their schools are a dumping ground for children in need of special education services that charter schools cannot or will not serve. It's not a baseless complaint. A significant tension between public schools and charter schools is the question of who bears the cost and responsibility for the hardest-to-teach students. On the one hand, it is demonstrably incorrect to say that public schools "educate all children." Even the wealthiest public schools routinely approve "out of district" placements for some students at public expense when a disability is serious, when the cost of servicing them in-house can't be justified, or simply to mollify pushy parents and their attorneys seeking a private school placement for a child with a learning disability. "The parents come in armed with lawyers, and they say, 'This is what we want, and you need to do this, or we are going to sue you,'" explains the former head of a major suburban school district. "You make a cost-benefit calculation. Am I going to spend the money on legal fees? Are people going to support me? Or am I just going to write the check and send the kid out of district?" When a charter school tells a parent that they do not offer services a child needs, or an appropriate setting, it is impossible to tell objectively if that is earnest advice offered in the child's best interest or an attempt to "counsel out" a challenging student, making that child the district's problem and its cost to bear.

The more challenging question is the moral one: If a child is seriously disruptive, whose interests should we prioritize? The one who needs extra attention and resources to succeed? Or his classmates, whose class time is reduced by his issues and outbursts? It is difficult to overstate how common this dilemma is in schools serving almost entirely low-income children—and how rarely it goes unresolved in schools where affluent Americans send their children.

CHAPTER 24

The "Likely" List

THE METAL DETECTOR WAS THE FIRST THING AYAN WILSON noticed. It made an indelible impression on her when she visited the neighborhood school where she was supposed to send her children. Born in Somalia and raised in Canada, Wilson came to the United States in 2003 with her husband. A few years later, when her first child, her daughter, Leah, was approaching school age, Wilson visited PS 29, her zoned DOE school a few blocks from her home. It left her shaken and unnerved. "Cops. Security. Metal detectors. Like you're going to the airport," she recalls. Her voice goes up an octave. "I'm like, Who goes here? *Jeffrey Dahmer?*" Wilson had never seen anything like it in Canada. "I was like, 'No.' I don't even know what their test scores were. I didn't even care." We're sitting at the kitchen table in her basement apartment on Melrose Avenue, halfway between Bronx 1 and Yankee Stadium. Wilson grows even more agitated. "Do you know what the security lady told me? She said, 'Don't put your kid here. *Don't you dare!*'"

Wilson had attended Catholic school, so she enrolled Leah in

Saints Peter and Paul, a nearby K–8 Catholic school. "It was hor-
rendous," she said. "It had no metal detectors, but they really didn't
do anything for her." Leah had difficulty sitting still and paying
attention; she ended up spending a lot of time out of the classroom.
"They would just put her in a corner or send her to the administrative office. She'd just sit there while everybody else was learning,"
Wilson says. Worse, she didn't even find out her daughter was
missing class time because of behavior problems until the end of the
year, when the school staff told Wilson they wanted her daughter to
repeat kindergarten. She enrolled her in Bronx Global Learning Institute for Girls, a charter school down the block, where Leah, now
in middle school, began doing much better once they suggested that
she be evaluated for attention deficit disorder. Wilson faults herself
for not being more aware of her daughter's early struggles. "She was
my first, so I didn't really know about hyperactivity or attention
deficit disorder or anything. I didn't ask the right questions, and I
didn't know the right course of action," she says. Wilson enrolled
Leah most summers in a supplementary reading program at
Fordham University. She is still about a half year behind, but has
closed the gap considerably. "I just want her to keep improving," she
says. "She's a work in progress, but she's doing very good."

Lesson learned. Her daughter's rocky start prompted Wilson to
do her homework when her son, Darren, approached school age.
She entered the lotteries for KIPP and Success Academy. "I didn't
care which one. I just knew that they were the top schools." She researched both. "I know they had a lot of positives and negatives,
especially Success," she tells me. Darren ended up on the "likely"
list for Bronx 1, and his mother ended up in the audience at Shea
Reeder's welcome meeting.

Reeder's talk left her excited about Success but also appre-
hensive. "Just sitting and listening to them, you can clearly see that
they're really strict," Wilson said. Darren is a bright, active, and
talkative little boy. He climbs all over his mom while we talk.
Reeder, she admits, "scared me a little bit. Because every child is
not . . ." She doesn't complete the thought, but her meaning is clear.

Would her son even fit in? She describes both her children as "independent" and "hardheaded." Even though she worries about how Darren would adapt, she likes what she heard. "I like structure. Just like everybody else—any normal parent, anyway," she says. "I want them to sleep at this time, I want them to get up at this time."

Wilson opens her laptop and shows me her "enrollment dashboard," where she tracks Darren's progress through the admissions process. "Step one is look at my account. Step two, lottery results. Step three, welcome meeting," she reads from left to right across the top of the screen. "Step four is 'confirm your interest.'" A check mark indicates that she's completed each of the required steps and that her application remains active and up to date. The next step is a mandatory uniform fitting, at 1:30 p.m. on Saturday at Bronx 1. A large orange-and-blue "Reschedule My Meeting" button gives her the option to choose an alternative date if she can't make the one she's been assigned. Below that is a long list of the documents she needs to provide before Darren can enroll. "It's part of the steps. If you don't do these, you will not be called," Wilson explains. "Birth certificate, proof of address, health exam? All those things had to be done prior." To be clear: Wilson's son has not even been offered a seat; he remains on the "likely" list. But she's still required to complete all the steps and bring her son to the uniform fitting to maintain her "active" status.

After a decade managing the front desk at a Starwood hotel in Manhattan, Wilson recently gave her notice. She's opening up a day care facility in her home. She already has half a dozen parents signed up. Compared with the paperwork and regulatory hurdles she has to clear to become a licensed day care provider, Success Academy's enrollment process does not feel burdensome to Wilson, who holds a bachelor's degree from Monroe College in the Bronx and worked as an executive secretary for the New York City Department of Health and Mental Hygiene before entering the hospitality industry ten years ago.

She shows me the rest of the dashboard. Parents on the "likely" list are instructed to check regularly for updated lottery results. And even though their children have not been admitted, they are told to "read at least one book with your child every night and record it on his/her reading log."

It's getting late. Darren has had his bath and exhausted his big sister's patience; he is eager for his mother's attention. He has been accepted in other local charter schools, but after looking at test scores and reading online reviews, Wilson decided against all of them. "Some of the ones where he got accepted were either starting this year or new. I don't want him to be a guinea pig," she explains. If he doesn't get off the waitlist for Bronx 1, she will enroll Darren in a neighborhood public school in the same building as his sister's charter school, Bronx Global Learning Institute for Girls. There are no metal detectors. "It's actually a really good school. The only problem is that it only goes up to fifth grade," she says. "So I don't want to be stuck after fifth grade and not know where he needs to go next. If I get Success, I will put him in Success." She admits, "I'm scared, but I will put him in Success."

Darren is number seventeen on the "likely" list. There's no way of knowing how realistic his chances are, which Wilson finds frustrating, but she remains hopeful. "It's almost like they're dangling something in front of you. You know what I mean?" I tell Wilson that I'll see if I can find out what "likely" actually means.

The next day, I ask Jen Fuoco about Ayan Wilson's chances of getting her boy off the waitlist. She doesn't know. Enrollment is handled entirely by the network until the new class of kindergarteners comes in for a dress rehearsal just prior to the start of the term. She suggests I call the network office, but I decide not to pursue it. Number seventeen seems like a long shot in a kindergarten class of ninety. My gut tells me that I already know the answer.

The following Saturday afternoon, a monsoon rain pelts the South Bronx. Cars disgorge small children and parents who sprint forty yards from the curb through the courtyard of Bronx 1. By the time they reach the safety of the overhang at the front entrance, it looks as if someone has opened a hose on them. Families who have been admitted to Success Academy for the fall, as well as those who remain in the purgatory of the "likely" list, are braving the deluge for the mandatory uniform-fitting day. Shaking out umbrellas and shedding soaked jackets, parents line up at a table in the cafeteria covered by a bright orange banner. They sign in by their child's last name and wait to be called. Representatives from FlynnO'Hara Uniforms measure boys and girls for pants, polo shirts, jumpers, and cardigans, adding one size for every item. "We kinda figure they'll grow up a size over the summer," says Jim Everett, the genial sales rep for the Philadelphia-based company, which landed Success as a client in the network's second year of existence, when Harlem 1 was its only school. Success is now the company's biggest account. Children in their distinctive Success Academy orange polo shirts and plaid jumpers are ubiquitous on New York City streets and subways. A full girl's uniform—jumper, short- and long-sleeved polo shirts, cardigan, and backpack—runs $242 with shoes; a boy's costs $206; the jumper accounts for most of the price difference. Shoes and socks are an optional purchase; compliance with the school's dress code is not. "It's a big outlay initially, but over the course of a year, you'd be spending that much easily on school clothes," adds Everett, who sounds used to defending the cost of his wares. The uniforms are guaranteed for a year but wear like iron. Families hand them down to younger siblings or pass them on to other parents as their kids grow out of them.

Success gives the poorest families vouchers to cover a substantial amount of the price. On top of their order forms is a capital letter "V" and a dollar amount, indicating the value of a voucher they have received to defray the cost. If a parent has three children at Success, the third uniform is free, but every family is expected to pay at least something. "There are instances where we will 'comp' a uniform—obviously if a parent is not working and can't put any money in," explains Jessie Diaz, senior manager of parent engagement, whom I first met at the Bronx 1 open house on Groundhog

Day. An upbeat young woman in a bright green dress, she is shepherding parents from station to station. After measurements are taken, admitted parents and children shuffle off to the next table with their completed order forms to pay. For families in "likely" list limbo, measurement is the last stop. There's no point in wait-listed families shelling out for a uniform until they know for sure that the bottom of a $45 pair of pants will be matched to a Success Academy seat come August. So why bother making wait-listed families attend the fitting at all? Diaz explains that it's for compliance. "We want to make sure that 100 percent of our students are in full uniforms the first day of school. If we have parents do it on their own, they're going to take their own time." If a family makes it off the "likely" list right before school starts or a few weeks into the year, the uniform can be ordered right away. "Waitlist pulls" happen past Thanksgiving. If a child's number comes up, the family can call FlynnO'Hara, which will have the child's measurement on file and expedite delivery.

Uniform-fitting day is also another step in the process, largely unspoken but well understood, whereby Success Academy ensures that every seat goes to a fully committed family. "If parents don't show, if they don't come to their reschedule [an alternative uniform-fitting day], if they don't call us and let us know, we move to the next child on the waitlist," Diaz says, adding that it would be unfair to families hoping for a seat if an expected student simply failed to materialize on the first day of school. Like every other step on the enrollment dashboard Ayan Wilson showed me at her kitchen table, it's another de facto screen for parental engagement, organization, and follow-through. Whether by design or happenstance, the multiple steps required of parents—attendance at the welcome meeting, the "confirm your interest" email, the uniform fitting—test their ability to show up, follow up, and stay on top of things.

As the fitting winds down, a teenage girl in a white hoodie with a child's tiny pink umbrella hooked over her arm approaches Diaz shyly. She introduces her mother, who speaks no English. Her sister is wait-listed at Shea Reeder's elementary school, Bronx 4. The girl in the hoodie translates, switching between English and a language I do not recognize. Most of what I can hear is Diaz's side of the conversation. "I can't guarantee that," she explains, "but the numbers move about every three weeks. The next waitlist pull is July 8." The mother's expression darkens; she grows agitated as the conversation continues. "No, the school she's likely for is Bronx 4," Diaz says, then, "I'll keep my fingers crossed." Finally, the girl asks, "Do you have a high school?" She's asking for herself. "We do," Diaz answers, "but we only accept kids from K–4, and then middle school and high school is for those kids."

Diaz tells them, "Don't lose hope," then turns and walks back to where she left me standing by the payment table, her jaw set. "That's a tough conversation to have," she says once the family is out of earshot. "The little girl is number seventy-eight right now. They were originally one hundred and forty-two, so they've moved halfway. But," her voice drops, "it's hard." It's unclear whether she's referring to the child's chances or giving disappointing news to the family.

I summon up the courage to ask on Ayan Wilson's behalf the question I've been avoiding: How likely is "likely"? Does her son, Darren, have a puncher's chance to get into Bronx 1? Diaz asks me for Ayan's name; after calling up data on her iPhone, she nods. Darren has moved up to number nine. "That's good," she says. Then she says something astounding. "She was originally number one hundred and six." Certain I've misheard, I ask her to repeat it. But there is no mistake. From 106 to 17 and now 9—Ayan Wilson's son has moved up more than *ninety slots* since the April lottery. It seems impossible.

There have been two waitlist pulls since the April lottery, and it's difficult to generalize or guess how deep into the waitlist any individual Success Academy school needs to go to fill every seat. The biggest falloff occurs in the first few weeks after the lottery. Some families might decide after the welcome meeting that they're not a good fit; some don't show up or they accept a seat at another school. People move. Plans change.

Neither are all waitlist numbers the same. A child who is number seventy for kindergarten may have a better chance than a kid with a single-digit number for third grade. Enrollment patterns also vary from school to school—a function of the quality of a neighborhood's public schools and the availability of other charter schools. Enrollment staff hints that "bad press" also plays a role in determining a child's chance to get off the "likely" list. The past few years have seen a number of broadside media hits to Success Academy's reputation: the now-infamous Charlotte Dial video[1] and "Got to Go" stories in the *New York Times*[2] and a PBS *NewsHour* piece questioning whether kindergarten is too young to suspend children from school.[3] "Bad press doesn't affect us so much here in the Bronx," Diaz says. Not only are the alternatives generally poor, but also "a lot of parents like the discipline. That's how they grew up." Schools such as Cobble Hill, where the Charlotte Dial video was made, are different. Cobble Hill has more "progressive" families, Diaz explains, suggesting that parental compliance demands and strict discipline don't play as well in trendy Brooklyn neighborhoods. On the other hand, the network's Upper West Side school, in a similarly upscale neighborhood, is the hardest to get into even for in-district parents.

Uniform fitting is over. Diaz goes off to pack up boxes and collect folders, order forms, and signage. The FlynnO'Hara reps, with no kids left to measure, break down their displays. Outside, it's raining even harder. On my way out, I see the Bronx 4 "likely" family standing under the overhang staring out into the rain. The little girl fidgets and twirls her umbrella. The teenager and her mother look miserable.

———

On July 8, there's a waitlist pull. Ayan Wilson's son moves from ninth on the "likely" list to sixth. Three weeks later, with the school year just weeks away, there's another round.

Darren is number five.

CHAPTER 25

Lessons Learned

I CAME TO SUCCESS ACADEMY TO SEE IF I COULD LEARN HOW IT has succeeded where so many have failed.

Guided by a single question—what do the kids do all day?—I expected to find a story about curriculum and instruction. If there was an explanation for how Success Academy has managed to achieve its exceptional—and exceptionally consistent—results, surely it would reside in rigorous teaching and learning, strong school leadership, or both. But the more plausible story turned out to be school culture, the role it plays in driving student achievement, and the signals it sends to children about the value of education in their lives and even their place in American society. This is surprising and troubling. Surprising because while my year at Success Academy reaffirmed my sense that what children learn is a matter of great importance, I've come to believe that the school culture, conditions, and expectations under which they learn are ultimately of even greater importance. Troubling because "culture" is a third rail in education: to talk about culture, much less try to influence it, dredges up deep-seated questions, convictions, and grievances related to history, tradition, race, social justice, economic opportunity, and more. School culture is freighted, hard to define, harder to impose, and nearly impossible to shape through public policy.

The current era of education reform began with *A Nation at Risk*,[1] the 1983 report from a commission assembled by President Ronald Reagan. In a stirring and memorable piece of phrasemaking, the report warned darkly of a "rising tide of mediocrity" that was threatening America's future and noted, "If an unfriendly foreign power had attempted to impose on America the mediocre educational performance that exists today, we might well have viewed it as an act of war." The first charter school in the United States was still nearly a decade away when those words were written, and while few of the recommendations of the landmark report ended up being enacted,[2] it served its larger purpose, ratcheting up concern over the desultory state of American education. Nearly two decades later, Joel Greenblatt was pouring money into PS 65 in Queens, and Eva Moskowitz was still a New York City Council member when President George W. Bush signed No Child Left Behind into law, enshrining test-driven, standards-based education as the default setting for American schools.

When the authors and architects of the education reform movement issued their various calls to action, codified their ambitions into state and federal laws and policies, and launched an era whose principal levers for school improvement were higher academic standards, standardized testing, teacher accountability, and enhanced school choice and charter schools, they surely imagined that two decades into the twenty-first century, schools like Success Academy would be closer to the norm than the exception, in student outcomes if not in school design. This raises a pivotal question: Is Success Academy a proof point that the reform playbook works and that professionally run schools with high standards and even higher expectations can set any child on a path out of poverty? Or does the rarity of Moskowitz's accomplishment suggest that however nobly intended it might have been, the reform impulse was doomed from the start? Perhaps the hurdles to overcome generational poverty are so complex and daunting—so many social and historical factors; so much beyond a school's sphere of influence—that only the rarest and most precise blend of conditions under a demanding and visionary leader is sufficient, making Success Academy not a blueprint to follow but something closer to a reverse perfect storm.

One lesson I draw from closely observing schools that appear to be succeeding where I and countless others have failed is that while it is obviously too much to expect schools to overcome every obstacle, it is certainly possible—to the degree that schools can do this at all—to put far more children than we do at present on a path to educational attainment and upward mobility. But there are things we know and do not say in education and education reform. One of them is that we expect too much of schools.

———

"Government cannot identify the worthy, but it can protect a society in which the worthy can identify themselves," observed Charles Murray in his 1984 book, *Losing Ground: American Social Policy, 1950–1980*.[3] If Murray's statement falls on the ears as too harsh and deterministic—an aspirational spirit makes us uncomfortable with the idea of schooling as a mere sorting mechanism—we must also recognize that aspiration is a poor substitute for rational policy-making and ask whether we have accidentally conspired to undermine the very outcomes to which we aspire. There is no moral reason for government at any level to prevent the children of engaged and invested Americans of any race, ethnic group, or income level from reaping the full rewards of their talents and ambitions, nor interfering with parents' best efforts to do what they deem best for their children. Yet the last several decades of education policy have set equity and excellence at war with each other. If you are wealthy, with the means to pay tuition or move to a community with great schools, you have ready access to excellence. If you are poor, black, or brown, you get equity and an impotent lecture: on fairness, on democracy, or, infuriatingly, on the need for patience and restraint.

The explicit end of much current education policy is raising academic achievement, measured principally through test scores. But if this end is disproportionately influenced by whom children go to school with and their parents' attitudes, beliefs, and commitment to education, it is a thorny issue for education policymakers to solve for. Even to suggest that school culture matters is significant or determinative—in this context meaning parental engagement, student motivation, and a focused and intentional effort to direct it by educators—violates the egalitarian impulses that undergird the education reform movement's lofty ideals and much current policy and practice. We may need to rethink nearly all of it.

By law, oversubscribed charter schools must admit students by lottery, which gives the appearance of a randomly selected, first-come, first-served student body. This, in turn, has helped create a halo effect over the best charter schools. Much of the support for them has been built on a narrative that holds that the same students attend traditional public schools and charters but achieve different outcomes based merely on which door they walk through each morning. This story is deeply satisfying to charter school advocates and anyone who wishes to believe that the best schools can overcome much of what takes place outside their walls. It is also misleading or even false. It removes student and parent engagement and ambition from the story line. The moment a parent in a district with struggling schools is motivated to enter a charter school lottery, she is distinguishing herself from her neighbor who bundles her child off to the neighborhood school, unaware or incurious about what else might be available. The simple act of volition at least suggests a nominally engaged family, dissatisfied or curious enough to at least explore other options.

Success Academy begins there and goes several steps further. It starts with the raw material of a self-selected group of mostly low-income parents who win a seat in the lottery, and then ensures and re-ensures multiple times prior to enrollment that they are sufficiently motivated, attentive, and organized to come to meetings, confirm their interest, get their children fitted for school uniforms, solve transportation logistics, and take other small but nontrivial steps, which test their commitment, motivation, and organizational skills, guaranteeing that the families who choose Success are walking in with their eyes wide open. The stage is now set to strive for—and mostly achieve—the most consistent and highest measurable academic achievement "at scale" among low-income children of color. That the sustained level of effort and engagement this requires proves too much for some parents and children to keep up with is undeniable. But the thousands of families who are buying what Success Academy is selling are served very well. More pertinent, under any other circumstances those families would likely not be encouraged or even permitted to band together to choose an academic program and school culture that works for the educational benefit of their children. What Eva Moskowitz appears to have created is something unprecedented in contemporary education: a mechanism for a critical mass of engaged and invested low-income families of color to self-select into schools where their attitudes, values, and ambitions for their children make them culture keepers and drivers, not outliers. The parental self-selection that occurs on the front end in no way diminishes the significance of Success Academy's outcomes, which compare favorably and even exceed New York City's gifted and talented schools, which actually *do* handpick their students, who are decidedly more advantaged socioeconomically.

—

Success Academy's outcomes may be remarkable. But are they transferable? Moskowitz concluded her 2017 memoir with a chapter titled "Extra Credit," which lists the features that she believes enable Success Academy to deliver the results that have made it an object of fascination. Some of her observations are anodyne, such as "management is key," which undersells the professionalism and level of detail with which her schools are run. She also defends some of her more controversial practices, such as student suspensions and large class sizes. At the end of my year at Success Academy, I asked Moskowitz how much of her model she believes could be exported broadly to American education. Her answer was "all of it." My best guess is less than that, but more than we might imagine. Success Academy is fundamentally a well-run shadow school district serving a small but significant percentage of New York City's 1.1 million schoolchildren. Its muscular adult culture and intense focus on test scores might be generally "replicable," but it would be impossible to make those features the default setting for every American school, or to get similar results even if we did so. You could not compel the level of parental support or compliance that Success demands and mostly appears to receive from its parents, and which contribute significantly to its school culture and outcomes.

If there is one instructional practice that is most transferable from Success Academy, it is this one: implementing a single curriculum across a school or district. American teachers spend an average of twelve hours per week gathering or generating instructional materials.[4] Those are hours *not* spent studying student work, developing questioning strategies, anticipating students' misunderstandings and challenges, working with individual children on their strengths and weaknesses, building relationships with parents, or any of dozens of other activities that are more valuable than spending hours on Google and Pinterest in search of lesson plans, or staring at an empty plan book and wondering, "What should I teach this week?" Lesson planning at Success Academy is "intellectual preparation." As the name implies, it means preparing to teach a lesson or unit, not creating one from scratch. It enables even relatively inexperienced teachers to achieve good results quickly without reducing them to automatons.

A common misconception is that Success Academy's curriculum is "scripted." Teachers do not read their lines from prepared scripts, but working from an established curriculum and lesson sequences, typically prepared by network-level staff, changes the teacher's role significantly. Most schools tend to expect teachers to be both curriculum designers and deliverers. To do either one of these tasks well is challenging. To do both expertly is simply too much to ask of all but a vanishingly small number of the nation's nearly four million classroom teachers. Success Academy's model asks teachers to focus on *teaching*, not on creating curriculum or gathering instructional resources. This frees up hours of capacity for teachers to look at data, to study student work, and to act, adapt, and intervene quickly when students are struggling or falling behind.

While it has been subject to intense criticism, Success Academy's focus on monitoring and shaping student behavior contributes to academic outcomes, too. If you see only children locking their hands, tracking the teacher, and walking through the halls in two straight lines, you fail to see that those things are in the service of maximizing attention and time spent on task. Here again, however, it must be acknowledged that it is not possible or desirable to impose this school culture or style of teaching on those who do not willingly embrace it, whether it's teachers, students, or parents.

For many years, our hopes for improving educational outcomes at scale in K–12 education have rested largely on attempts to improve teacher quality and effectiveness through various mechanisms, including merit pay, raising the bar for entry into the profession, and an aggressive test-driven accountability aimed at identifying the least effective teachers and either improving their performance through coaching and professional development or counseling them to exit the profession. The unavoidable fact is that if nearly four million people do any job, there will always be a broad range of talent and ability. There are not, and never will be, enough classroom saints and superstars to ensure that every American child will have one, an insight that Joel Greenblatt and John Petry arrived at even before hiring Moskowitz to run Success Academy. We already spend more money per pupil to educate our children than nearly all other Organization for Economic Cooperation and Development nations.[5] It is fantasy to think that teacher salaries can ever be generous enough to draw the cognitively elite away from other, more remunerative professions in large numbers. At scale, teaching *must* be a job that can be done well and competently by people of average sentience and talent. That is who we have in our classrooms and *all we are likely ever to have.*

Some aspects of Success Academy's model are obviously not universally applicable, notably the parental self-selection and the effects of building a clear (some will say rigid) high-expectation culture around families who are invested in those values. Neither could Success Academy's no-backfill policy after fourth grade be universally applied. One former Success Academy administrator notes that if the same expectations were present in every school in the country, then those conditions would become the default setting for all schools. It's a fair point, but a fanciful one. While there is a demand for that culture and rigor among a significant subset of parents, for many others it is unacceptably strict, burdensome, paternalistic, or simply in conflict with their tastes. This acts as a speed limit, ensuring the model cannot be imposed on families who do not willingly sign up for it. However, a comprehensive and equitable system of public education does not require that every school be exactly the same; it requires an ecosystem of schools that collectively can serve the need of every child. If you accept the idea that families at all income levels ought to have some choice in who educates their children—and not everyone does—then it is unfair to deny families who want the kind of education and culture Success Academy offers from having access to it. Genuine education equity will be achieved only when schools serving low-income children mirror in number, variety, and access the options that affluent parents have come to expect for their children. This alone could increase the likelihood of "culture matches" among larger numbers of schools and families, with beneficial effects for both.

Finally, there is Eva Moskowitz herself. The reliably high level of student outcomes she has achieved across dozens of schools is an accomplishment that is without precedent in American education. She is without question a prodigiously gifted leader who has built and maintained a coherent vision across her network. Eva Moskowitz is not "scalable." Watching her closely and steeping myself in the kind of education she offers has convinced me that she could easily run a mid-size corporation successfully, and I would buy stock the day she was hired. However, if you put her in charge of a large public school district, in Atlanta or Baltimore, for example, she might do well by the standards of such places. But the results would likely pale in comparison with what she's engineered at Success Academy, which she runs more like a corporation than a school district, controlling to the maximum amount possible its product, employees, brand, and, yes, its customers. A large public school district has too many moving parts for even the most talented and dynamic leader to impose her vision and will, or to make it stick for long.

———

Success Academy's most important lesson may be about repairing the strained relationship between low-income families of color and the school system. The lesson is that we can make this relationship fruitful, if not for every disadvantaged child—schools don't "work" for every privileged child, either—then for geometrically more than we do at present. But this is possible only if we are clear-eyed and candid about what it takes and willing to be guided by pragmatism rather than by aspiration and idealism. That lesson is unambiguous: culture matters. But it cannot be imposed. If a government takes its legitimacy from the consent of the governed, so does a school. The full benefit and effect is obtained only when all parties involved share a common vision, entered voluntarily and by choice.

There is no one correct way to educate children. Any pedagogy reaches its fullest expression and maximum effectiveness when children learn within a school culture that supports it, particularly when it's reinforced by all the adults in a child's life, in school and at home. If the culture of any organization is defined as "how we do things here," Success Academy students cannot fail to get the message that working hard, getting good grades, and following certain behavioral norms is how things are done. What makes Success different from other schools that mostly serve low-income families is a muscular adult culture that is well understood not just in its schools but beyond: the reach of its expectations and norms extend deep into students' homes and lives. "This is how we do things here," Success Academy functionally tells parents, *and so will you.* It is not possible—or desirable—to impose a school's "culture demands" on parents who are unwilling or unable to comply.

Again, culture is a fraught topic, in both education and in American society at large. Many educators, policymakers, and parents are deeply uncomfortable with a vision of schooling that seeks to impose a set of values on children. But schools are not values-neutral. Nearly every aspect of a child's schooling is a manifestation of *someone's* values. From curriculum, pedagogy, and discipline practices to whether children are expected to say "please" and "thank you" to cafeteria workers, it all reflects norms and values that may or may not align with those of every family in a given community. In many schools, perhaps most, those values can vary wildly from room to room. At Success Academy, adults speak with one voice. One need not value or agree with the school-culture demands it places on children, but their effect is unmistakable. Color-coded behavior charts, codes of conduct, data walls with children's reading levels, and "effort parties" to which a child is either invited or excluded leave no room for doubt about what is expected, praised, or frowned upon.

If behavior management for its own sake were the alpha and omega of Success Academy's culture and curriculum—behavior management for its own sake; student compliance and performance on full public display—then Moskowitz would deserve the scorn from her many and voluble critics. But superficial critiques of Success Academy's routines—tracking the teacher, sitting in Magic Five—overlook the warmth, joy, and investment in children displayed by teachers and staff. Classroom culture mirrors parenting styles; no one suggests that "tough love" parents don't love their children. The best teachers everywhere care deeply for their students. But that caring is the starting line, not the finish line. The payoff is academic performance and is most conspicuous when students prepare and sit for state tests.

We can debate endlessly, and to no one's satisfaction, whether earning a high score on a standardized test is an appropriate focus of public education; however, tests are a condition imposed on every public school in the country in the name of public stewardship and accountability. At Success Academy, a student's experience of a place called school is to be surrounded by adults who seem deeply invested in him and his test scores. You get pushed and encouraged with "attack strategies," positive reinforcement, and, yes, a megadose of test prep. There are phone calls from your teacher, often nightly; handwritten notes of encouragement from your principal or your teacher from last year; and pep rallies, prizes, and effort parties. No attempt is made to suggest that the bar is low and the test is easy. It is quite the opposite. The bar is *high.* You are given a challenging task by supportive adults, pushed, prodded, cajoled for months, and told, "You can do this!"

And then *you actually do it.*

Consider for a moment how this experience must feel to a low-income child of color: You have been the obsessive focus for months of every adult in your school. You earn a test score that not just your teachers, parents, and friends, but also your state, says equals or exceeds those of children anywhere in the state—an externally validated outcome affirming that you are the equal of any of your peers, rich or poor; black, white, or brown. Even more powerfully, you are part of a school community where nearly all your friends do just as well as you, and all your friends' parents value education every bit as much as your own do. Very little in the history, experience, or memory of low-income African American or Hispanic families in this country would lead one to expect this level of investment, this consistency of achievement, or this outcome. It's not possible to overstate the astonishing normalizing power of this school culture or the degree to which it is at odds with the experience of the majority of low-income children of color in the United States of America of a place called a school.

One cannot be blithe about it, or cynical.

Critics will immediately seize on this and protest that this isn't so. Not every child is successful at Success Academy. This is a substantial and important critique. But not every child is successful at an elite private school or the best-resourced school in our most affluent neighborhoods either. If we define a good school as one that serves all children equally well and effectively, we might as well concede there is no such thing as a good school and never will be.

———

What surprised me most, and I suspect will surprise others, is how far Success Academy reaches into its waitlist to fill its seats. It defies conventional wisdom, the standard education reform narrative, and the story Success Academy tells about itself. A charter school that produces such exemplary results, with six applicants for every seat, is surely one that parents would kill to enroll their children in. I did not appreciate the winnowing effect that the enrollment process has on prospective families to ensure a "culture match."

Recall that at the April lottery, director of enrollment Holly Saso noted in passing that of the seventeen thousand families who had entered, roughly three thousand would be immediately offered seats while about "six or seven thousand" would be deemed unlikely to be enrolled. The remainder would be notified that they were on the "likely" list. Simple subtraction suggests that seven thousand to eight thousand families who did not win a slot outright still had a good chance to be offered a seat. The significance of this didn't dawn on me—neither did the math—until I met Ayan Wilson. Even though her son was number 106 on the waiting list after the lottery, Success Academy's enrollment algorithm deemed him "likely" to be offered a seat at Bronx 1. Immediately after the welcome meeting and the network's requirement that parents reaffirm their interest in attending Success Academy, Darren Wilson went from 106 to 17. Virtually overnight, enough children to fill the entire kindergarten class at Bronx 1 fell away. What became of them? Some parents may have listened to Shea Reeder's unsparing "Is Success Academy right for you?" speech and decided it was not. Others may have won seats at a different school, perhaps one closer to home. The lack of transportation and after-school activities might have been an insurmountable hurdle for parents without the wherewithal to drop children off every morning at 7:30 and pick them up at 3:45 in the afternoon, and at 12:30 on Wednesdays. Either way, the upshot is clear: when school started in August, the kindergarten class was filled with children of parents who were fully engaged, aware of what they were getting into, and had voted with their feet not once but repeatedly, demonstrating their ability and willingness show up and follow through. The enrollment process is a de facto screen for parental engagement, enthusiasm, and competence. It is pointless, even dishonest, to deny it.*

Critics will no doubt view this as a smoking gun and proof of "creaming"—a deliberate practice of ensuring that only the easiest-to-teach students emerge. But if you wish to say that all of this is unfair or inequitable, then you must also answer why low-income families of color should not have the ability to send their children to school with the children of other parents who are equally engaged, committed, or ambitious. This is what affluent parents do when they send their kids to private schools. It's what striving middle-class families do when they move to the suburbs. If Eva Moskowitz is to be charged with creating an opportunity for parents like Ayan Wilson, Evelyn Ortega, Vanessa and Andre Farrer, and other families with more ambition for their children than means, it is a curious charge. If you demand that engaged and committed parents send their children to school with the children of disengaged and uncommitted parents, then you are obligated to explain why this standard applies to low-income black and brown parents—*and only to them.*

---

* The substantial number of lottery winners who end up not enrolling at Success Academy fits a long-standing pattern at the network. An independent analysis of Success Academy's academic achievement conducted by MDRC as part of a federal Investing in Innovation (i3) grant application noted that in the 2010–2011 school year "about 82 percent" of lottery winners attended a welcome meeting. "Approximately 61 percent of lottery winners attended student registration, 54 percent attended a uniform fitting, and 50 percent attended a dress rehearsal. With few exceptions, lottery winners who did not attend an activity did not attend subsequent activities. Ultimately, about 50 percent of lottery winners enrolled in Success Academy schools in the 2010–2011 school year." Source: Unterman, R. (August 2017). An Early Look at the Effects of Success Academy Charter Schools. Retrieved from https://www.mdrc.org/sites/default/files/2017 _Success_Academy.pdf

Moskowitz's many critics will almost certainly read much of what has been discussed in the preceding pages as an indictment. Her schools systematically favor the functional and easiest to teach, they have argued. If the "culture matching" and parental engagement Success Academy demands and enforces aren't creaming, it's close enough. Others, perhaps far more numerous, will simply say, "Well, what's wrong with that?" and perhaps, "It's about time." A significant number of American parents, probably a majority, would prefer to send their children to schools where discipline is tight, adult authority respected, and academic expectations high. In their imagination, this is simply what school is or ought to be. If Moskowitz has created something like the poor man's private school, a means for engaged and ambitious low-income families to surround themselves with like-minded souls, raising their children in a cocoon of high expectations and academic achievement in places where it has seldom existed, many will likely applaud the effort and share her view that she is, in fact, serving the cause of equity and working for the common good.

It would be dishonest to pretend that Success Academy is not a self-selection engine that allows engaged families who happen to be poor or of modest means to get the best available education for their children. But it is equally dishonest and close to cruel to deny such families the ability to self-select in the name of "equity." Indeed, it is nearly perverse to deny low-income families of color—and *only* those families—the ability to choose schools that allow their children to thrive, advance, and enjoy the full measure of their abilities. As Evelyn Ortega once said of Success Academy critics, "Do they *want* to keep us down?"

Likewise, in the final analysis, it misses the mark to say Success Academy is a sorting mechanism that chases away weak students to increase test scores. A more nuanced view is that they leverage parent demand to increase academic rigor and to enshrine a culture that drives student achievement—and that drives some away. When you have a long line of people waiting for a seat, you have the latitude to say, directly or implicitly, "my way or the highway." When so many are willing, even desperate, to get in, it gives that school leverage that the neighborhood school across the street cannot hope to match and should not be expected to. Thus, when charter school critics insist comparisons between the two are unfair, they are correct.

But this also places neighborhood schools on the horns of an ethical dilemma. When *opponents* make the argument that savvy parents will obviously want their children to attend a charter school, this speaks volumes about the schools and situations those parents are seeking to flee. If the smartest, best informed, and most motivated are the first ones out the door when you unlock it—if the more you know, the more you want out—what does that tell you about the conditions inside? If it's "cheating" to appeal to and draw off the most motivated families, who is cheating and who's being cheated when we make it difficult or impossible for them to leave?

The same argument applies to competing charter schools that accuse Success Academy of getting their stellar results by putting hurdles in front of low-income families that only the strongest and most committed parents can clear after winning a seat in the lottery. A veteran charter school educator offers an analogy. Imagine two lifeboats floating off the bow of a sinking ship. The first allocates seats by lottery. The second one allocates seats via a test: *Ready? Set? Swim to the boat!* The passengers in the second boat are strong swimmers and the most likely to be able to row safely to the distant shore; it's a boat full of strong swimmers. "That's the best place to be. Do everything you can to get in that second boat," he said. "But you'd rather be in either one. The captain shouting that everyone has to stay on the sinking ship somehow ain't quite right."

One Last Visit

ON THE FIRST DAY OF THE NEW SCHOOL YEAR, I MADE ONE LAST visit to Bronx 1. I wanted to see Darren Wilson's first day of kinder-garten after his long journey there. After more than four months in likely-list limbo, he was seated just days ago. His mother emailed me the news in all caps, "HE GOT ACCEPTED TODAY!!!!!" with more exclamation marks than words. Darren shook Liz Vandlik's hand and entered the building without as much as a backward glance at his mom. He will be in Ms. Skinner's kindergarten class.

Another boy named King'Anthony was stopped at the door. He was wearing a Success Academy name tag but different in ap-pearance from those worn by the other children, perhaps for the previous week's dress rehearsal, when kindergarteners who have been admitted but are not yet officially enrolled come to school to meet their teachers and learn classroom routines. King'Anthony didn't come to school that day. There was no call from his mother to explain the absence. Vandlik calls over Noreen Cooke-Coleman, who takes the child's caregiver, apparently his grandmother, off to one side. The woman claims the boy's mother *did* call, but Ms. CeeCee is firm. She shakes her head. After a long conversation, she tells her, "Right now, we don't have a place for him."

His seat was given away.

Vandlik turns away another child who doesn't have his orange tie—but just for today. "I'm going to get him one right now," says the boy's mother. Vandlik responds that they are looking forward to having the boy in school the moment he's in uniform and ready. The mother, visibly agitated, whips out her cell phone. Seconds later, she is theatrically complaining to whoever she called, but the intended audience is Vandlik, who is still five feet away welcoming students. "I guess a tie is more important than his education," the mom says more than once. The comment gets no immediate response, but a few moments later, Vandlik is uncharacteristically curt with Ms. CeeCee for admitting a student who was wearing black socks instead of navy blue ones. It makes Vandlik look like a hypocrite in front of the mother who was angry about her son's missing tie.

The boy's tie and his education cannot be unknotted. It is a tool that Bronx 1—and every other Success Academy school welcoming students at this hour—uses to set, maintain, and even screen for its expectations of parents. The first day of school is merely an occasion for them to demonstrate that they mean what they say. No uniform, no admittance, no exceptions. No, *seriously*.

One child is let in who is not in uniform, however. His name is Langston Boyce, and he is five years old. He got his seat even later than Ayan Wilson's son. His shirt, tie, and khaki pants haven't arrived yet, but because his parents communicated the issue to the school when they were admitted over the weekend, Langston shakes Vandlik's hand and strolls right in wearing a bright crimson polo shirt. He is literally the last kid in the door. As he goes up the stairs, his father, Duane Boyce, who drives tourist buses in Manhattan, looks thunderstruck. "Wow," he sighs to his wife, Natara Hamilton, "he made it." The door closes behind their son.

I spend several minutes talking to the couple. She is a special education teacher at PS 103 at the opposite end of the Bronx, a few blocks from the Westchester County line, where fewer than one in four students are on grade level in math and reading. They applied to forty-seven charter schools for kindergarten. I asked her to repeat the number, but there is no mistake. A veteran DOE teacher with more than a decade in the classroom and a member of the United Federation of Teachers, she applied to *forty-seven* charter schools. Success Academy and Bronx 1 were their first choice. When I explain that I'm writing a book about Success Academy and spent the previous year embedded at Bronx 1, Duane, his voice betraying a touch of anxiety, asks me if it's a good school. I start to explain that I need to be objective and careful in what I say, then I stop myself and close my notebook. We're just two dads talking on a South Bronx sidewalk. "It's a great school," I say. "You're really lucky." He and his wife look instantly relieved. They will have to travel a long way to get Langston here every day, and Duane's work schedule will be disrupted, costing him bids for the best bus routes and taking money out of the family's pocket. "Just do whatever you need to do to keep him here," I say. Hamilton explains that the easiest thing in the world would have been to enroll her son at the school where she works. But she went to Catholic school; her husband went to a Montessori school. There was simply *no way* they were not going to get the best possible education for Langston.

They are the Success Academy family from central casting. Their son has won two lotteries: He's got a seat at Bronx 1 and, from all appearances, a golden ticket in the parent lottery. His mother is already impressed with the school. Last night, Sunday, she was at the Yankees game when Mr. Carnaghi, her son's kindergarten teacher, called them to welcome them and review expectations. "He told me, 'Your son *will* learn to read this year,'" she says. "It was reassuring to hear."

The thought doesn't occur to me until nearly an hour later when I'm sitting over a plate of eggs in a storefront Mexican restaurant reading my notes. I may just have witnessed two lives take very different directions at the same moment. King'Anthony had a seat in the best elementary school in the South Bronx and lost it. Is it the seat that Langston Boyce now occupies? One little boy is inside with Mr. Carnaghi and Ms. Kowalski. The other is left standing on the sidewalk.

Is it unfair? *Of course* it's unfair. Children shouldn't be penalized or disadvantaged for the actions or inactions of their parents. But a moment of parental inattention, disengagement, indifference, a lack of communication, an honest mistake, or God knows what opened a door of opportunity just a crack, and Duane Boyce and Natara Hamilton, a deeply engaged and motivated couple, barreled through it, trailing Langston behind. Five-year-old King'Anthony is on the sidewalk without the first clue about what is happening or about the stakes involved, while his grandmother mutters apologies and excuses. The school year—and perhaps a lifetime of attainment and accomplishment—started without him.

Would it be less unfair if it were Langston Boyce and his parents on the outside looking in? Any mother who is willing to sit up late into the evening after work applying to forty-seven different schools is obviously diligent and dedicated, a fierce advocate for her child. Isn't that enough?

Are you enough for your child? Is *any* parent enough? And if a parent is enough, then why are we so obsessed with schools? Why do the wealthiest mothers and fathers in Manhattan go to such extraordinary lengths to get their children into just the right preschool, which feeds into just the right private school, where they will spend more money on tuition for kindergarten than the average American earns in a year—all in the hope of making their kids' path straight into elite colleges and universities—an academic arms race, which *New York* magazine christened in a cover story as "Give Me Harvard or Give Me Death"?[1] And if they fail to get their children, born with every conceivable advantage of race, class, and privilege, into the best private school, who begrudges them when they move to Greenwich, Scarsdale, or Montclair, New Jersey? Why does it offend our egalitarian impulses when Eva Moskowitz engineers a way for families of color with more ambition than means to pursue—to the degree to which they are permitted at all to pursue—the same ends for their children as the white families two subway stops away? Evelyn Ortega's words echo in my head:

"Do they *want* to keep us down?"

I'm thinking once again about Tiffany, the fifth grader I had in my second year at PS 277 a few blocks from Bronx 1. I see her now as the ur–Success Academy student, spending a year in my classroom in the spotless school uniform that the rules insisted she didn't have to wear but her mother did; her homework neatly done every night, never missing a day of school or a single assignment. She personified grit years before we began fetishizing it. But *she* was an outlier—solidly on grade level and perfectly behaved in a school where most of her peers were well behind and far less focused. What message did we send as teachers—as a nation—to a kid who bought in and was dialed in to the promise of education, playing by the rules, doing her best, but largely ignored for her dutiful, compliant nature, not by mistake or oversight but intentionally, virtually as public policy?

Tiffany eventually graduated from a state university in Pennsylvania. Any debate about excellence and equity must also include her. Based on the way we keep score in education policy, we congratulate ourselves for her accomplishment. As a low-income kid of color growing up in the South Bronx, she had, from birth, perhaps a 6 to 8 percent chance of graduating college. She made it. She beat the odds. We did right by her. Mission accomplished.

But that's a lie. I did nothing for her. We did nothing for her. Nothing to maximize her God-given potential and her mother's aspirations. In a fair system, one that cultivated her gifts rather than taking advantage of them, she might have graduated from Harvard, Yale, or Stanford. Your children might be working for her right now.

Tiffany was a dandelion pushing up stubbornly through a sidewalk crack. In that school, she defied and resisted the culture; at Bronx 1, she would have *personified* it. At Bronx 1, every seat is filled with a kid just like her, whether they were born that way or become that way. If you think that can be done without creating a mechanism for families like the Boyces—or the Ortegas, or the

Farrers, or the McKinnons—to self-select into a school where they learn alongside the children of other parents like themselves, you're crazy, a dreamer, or both.

Unlovely and undemocratic, you say? Every child should go to school with the broadest range of children—black, white, and brown; rich and poor; well behaved and profoundly disruptive; academically engaged and utterly indifferent. So what's stopping you from sending your child to such a school today? Such schools are legion.

What precisely?

NOTES

Chapter 1 | The Tiffany Test

1. Sanchez retired in December 2016 after twenty-seven years serving as the executive director of East Side House Settlement.

2. Core Knowledge Foundation, 801 East High Street, Charlottesville, Virginia, 22902. https://www.coreknowledge.org/

3. Hirsch, E. D., Kett, J. F., & Trefil, J. (1998). *Cultural literacy: What every American needs to know.* New York: Vintage.

4. Common Core State Standards Initiative. http://www.corestandards.org/about-the-standards/

Chapter 2 | "We Have an Army Coming"

1. According to Success Academy, "across the network, 76% of students are from low-income households; 8.5% are current and former English Language Learners, and 15% are current and former special-needs students. About 93% of students are children of color." https://www.successacademies.org/about/

2. Most recent numbers are as impressive. According to Success Academy, "Among the 6,800 scholars who were age-eligible to take the tests, 98% were proficient in math and 91% proficient in ELA. In both subjects, students with disabilities and English Language Learners at Success Academy schools not only

surpassed their peers statewide, but also outperformed students without disabilities and native English speakers, respectively, across New York City." https://www.successacademies.org/results/

3. Taylor, K. (2015, October 29). At a Success Academy charter school, singling out pupils who have "got to go." *New York Times*. Retrieved January 3, 2019, from https://www.nytimes .com/2015/10/30/nyregion/at-a-success-academy-charter-school -singling-out-pupils-who-have-got-to-go.html

4. In its own words, "Success Academy is redefining what's possible in public education. Our dual mission is to: Build exceptional, world-class public schools that prove children from all backgrounds can succeed in college and life; and advocate across the country to change public policies that prevent so many children from having access to opportunity." https://www .successacademies.org/about/

5. See "The Facts about Success Academy." https:// successacademies.org/app/uploads/2013/10/The-FACTS-About -Success-Academy-CSD27-Final.pdf

6. Success Academy. (2015, October 13). Success Academy students soar to top of New York State in results of proficiency exams. Retrieved from https://www.successacademies.org/press -releases/success-academy-students-soar-to-top-of-new-york -state-in-results-of-proficiency-exams/

7. Moskowitz, E. (2018, November 16). Fanning flames of partisanship hurts kids. Retrieved from https://www .successacademies.org/education-blog-post/fanning-flames -of-partisanship-hurts-kids/

Chapter 3 | Bronx 1

1. Howard Cosell's "The Bronx is Burning" Comments During 1977 World Series. Retrieved from https://www.youtube.com /watch?v=bnVH-BE9CUo

2. Ibid.

3. Fernandez, M. (2007, October 5). In the Bronx, blight gave way to renewal. *New York Times*. Retrieved from https://www.nytimes.com/2007/10/05/nyregion/05charlotte.html

4. Community School District 7 Data. https://data.nysed.gov/profile.php?instid=800000046647

5. Kozol, J. (1995). *Amazing grace: The lives of children and the conscience of a nation*. New York: Crown.

6. Cody, A. (2011, July 18). Confronting the inequality juggernaut: A Q&A with Jonathan Kozol. *Education Week*. Retrieved from http://blogs.edweek.org/teachers/living-in-dialogue/2011/07/time_to_get_off_our_knees_why.html

7. Taylor, K. (2016, February 12). At Success Academy school, a stumble in math and a teacher's anger on video. *New York Times*. Retrieved from https://www.nytimes.com/2016/02/13/nyregion/success-academy-teacher-rips-up-student-paper.html

8. Taylor, K. (2015, October 29). At a Success Academy charter school, singling out pupils who have "got to go." *New York Times*. Retrieved March 5, 2019, from https://www.nytimes.com/2015/10/30/nyregion/at-a-success-academy-charter-school-singling-out-pupils-who-have-got-to-go.html

9. Tyre, P. (2018, October 26). Yes, there's a right way to teach reading. Retrieved from https://www.greatschools.org/gk/articles/importance-of-reading-success/

10. Annie E. Casey Foundation. (2002, January 1). Double jeopardy. Retrieved from https://www.aecf.org/resources/double-jeopardy/

11. Scott, N. (2010, September 6). KIPP is the way the white and powerful want the poor of color to be educated—a question for Obama: Why does KIPP not look like Sidwell? *Substance News*. Retrieved from http://www.substancenews.net/articles.php?page=1653

Chapter 4 | No Excuses

1. Wong, A. (2017, September 25). The most polarizing education reformer in New York City. *Atlantic*. Retrieved February 9, 2019, from https://www.theatlantic.com/education/archive /2017/09/the-education-of-eva-moskowitz/540690/

2. Carter, S. C. (2000). *No excuses: Lessons from 21 high-performing, high-poverty schools*. Washington, DC: Heritage Foundation.

3. CREDO. (2015). Urban charter school study report on 41 regions. Retrieved January 11, 2019, from http://urbancharters .stanford.edu/summary.php

4. Prothero, A. (2017, December 13). Charter networks show big gains over other New York City schools. *Education Week* blog. Retrieved January 11, 2019, from http://blogs.edweek.org /edweek/charterschoice/2017/10/charter_management _organizations_show_big_gains_over_other_school_types _in_new_york_city.html?cmp=RSS-FEED&print=1

5. Whitman, D. (2008). *Sweating the small stuff: Inner-city schools and the new paternalism*. Washington, DC: Thomas B. Fordham Institute.

6. Ravitch, D. (2011, June 1). Waiting for a school miracle. *New York Times*. Retrieved January 11, 2019, from https://www .nytimes.com/2011/06/01/opinion/01ravitch.html

Chapter 5 | Whack-a-Mole

1. NYSED. (2014, April 15). Student support services: Educational neglect. Retrieved January 12, 2019, from http://www.p12 .nysed.gov/sss/pps/educationalneglect/

2. NYC Administration for Children's Services. (n.d.). About ACS. Retrieved January 12, 2019, from https://www1.nyc.gov/site/acs /about/about.page

Chapter 6 | "I Want to Slit My Wrists"

1. Moskowitz, E. S. (2018). *The education of Eva Moskowitz: A memoir*. New York: Harper.

2. Kolker, R. (n.d.). How is a hedge fund like a school? *New York* magazine. Retrieved from http://nymag.com/news /businessfinance/15958/index5.html

3. Board of Directors. (2018, June 26). Retrieved February 9, 2019, from https://www.successacademies.org/about/board-of-directors/

4. Gotham Funds. (n.d.). Retrieved February 9, 2019, from https:// www.gothamfunds.com/default.aspx

5. Robert Slavin, Ph.D. (n.d.). Retrieved February 9, 2019, from https://education.jhu.edu/directory/robert-e-slavin-phd/

6. Kolker, R. (n.d.). How is a hedge fund like a school? *New York* magazine. Retrieved February 9, 2019, from http://nymag.com /news/businessfinance/15958/

7. Andrew Tobias. (n.d.). Retrieved February 9, 2019, from https:// andrewtobias.com/

8. Otterman, S. (2017, December 21). Joel Klein, ex-New York schools chancellor, to join health insurance start-up. *New York Times*. Retrieved February 9, 2019, from https://www.nytimes .com/2016/01/15/nyregion/joel-klein-ex-new-york-schools -chancellor-to-join-health-insurance-start-up.html

9. About Eric Grannis. (n.d.). Grannis Law. Retrieved February 9, 2019, from http://www.grannislaw.com/about.html

10. About Scott M. Stringer. (n.d.). New York City Comptroller. Retrieved February 9, 2019, from https://comptroller.nyc.gov /about/about-scott-m-stringer/

11. *New York Times*. (2005, August 28). For Manhattan borough president. Retrieved February 9, 2019, from https://www .nytimes.com/2005/08/28/opinion/nyregionopinions/for -manhattan-borough-president.html

12. Interview with the author, March 28, 2017.

13. *New York Times*. (2016, February 12). A momentary lapse or abusive teaching? Retrieved February 9, 2019, from https:// www.nytimes.com/video/nyregion/100000004159212/success -academy-teacher-rip-and-redo-video.html

Chapter 7 | "Just Let This Latina Pass"

1. Jeynes, W. H. (2005). A meta-analysis of the relation of parental involvement to urban elementary school student academic achievement. *Urban Education*, 40(3), 237–269. doi:10.1177/0042085905274540

2. Jeynes, W. H. (2007). Religion, intact families, and the achievement gap. *Interdisciplinary Journal of Research on Religion*, 3, article 3. Retrieved from http://www.religjournal .com/pdf/ijrr03003.pdf

3. Elementary School Handbook. (n.d.). Retrieved February 10, 2019, from https://www.successacademies.org/handbooks /elementary-school-handbook/

4. All quotations in this section are from Stories from current and former Success Academy parents. (2015, April 17). *New York Times*. Retrieved February 10, 2019, from https://www.nytimes .com/interactive/2015/04/17/nyregion/success-academy-parents -voices.html

5. Sparks, S. D. (2012, December 11). Students who struggle early rarely catch up, study says. *Education Week*. Retrieved February 10, 2019, from https://blogs.edweek.org/edweek/inside-school -research/2012/12/Helping_struggling_students_catch_up.html

6. Parker, E., Diffey, L., & Atchison, B. (2016). *Full-day kindergarten: A look across the states.* https://www.ecs.org/wp-content/uploads /Full-Day-Kindergarten-A-look-across-the-states.pdf

7. Preschool and kindergarten enrollment. (2018, April). Retrieved February 12, 2019, from https://nces.ed.gov/programs/coe /indicator_cfa.asp

8. 50-State Comparison: State Kindergarten-Through-Third-Grade
    Policies. (n.d.). Retrieved May 6, 2019, from https://www.ecs
    .org/kindergarten-policies/

9. Snow, K. (2015, August 21). 15 states require kids to attend
    kindergarten and other kindergarten facts. Retrieved February
    12, 2019, from https://www.naeyc.org/resources/blog/15-states
    -require-kids-attend-kindergarten

10. New York School Rankings. (n.d.). Retrieved May 6, 2019, from
    https://www.schooldigger.com/go/NY/schoolrank.aspx

Chapter 9 | The Window and the Mirror

1. Lavinia, A., & Moskowitz, E. (2012). *Mission possible: How the
    secrets of the Success Academies can work in any school* (p. 72).
    San Francisco: Jossey-Bass.

2. Ibid, p. 71.

3. 10454 Income Statistics. (n.d.). Retrieved August 19, 2018, from
    https://www.incomebyzipcode.com/newyork/10454

4. Hart, B., & Risley, T. R. (1995). *Meaningful differences in the
    everyday experience of young American children.* Baltimore,
    MD: Paul H. Brookes Publishing.

5. Hart, B., & Risley, T. R. (2003). The early catastrophe: The 30
    million word gap by age 3. *American Educator* (Spring).
    Retrieved March 4, 2019, from https://www.aft.org/sites
    /default/files/periodicals/TheEarlyCatastrophe.pdf

6. Popham, W. J. (1999). Why standardized tests don't
    measure educational quality. *Educational Leadership*, 56(6).
    Retrieved March 4, 2019, from http://www.ascd.org
    /publications/educational-leadership/mar99/vol56/num06
    /Why-Standardized-Tests-Don't-Measure-Educational-Quality
    .aspx

7. Stanford Education Data Archive. (n.d.). Retrieved March 4,
    2019, from https://cepa.stanford.edu/seda/overview

8. Kamenetz, A. (2018, June 1). Let's stop talking about the "30 million word gap." *NPR*. Retrieved March 4, 2019, from https://www.npr.org/sections/ed/2018/06/01/615188051/lets-stop-talking-about-the-30-million-word-gap

9. Bellafante, G. (2012, October 6). Before a test, a poverty of words. *New York Times*. Retrieved March 4, 2019, from https://www.nytimes.com/2012/10/07/nyregion/for-poor-schoolchildren-a-poverty-of-words.html

10. Lareau, A. (2003). *Unequal childhoods: Class, race, and family life*. Berkeley: University of California Press.

11. Hirsch, E. D. (2013). A wealth of words: The key to increasing upward mobility is expanding vocabulary. *City Journal* (Winter). Retrieved March 4, 2019, from https://www.city-journal.org/html/wealth-words-13523.html

12. Recht, D. R., & Leslie, L. (1988). Effect of prior knowledge on good and poor readers memory of text. *Journal of Educational Psychology, 80*(1), 16–20. doi:10.1037/0022-0663.80.1.16

13. Willingham, D. T. (2017). *The reading mind: A cognitive approach to understanding how the mind reads*. San Francisco: Jossey-Bass.

14. Wexler, N. (2017, December 10). The mystery of Success Academy's success. Retrieved March 4, 2019, from http://www.dceduphile.org/uncategorized/the-mystery-of-success-academys-success/

15. Cunningham, A. E., & Stanovitch, K. E. (1998). What reading does for the mind. *American Educator* (Spring/Summer). Retrieved March 4, 2019, from https://www.aft.org/sites/default/files/periodicals/cunningham.pdf

16. Fertig, B. (2011, October 3). Soul searching at a struggling school where teachers see progress. *WNYC*. Retrieved May 6, 2019, from https://www.wnyc.org/story/302667-soul-searching-at-a-struggling-school-where-teachers-see-progress/

17. Hirsch, E. D., & Pondiscio, R. (2013, June 13). There's no such thing as a reading test. *American Prospect*. Retrieved March 4,

2019, from https://prospect.org/article/theres-no-such-thing
-reading-test

Chapter 11 | The Math Lesson

1. Gary Rubenstein, an education blogger and math teacher at New York City's elite Stuyvesant High School, and a former Teach For America corps member, is a persistent critic of Success Academy who has analyzed the schools' attrition rates and its students' performance on standardized tests. In a May 2018 blog post, he noted that of the sixteen high school students in Success Academy's inaugural graduating class who took the New York State Algebra II Regents test, "none of them were able to achieve the level 5" (the highest score). Two more earned a level 4 officially meeting the standards. "Eleven partially met the standards with a level 3," Rubenstein wrote. "This is a pretty poor showing for a school that prides themselves on their math standardized test scores for the state 3-8 tests," he concluded.

2. Investigations: Center for Curriculum and Professional Development. (n.d.). Retrieved March 4, 2019, from https:// investigations.terc.edu/

3. Contexts for Learning Mathematics. (n.d.). Retrieved March 4, 2019, from https://www.heinemann.com/contextsforlearning/

4. Lemov, D. (2013, May 29). On abuelita and the perils of "rounding up." Retrieved March 4, 2019, from http:// teachlikeachampion.com/blog/teaching-and-schools/on-abuelita -and-the-perils-of-rounding-up/

Chapter 12 | "Catholic School on the Outside, Bank Street on the Inside"

1. Interview with the author, November 6, 2017.

2. Wolpert-Gawron, H. (2015, August 13). What the heck is project-based learning? Retrieved March 4, 2019, from https://

www.edutopia.org/blog/what-heck-project-based-learning
-heather-wolpert-gawron

3. Moskowitz, E. S. (2018). *The education of Eva Moskowitz: A memoir* (p. 342). New York: Harper.

4. Ravitch, D. (2014, September 24). The secret to Eva Moskowitz's "Success." *Nation.* Retrieved March 4, 2019, from https://www
.thenation.com/article/secret-eva-moskowitzs-success/

5. Gonzalez, J. (2014, June 18). Gonzalez: Students of much-touted Success Academy charter school score too low on entrance exam for top city high schools. *New York Daily News.* Retrieved March 4, 2019, from https://www.nydailynews.com/new-york
/education/gonzalez-success-charter-students-fail-top-city
-schools-article-1.1833960

6. Chapman, B. (2016, June 17). Exclusive: Success charter students nab slots at elite specialized NYC high schools. *New York Daily News.* Retrieved March 4, 2019, from https://www
.nydailynews.com/new-york/education/success-charter-kids-nab
-elite-nyc-high-school-slots-article-1.2677005

7. Brody, L. (2018, March 22). How Success Academy got its first seniors to college. *Wall Street Journal.* Retrieved March 4, 2019, from https://www.wsj.com/articles/how-success-academy-got
-its-first-seniors-to-college-1521711000

8. Whitmire, R. (2016, September 12). How KIPP learned the truth about its students' college completion and inspired others to do the same. Chalkbeat. Retrieved March 5, 2019, from https://
www.chalkbeat.org/posts/us/2016/09/12/how-kipp-learned-the
-truth-about-its-students-college-completion-and-inspired
-others-to-do-the-same/

9. Ibid.

Chapter 13 | Survival Mode

1. Success Academy. (2017). Expanding Success for NYC children. Retrieved from https://innovation.ed.gov/files/2017/09/
successacademycharterNAR.pdf

Chapter 14 | Releasing the Beast

1. Hernandez, J. C., & Gebeloff, R. (2013, August 7). Test scores sink as New York adopts tougher benchmarks. *New York Times*. Retrieved March 5, 2019, from https://www.nytimes .com/2013/08/08/nyregion/under-new-standards-students-see -sharp-decline-in-test-scores.html?mcubz=0

2. Simon, S. (2013, August 7). N.Y. fails Common Core tests. *Politico*. Retrieved March 5, 2019, from https://www.politico .com/story/2013/08/new-york-fails-common-core-tests-095304

3. Families for Excellent Schools. (n.d.). A tale of two school systems. Retrieved from http://www.familiesforexcellentschools .org/wp-content/uploads/2015/08/TaleofTwoSchoolSystems _Final.pdf

4. Interview with the author, August 29, 2016.

5. Moskowitz, E. S. (2017). *The education of Eva Moskowitz: A memoir* (p. 103). New York: Harper.

6. See, for example, Taylor, K. (2015, October 29). At a Success Academy charter school, singling out pupils who have "got to go." *New York Times*. Retrieved March 5, 2019, from https:// www.nytimes.com/2015/10/30/nyregion/at-a-success-academy -charter-school-singling-out-pupils-who-have-got-to-go.html

7. Fertig, B., & Lewis, R. (2015, December 30). New data: White and Asian children far outpace city population in gifted programs. WNYC. Retrieved March 5, 2019, from https://www .wnyc.org/story/city-data-shows-diversity-varies-greatly-across -within-schools/

8. Harris, E. A. (2017, June 12). New York to shorten standardized tests in elementary and middle schools. *New York Times*. Retrieved March 5, 2019, from https://www.nytimes.com/2017 /06/12/nyregion/new-york-to-shorten-standardized-tests-in -elementary-and-middle-schools.html

9. Zimmerman, A. (2016, April 20). Eva Moskowitz: Opt-out movement will leave students unprepared. Chalkbeat. Retrieved

March 5, 2019, from https://www.chalkbeat.org/posts/ny/2016
/04/01/eva-moskowitz-opt-out-movement-will-leave-students
-unprepared/

10. Taylor, K. (2015, April 06). At Success Academy charter schools,
high scores and polarizing tactics. *The New York Times*.
Retrieved from https://www.nytimes.com/2015/04/07/nyregion
/at-success-academy-charter-schools-polarizing-methods-and
-superior-results.html

Chapter 15 | Come to Jesus

1. Cunningham, A. E., & Stanovitch, K. E. (1998). What reading
does for the mind. *American Educator* (Spring–Summer).
Retrieved March 4, 2019, from https://www.aft.org/sites/
default/files/periodicals/cunningham.pdf

Chapter 16 | Plan of Attack

1. See TRIAND (2013). Test booklet, LA grade 6. Retrieved from
https://my.triand.com/ncc/production/testbundle/0018/2059/
test_watermark/testbooklet.pdf?1370639472

2. Campbell, D. T. (1976). Assessing the impact of planned social
change. Paper 8, Occasional Paper Series. Retrieved from http://
citeseerx.ist.psu.edu/viewdoc/download?doi=10.1.1.170.6988&
rep=rep1&type=pdf

3. Carter, S. C. (2001). *No excuses: Lessons from 21 high-
performing, high-poverty schools*. Washington, DC: Heritage
Foundation.

4. American Association of School Administrators. (2009, February
20). Atlanta school leader Beverly Hall named 2009 national
superintendent of the year. Retrieved March 5, 2019, from
http://www.aasa.org/content.aspx?id=1592

5. *Atlanta Journal-Constitution*. A timeline of how the Atlanta
school cheating scandal unfolded. (2018, May 4). Retrieved

March 5, 2019, from https://www.ajc.com/news/timeline-how
-the-atlanta-school-cheating-scandal-unfolded/
jn4vTk7GZUQoQRJTVR7UHK/

6. Koretz, D. (2017). *The testing charade: Pretending to make schools better.* Chicago: University of Chicago Press.

7. Banilower, E. R., Smith, P. S., Weiss, I. R., Malzahn, K. M., Campbell, K. M., & Weis, A. M. (2013, February). 2012 NSSME report of the 2012 National Survey of Science and Mathematics Education. Retrieved March 5, 2019, from http://www.horizon-research.com/2012nssme/research-products/reports/technical-report/

8. Koretz, D. (2017). *The testing charade: Pretending to make schools better.* Chicago: University of Chicago Press.

9. Interview with the author, September 22, 2017.

Chapter 17 | "Teach Me!"

1. Whitman, D. (2008). *Sweating the small stuff: Inner-city schools and the new paternalism.* Washington, DC: Thomas B. Fordham Institute.

2. Louis, E. (2010, April 28). "The Lottery" documentary shows education is a sure bet. *New York Daily News.* Retrieved March 5, 2019, from https://www.nydailynews.com/opinion/lottery-documentary-shows-education-bet-article-1.163454

3. Peterson, P. E. (2011). *Saving schools: From Horace Mann to virtual learning* (p. 70). Cambridge, MA: Belknap Press of Harvard University Press.

4. Haskins, R., & Sawhill, I. V. (2009). *Creating an opportunity society.* Washington, DC: Brookings Institution Press.

5. Ross, N. (2014, July 28). Teach Me. Retrieved from http://www.raiseupproject.org/contest-entries/teach-2/

Chapter 18 | Joy and Vomit

1. See F&P Text Level Gradient. https://www.fountasandpinnell
   .com/textlevelgradient/

2. Willingham, D. T. (2009). *Why don't students like school?
   A cognitive scientist answers questions about how the mind
   works and what it means for the classroom.* San Francisco:
   Jossey-Bass.

3. Shanahan, T. (2011, April 17). Rejecting instructional level
   theory. Retrieved June 7, 2019, from https://shanahanonliteracy
   .com/blog/rejecting-instructional-level-theory

4. Parrott, K. (2017, October 13). Fountas and Pinnell say
   librarians should guide readers by interest, not level. *School
   Library Journal.* Retrieved March 5, 2019, from https://www.slj
   .com/?detailStory=fountas-pinnell-say-librarians-guide-readers
   -interest-not-level

Chapter 19 | Testing Day

1. Bakeman, J. (2018, August 25). The rise and fade of education's
   "opt out" movement. Medium. Retrieved March 5, 2019, from
   https://medium.com/s/new-school/the-rise-and-fade-of
   -educations-opt-out-movement-13250787e7f4

Chapter 21 | The GAS Factor

1. See, for example, Pondiscio, R. (2018, November 20). It's time to
   end the testing culture in America's schools—and start playing
   the long game to produce better life outcomes for at-risk kids.
   The 74. Retrieved May 6, 2019, from https://www.the74million.org
   /article/pondiscio-its-time-to-end-the-testing-culture-in-americas
   -schools-and-start-playing-the-long-game-to-produce-better
   -life-outcomes-for-at-risk-kids/

2. Ibid.

3.   Akerlof, G. A., & Kranton, R. E. (2002). Identity and schooling: Some lessons for the economics of education. *Journal of Economic Literature*, 40(4), 1167–1201. doi:10.1257/.40.4.1167

4.   Interview with the author, October 24, 2017.

5.   Akerlof, G., & Kranton, R. (2010). *Identity economics: How our identities shape our work, wages, and well-being.* Princeton, NJ: Princeton University Press.

6.   Farr, S., Kamras, J., & Kopp, W. (2010). *Teaching as leadership: The highly effective teacher's guide to closing the achievement gap.* San Francisco: Jossey-Bass.

7.   Houchens, G. (2018, February 16). Does giving parents education options "divert" money from schools? My TeachThought podcast discussion on scholarship tax credits. Retrieved March 5, 2019, from https://schoolleader.typepad .com/school-leader/2018/02/my-teachthought-podcast -discussion-on-scholarship-tax-credits.html

Chapter 22 | Proof Point

1.   Interview with the author, May 17, 2017.

2.   Hernández, J. C. (2017, December 20). New York schools chief advocates more "balanced literacy." *New York Times*. Retrieved March 5, 2019, from https://www.nytimes.com/2014/06/27 /nyregion/new-york-schools-chancellor-carmen-farina-advocates -more-balanced-literacy.html

3.   Shapiro, E. (2017, February 22). Success faculty question Moskowitz's ties to Trump, support for DeVos. *Politico*. Retrieved March 5, 2019, from https://www.politico.com/states /new-york/city-hall/story/2017/02/success-staff-question -moskowitzs-ties-to-trump-109792

4.   Chapman, B. (2018, April 8). Exclusive: City's Success Academy charter schools come out in support of transgender

students. *New York Daily News*. Retrieved March 5, 2019, from https://www.nydailynews.com/new-york/success -academy-schools-support-transgender-students-article -1.2984127

Chapter 23 | Culture Clash

1. Success Academy wins 2017 Broad Prize for public charter schools. (2017, June 12). Retrieved March 5, 2019, from https:// broadfoundation.org/success-academy-wins-2017-broad-prize -public-charter-schools/

2. Interviews with the author.

3. Fertig, B., & Ye, J. (2016, March 15). NYC charters retain students better than traditional schools. WNYC. Retrieved March 5, 2019, from https://www.wnyc.org/story/nyc-charter -school-attrition-rates/

4. Winters, M. A. (2015). Pushed out? Low-performing students and New York City charter schools (Report 95). Manhattan Institute. Retrieved from https://media4.manhattan-institute .org/pdf/cr_95.pdf

5. Ravitch, D. (2017, June 12). Success Academy, known for harsh discipline and skimming students, wins Broad Prize. Retrieved March 6, 2019, from https://dianeravitch.net/2017/06/12 /success-academy-known-for-harsh-discipline-and-skimming -students-wins-broad-prize/

6. Federal Civil Rights Complaint vs Success Charter Academy's Systematic Violation of Disabled Students' Rights. (2016, January 20). Retrieved March 6, 2019, from https:// nycpublicschoolparents.blogspot.com/2016/01/federal-civil -rights-complaint-vs.html?spref=tw

7. Veiga, C. (2019, February 27). Success Academy violated the civil rights of students with disabilities, New York state investigation finds. Chalkbeat. Retrieved May 6, 2019, from https://www.chalkbeat.org/posts/ny/2019/02/27/state-faults

-success-academy-nyc-education-department-for-violating-civil
-rights-of-students-with-disabilities/

8.   Bush, G. W. (2000, July 10). Text: George W. Bush's Speech to the NAACP. *Washington Post.* Retrieved March 6, 2019, from http://www.washingtonpost.com/wp-srv/onpolitics/elections /bushtext071000.htm

9.   Schott Foundation. (2014). *Restorative practices: Fostering healthy relationships and promoting positive discipline in schools: A guide for educators.* Quincy, MA. http://schottfoundation.org/ sites/default/files/restorative-practices-guide.pdf

10.   Moskowitz, E. S. (2015, April 1). Turning schools into fight clubs. *Wall Street Journal.* Retrieved March 6, 2019, from https://www.wsj.com/articles/eva-moskowitz-turning-schools -into-fight-clubs-1427930575

11.   Interview with the author.

Chapter 24 | The "Likely" List

1.   *New York Times.* (2016, February 12). A momentary lapse or abusive teaching? Retrieved February 9, 2019, from https:// www.nytimes.com/video/nyregion/100000004159212/success -academy-teacher-rip-and-redo-video.html

2.   Taylor, K. (2015, October 29). At a Success Academy charter school, singling out pupils who have "got to go." *New York Times.* Retrieved March 5, 2019, from https://www.nytimes .com/2015/10/30/nyregion/at-a-success-academy-charter-school -singling-out-pupils-who-have-got-to-go.html

3.   PBS *NewsHour.* (2015, October 13). Is kindergarten too young to suspend a student? Retrieved March 6, 2019, from https:// www.pbs.org/newshour/show/charter-schools

Chapter 25 | Lessons Learned

1.   *A Nation at Risk.* (1983). Retrieved February 27, 2019, from https://www2.ed.gov/pubs/NatAtRisk/risk.html

2. Graham, E. (2013, April 25). "A Nation at Risk" turns 30: Where did it take us? National Education Association. Retrieved March 6, 2019, from http://neatoday.org/2013/04/25/a-nation -at-risk-turns-30-where-did-it-take-us-2/

3. Murray, C. A. (1984). *Losing ground: American social policy, 1950–1980*. New York: Basic Books.

4. Lebel, S. (2017, October 12). EdReports Whiteboard Wisdom: Steve Lebel (video). Retrieved February 27, 2019, from https:// www.youtube.com/watch?time_continue=8&v= TiUVKvRRNXQ

5. Feldman, S., & Richter, F. (2018, September 10). Infographic: U.S. outspends other developed nations in the classroom. Retrieved February 27, 2019, from https://www.statista.com /chart/15404/us-outspends-other-developed-nations-in-the -classroom/

Epilogue | One Last Visit

1. Gardner, R. (March 18, 1996). Give me Harvard or give me death. *New York* magazine, Issue 33.

ACKNOWLEDGMENTS

This book is, at least in part, an act of contrition. As a teacher, I was poorly prepared for the challenges that I faced in my South Bronx classroom. In the years since, I have tried my best to learn and write about the things I should have been taught before being put in front of a class of children whose margin for error—my errors as a teacher; education's inattention to properly preparing educators for classroom success; our collective error in limiting families' schooling options—was nonexistent. Thus my acknowledgments must begin not by giving thanks but with an apology to my former students. You deserved better and you had no choice. I cannot repay the debt I owe for having learned so much; I cannot apologize enough that so much of my education came at your expense. We must do better for your children and grandchildren.

I am blessed to work for the Thomas B. Fordham Institute under its president, Michael Petrilli. More than most education "think tanks" and many news organizations, Fordham welcomes and even encourages heterodox views about education and education policy—a contrarian spirit that owes much to its president emeritus and intellectual north star, Checker Finn. I'm deeply indebted to both Mike and Checker for their early and sustained enthusiasm for this project, and their unending wise counsel throughout, and to my Fordham colleagues past and present, particularly Brandon Wright, Gary LaBelle, Amber Northern, David Griffith, Victoria McDougald, Andrew Scanlan, Alyssa Schwenck, and Caryn Morgan.

The generous support of the William E. Simon Foundation and the Achelis & Bodman Foundation enabled me to devote nearly two years to reporting and writing this project.

Miriam Joelson was an indispensable assistant, offering essential research assistance and timely feedback throughout the process. Julianna Rauf contributed capable fact checking and research help. Jessie McBirney lent valuable last-minute assistance organizing the endnotes.

Over the years, I have leaned heavily on friends, colleagues, and respected authorities whose ideas and work have defined and focused my own views on education practice and policy, and who were particularly helpful with this book. Chief among them are Dan Willingham, Doug Lemov, Stefanie Sanford, David Steiner, Ashley Berner, Kathleen Porter-Magee, James Merriman, Erica Woolway, Tim Shanahan, Mike Goldstein, Joel Klein, Jay P. Greene, Patrick J. Wolf, Chris Cerf, Eric Kalenze, Seth Andrew, and Joshua P. Starr. John Sanchez and Daniel Diaz of East Side House Settlement have offered helpful insights into Mott Haven and its schools, during the reporting of this book and when I was a teacher in the South Bronx.

Among those who read the entire manuscript at various stages and offered thoughtful feedback were Martin Bounds, Nelson Smith, Andy Smarick, Benjamin Feit, Rachel Gleischman, Peter Greene, Adela Jones Holda, Colleen Dippel, and Erika Donalds.

Others who were generous with their time and insights included Macke Raymond, Richard Kahlenberg, Kimberly Quick, Susie Miller Carello, Leo Casey, Nytesia Ross, Robert Slavin, Nelson Mar, Colleen Driggs, Nina Rees, Tom Loveless, Nat Malkus, Tara Marlovits, Bill Phillips, Corey Callahan, Scott Seider, Andy Porter, Richard Barth, Jeremiah Kittridge, Lester Long, Susan Aud

Pendergrass, Gary Houchens, Anne Burns, Dan Koretz, Bob Bellafiore, Stephanie Smith, Ali Annunziato, Jane Martinez Dowling, and Steve Mancini.

The vast majority of America's schools run on public tax dollars. Thus it is inevitable, even appropriate, that opinions will be sharply divided on the kind of education on offer at Success Academy and similar charter schools. Education is not "above the fray." But any of our fellow citizens who devote a portion of their lives to teaching other people's children deserve some measure of our gratitude, notwithstanding our opinions about their school's curriculum, governance structure, or instructional model. Thus I owe a debt of gratitude to the staff of Success Academy Bronx 1, particularly Elizabeth Vandlik, Jennifer Fuoco, Carolyn Syskowski, Albert Barabas, and Kerri Lynch, for cheerfully allowing me into their lives and work. They were, without exception, warm, welcoming, and forthcoming, always making time, including evenings and weekends, to answer questions and to discuss their practice. Their colleagues Matthew Morales, Constance Smith, Laura Belkin, Alanna Kowalski, Brandon Whitaker, Charita Stewart, Alexandra Gottlieb, Matt Carnaghi, Alexandra Margolis, Carson Rockefeller, Josh Rothman, Katie Kolenda, and Brandon Richter, were similarly gracious and helpful. The leadership team of Bronx 1, Noreen Cooke-Coleman, Kerrie Riley, Amy Young, and Nick Carton, were patient and generous with their time. Collectively, Bronx 1's teachers and staff have chosen among the very hardest jobs not merely in education but in American life. Their willingness to go about their work in full public view speaks volumes about their belief in what they are doing. For this they deserve respect and admiration. They have mine, unreservedly.

Eva Moskowitz made time throughout the project to share her thoughts and allowed me to shadow her on numerous occasions; her cheerful assistant Jocelyn Galvez was a pleasure to work with. Ann Powell fielded endless fact-checking questions and arranged access to several Success Academy schools and dozens of staff professional-development sessions. Senior staffers, past and present, who shared their thoughts, allowed me to visit their schools, attend their training sessions, or who were otherwise helpful included Michelle Caracappa, Kaitlin McDermott, Jim Manly, Jessica Sie, Shea Reeder, Danielle Hauser, Jennifer Haynes, Vanessa Bangser, Georgia West, Sean O'Hanlon, Trevor Baisden, Stacey Gershkovich, Lisa Sun, Richard Ziegler, Jessica Azani, Tamika Tretu, Marc Meyer, and Nick Simmons. My thanks to all of them, as well as Success Academy board members John Petry, Joel Greenblatt, Derrell Bradford, Sam Cole, and Campbell Brown.

The parents who welcomed me into their homes, churches, and lives while reporting this book have not just my thanks but admiration. They include Camille McKinnon, Evelyn Ortega, Vanessa and Andre Farrer, Ayan Wilson, Maimouna Wouattara, Saiba Sanga, Michael Ackom, and Lori Fleming. Those of us who take for granted safe and well-run schools for our children should never forget that millions of our fellow parents do not have that luxury.

I am grateful to the McCormick Literary Agency for their efforts on my behalf (and for Sara Mosle for introducing me to David McCormick). Megan Newman at Penguin is deeply knowledgeable about education; her enthusiasm and support made this project not just possible but pleasurable. Editor Nina Shield sharpened my insights, and Mauren Klier expertly polished my prose. Nellys Liang provided the lovely cover; the elegant interior design is the work of Elke Sigal. I'm indebted to the entire team at Penguin, particularly Hannah Steigmeyer, Anne Kosmoski, Emily Fisher, and Sara Johnson.

I've never had a worthwhile thought about education that E.D. Hirsch, Jr. didn't have first and more comprehensively. His insights, peerless work, and high ideals inspire and guide me daily. Lastly, my greatest debt is to my wife, Liza Greene, and our daughter, Katie Pondiscio. Their love, patient support, and good humor sustain and nourish me. This book is dedicated to each of them.

INDEX

Printed in the United States
by Baker & Taylor Publisher Services